PREXIT:

Forging Puerto Rico's
Path to Sovereignty

PREXIT:

Forging Puerto Rico's Path to Sovereignty

Author: J.A. Hernández
Publisher: Editorial Libros El Telégrafo
Year of Publication: 2019
English Language Edition

For additional resources, articles, publications, information, and videos regarding PREXIT and the Puerto Rican sovereignty movement, please go to:

www.PrexitBook.com

Copyright © 2019 by J.A. Hernández

All rights reserved. No part of this publication may be reproduced, distributed, or transmitted in any form or by any means, including photocopying, recording, or other electronic or mechanical methods, without the prior written permission of the publisher, except in the case of brief quotations embodied in critical reviews and certain other noncommercial uses permitted by copyright law.

"The views and opinions expressed in this book are those solely of the author, and do not reflect those of the Puerto Rico Government, the U.S. Government, any of its government agencies, any government, any business, or any institution." For permission requests, e-mail the publisher, addressed "Attention: Permissions Coordinator," at the e-mail address below.

Editorial Libros El Telégrafo

San Juan, Puerto Rico

E-mail: libroseltelegrafo@gmail.com

First Printing, 2019

ISBN 9781676722182

Ordering Information:

Quantity sales. Special discounts are available on quantity purchases by corporations, schools, associations, and others. For details, contact the publisher at the e-mail address above.

Editorial Libros El Telégrafo

Copyright © 2019 Editorial Libros El Telégrafo

Dedication

To my beautiful and amazing wife Jessica, thank you for all your patience, support, and coffee during the writing of this book.

To my great and inquisitive children, thank you for your smiles and making me go outside to play with everyone.

To Puerto Rico, thank you for being such an amazing country. I can only hope that this book will help you reach the freedom and democracy that you deserve. I am so honored to have been born a Puerto Rican and cannot fathom being anything else.

Thank you

Table of Contents

Dedication v

Preface ix

Acknowledgments xiii

Introduction xvii

Section 1: FAQs About Puerto Rico Sovereignty &
    Free Association 1

Section 2: The Ten Major Reasons Why Puerto
    Rico Will Never Become A U.S. State 17

Section 3: List Of Colonial Atrocities, Repression,
    And Policies Committed On Puerto
    Rico By U.S. Colonial Rule 83

Section 4: Invalidating The Statehooder
    & Colonialist Narratives 157

Section 5: Why Americans Must Oppose Statehood &
    Support Sovereignty For Puerto Rico 169

Section 6. Developing A PREXIT Strategy
    & Why National Sovereignty Is The Only
    Viable Option For Puerto Rico 203

PREXIT Strategies: Roadmaps And Proposals For
                Decolonization & Sovereignty 209

Conclusion 301

Afterward: An Exhortation To Liberate Puerto
           Rico From The Barbarians 311

Author Bio 335

Addendum: List Of Ways To Support Puerto Rico's
          Path To Sovereignty And Democracy 337

A Concise List Of Colonial Atrocities 347

Proposed Map Of Puerto Rican Autonomous Regions 351

Coming Soon 353

Editorial Libros El Telégrafo 355

Endnotes & References 357

PREFACE

Firstly, I would like to thank you, the reader, for taking the time and having the interest to learn more about this very contentious topic and having an open mind regarding the proposals and opinions presented in this book. Many books have been written on this subject, but never one quite like this. I have read almost every book about Puerto Rican politics, history, and the colonial dilemma, yet there was always something missing, a book that not only spoke about what has happened in the past, but a book that explained sovereignty in detail, presented a way forward, and presented various proposals on how to make Puerto Rico a stable, democratic, and economically prosperous sovereign Republic. This *is* that book.

I began writing drafts of this book in 2009, always adding more information and researching specific topics. In those years, I had to research more about economics, comparative politics, government structures and institutions, parliamentary systems, comparative tax and fiscal systems, and various other topics and fields. Regarding the title term "*PREXIT*", I'm not sure if I coined it, but I remember using it in 2012 with friends and family as soon as I heard about the "Brexit" situation in the UK. Parts of this book were written in Washington, DC; Miami; Burma; Brazil; Peru; Puerto Rico; Mexico; Tunisia; The Philippines; New Jersey; and in many airplanes and hotels over many years. In 2017, I planned on finishing and publishing the book in Mayagüez, Puerto Rico until

Hurricanes Irma and Maria changed our plans and forced my family and I to relocate to New Jersey near family.

For a few months, while my family and I resettled, nothing was done on the book, and it sat idle in my computer, although I frequently made notes on topics and other information I wanted to add. Finally, in 2019, I had the time and focus to finish the book, until my computer crashed and I thought I had lost the book draft forever. Thankfully, I recovered a version of the book that I could rewrite and continue on the goal of publishing on schedule. This book has had a long journey, and it is with excitement and joy that I finally bring this to the public, particularly the Puerto Rican people.

I believe this book is essential because it fills a void in the literature regarding Puerto Rico and the colonial dilemma. This book allows Puerto Ricans and others to see the awesome political, democratic, and economic potential that Puerto Rico has, along with showing how a future sovereign Republic could be structured. It also outlines how this new government can create wealth and economic development via various policies that aim on making Puerto Rico a part of the world economy, instead of relegating Puerto Rico to another hundred years of humiliating U.S. colonial rule.

This book also describes, in detail, the major reasons why Puerto Rico cannot, will not, and should not ever become a U.S. state, explained from the perspectives of both the United States and Puerto Rico. This book is going to be used by many people to learn more about Puerto Rico, colonial history, and the ever-growing pro-sovereignty movement, particularly after the massive Summer Revolution of 2019 that ousted the corrupt pro-statehood governor from office and demonstrated to many the true power of Puerto Ricans.

This book destroys many myths and virtually annihilates the statehooder and colonialist narratives that "Puerto Rico cannot be free." After reading this book, I'm sure you too will be inspired to storm the barricades of Calle Resistencia in Old San Juan with Puerto Rican flags in the upcoming protests. Believe me; they are coming. Yes, there are many controversial and contentious parts, opinions, and assertions in this book that will surely generate debate, but it's a debate that needs to happen. I hope that the many people who will read this book take something from it and view the Puerto Rican colonial dilemma with a different lens, a lens that is not always promoted by the media or the government itself.

Due to the topic and nature of this book and my views, I'm sure there will be a few statehooders and colonialists who will instantly label me a "separatist" and an "anti-American" in order to discredit me and this book, although they would not be able to refute the facts nor content presented in this book. Let me address this properly. If advocating for Puerto Rico's freedom, liberty, and sovereignty makes me a "separatist", then yes, I am a separatist. Being labeled a "separatist" by people whom I consider colonialists is fine by me because it means that my views are more in line with those of George Washington, Thomas Jefferson, Benjamin Franklin, and Thomas Paine, than the views of Benedict Arnold and the other loyalist Tories that preached colonialism. Thankfully, American currency is graced with the faces of such patriotic "separatists" and not the loyalists.

I am a Puerto Rican who was born in San Juan, yet raised in the United States and among Americans most of my life. I love Puerto Rico, consider Puerto Rico my only nation, value my Puerto Rican nationality, and I identify solely as a *"Puerto Rican"* whenever I travel around the United States and the world. I am part of the Puerto Rican diaspora, yet strongly identify with and participate in Puerto Rican affairs. In fact, I wish to return to Puerto Rico one day to support my country's path to sovereignty. I went to American public schools and public universities. I served in the federal government, have many American friends and colleagues, and even have American family members. At no point in my life have

I or any one of my American friends or family ever considered me an "anti-American" because of my views on Puerto Rico. Only statehooders and colonialists back in Puerto Rico would say such a *disparate* (ridiculous comment).

My struggle is not one against the United States, but against *U.S. colonial policies* in Puerto Rico that I believe need to be recognized, rectified, and changed to support decolonization and sovereignty, not continued colonial rule. Colonialism humiliates and demeans the United States just as much as it does Puerto Rico. I want Puerto Rico to aspire to the same freedom, liberty, and sovereignty enjoyed by the very United States, the country I believe Puerto Rico can associate with, and develop a strong bilateral relationship with in the international arena.

This book is not meant to be an ivory tower academic paper or dissertation only for the eyes of political scientists, but for everyone, young and old, liberal and conservative among others. I consider this book a conversation between you and I, where I attempt to not only explain the Puerto Rican colonial dilemma, but also answer all the questions you may have regarding Puerto Rico's decolonization, sovereignty, and future as a free country in the world. Hopefully, we can all contribute to and ensure Puerto Rico's "*PREXIT*" from stagnant and humiliating colonial rule and towards a future of freedom.

Thank you – Muchas Gracias – Bo-Matúm
Javier A. Hernández
November 19, 2019
Puerto Rican Diaspora in North America

ACKNOWLEDGMENTS

I would like to thank and express my gratitude to my family; to Jessica, Yosiat, and Luis for reading the draft and providing great feedback; Edil for the beautiful photos; to Jesús Omar for his guidance and inspiration; and to all those brave Puerto Ricans throughout the centuries who have fought, struggled, and died for our nation's freedom and liberty in the face of trying and overwhelming odds. Thank you for your sacrifices and ensuring the survival of the Puerto Rican Nation.

To my father, Rubén, thank you for your love and introducing me to Puerto Rican history and my self-awareness as a Puerto Rican. To my mother, Daisy, thank you for all your love, patience, sacrifices, and creating that loving Puerto Rican family environment even when we were living a thousand miles from Puerto Rico. To my brother and sisters, I love you all. To Angel and Geri, thank you for your support, love, and being a part of my life.

To abuela Angie and abuela Virginia, thank you for being pillars of strength and family, particularly in the harsh periods in which you both lived. Both of you were, as abuela Virginia would say, "*Boricuas de raza y cría.*"

To Aniceta Jiménez and Amparo Casanova, my great-grandmothers, thank you for all your hard work, patience, sacrifice, and being the personification of the strong no-nonsense Puerto Rican woman defying all odds. Aniceta was poor, widowed in the 1920s, and yet raised seven children in rural Quebradillas by herself.

Amparo was poor and raised eleven children in rural Manatí. Having raised families through the depression and decades of poverty is a feat that your descendants appreciate and thank you for. I am honored to have met both of you as a child, but I wish we could have had more time together.

To abuelo Ché and abuelo Tomás, thank you for your dedication, love of Puerto Rico, and not having been killed in all those wars you both had to go to. I am here because you survived.

To my tío Nestor, thank you for being the first person to have me realize as a child that Puerto Rico was under colonial rule. In that precise moment, I woke up, opened up the pod, and realized the existence of the "colonial" Matrix I did not know I was living in. You opened up my eyes, not just with your music and conversations, but with your love and dedication to Puerto Rico.

To my wife, thank you for always being there and supporting me throughout this journey. Your feedback, perspectives, and opinions were always important to me and were duly integrated into this book.

To my children, thank you for being my inspiration to write this book. You are too young to read this or understand its content, but one day, you will read this book and realize how "cool" and "awesome" your father was. When you read this book, you will better understand why I was often writing late at night and so adamant about speaking to you all only in Spanish. Every time I spoke Spanish to you, it was a small daily act of defiance to a whole system and colonial policy that aimed for decades to destroy our heritage as a people and our Spanish language.

One day you will understand why I always had a Puerto Rican flag at hand, tried to teach you Taino language and symbols, and always spoke to you about Puerto Rico, our family, and our great heroes and patriots. My hope is that one day, you all can witness, contribute, and experience the freedom of our Puerto Rican Nation and the birth of our third Republic so that you, unlike your ancestors and me, will never again see our beloved Puerto Rico under such humiliating colonial rule.

Remember that no matter where you live and where you were born, you are *Boricuas*, heirs to a long lineage of a proud people that survived, of beautiful revolutions, and civilizations that span not just Puerto Rico, but the Caribbean, Europe, Africa, and the Americas. Thank you for being such amazing children and I hope to give you not just the life you deserve, but the love that any proud father can give.

To Dr. Pedro Albizu Campos, thank you for your sacrifice and valiant efforts at trying to liberate our nation from colonial rule. Although I never had the honor to meet you in person, I feel that you are part of my spirit and consciousness as a Puerto Rican. As a teenager in the diaspora, you inspired me to be like you, to learn about the world, to learn languages, to accept and embrace my Puerto Rican nationality, and to become an excellent ambassador for the Puerto Rican Nation.

To Nelson A. Denis, thank you for writing "War Against All Puerto Ricans." You are truly a great author and an inspiration as a Puerto Rican.

To Adela López, thank you for your friendship over the years and pushing me to finish this book on time. You are an inspiration and a true leader of the Puerto Rican community in Florida.

To Luis Delgado, thank you for your service and dedication to Puerto Rico's freedom, and having introduced me to the idea of free association as a viable option for Puerto Rico.

Finally, I want to recognize and thank the editors and graphic designers that helped me make this book not only grammatically correct and formatted, but beautiful as well. I would also like to thank Roxana J. Clark for her great marketing and book launch ideas.

A special thank you to Micah, the amazing and talented computer specialist who retrieved the book draft file after my computer had crashed. Without you, I would have had to rewrite the entire book.

Thank you all for making this book possible.

INTRODUCTION

This book, "PREXIT: Forging Puerto Rico's Path to Sovereignty," is long overdue. It is intended not only to educate Puerto Ricans, Americans, and others around the world about the colossal mistake it would be to annex Puerto Rico as a U.S. state and the inner workings and legacies of U.S. colonial rule in Puerto Rico, but also to propose the viable option of National Sovereignty. This book will attempt to outline and detail a viable plan to support Puerto Rico's path to sovereignty and goals of economic and political development.

This book, which will be considered very controversial, aims to be concise, informative, and will be divided, apart from this Introduction, into the following seven sections and an afterward:

- FAQs about Puerto Rico Sovereignty & Free Association
- The Ten Major Reasons Why Puerto Rico will Never become a U.S. State
- List of Colonial Atrocities, Repression, and Policies Committed on Puerto Rico by U.S. Colonial Rule
- Invalidating the Statehooder & Colonialist Narratives
- Why Americans must Oppose Statehood & Support Sovereignty
- Developing a PREXIT Strategy & Why National Sovereignty is the Only Viable Option
- An Exhortation to Liberate Puerto Rico from the Barbarians

Americans and Puerto Ricans seriously need to consider the political, economic, and cultural ramifications of statehood for Puerto Rico, not just for Puerto Rico, but for the United States as well. Annexing and incorporating Puerto Rico, a Latin American and Caribbean nation, into the United States is not and will not be the same as incorporating Washington, DC, or Wisconsin. Many Puerto Ricans would consider statehood as a continuation and culmination of colonialism and would actively oppose and struggle against it.

Plebiscite after plebiscite continues to demonstrate that the majority of Puerto Ricans continue to reject statehood. In the 2012 status plebiscite, pro-sovereignty forces received 39% of voter support, a large increase after being a persecuted and repressed minority. In fact, as of the Puerto Rican status referendum of 2012, sovereignty via free association is the option with the largest growth margin among all other status options, experiencing a hundredfold (4,536 to 454,768) expansion in only 14 years[1].

In the most recent 2017 status plebiscite, pro-statehood forces only managed to pull 23% of the vote[2], in large part due to the electoral boycott led by pro-sovereignty forces who opposed the "territorial" colonial option being included in the plebiscite by the United States.

After the Puerto Rican Summer Revolution of 2019 that led to the resignation of the corrupt pro-statehood governor and the subsequent political crisis and debacle of the corrupt pro-statehood colonial government, one can safely say that statehood has been *discredited* and has *failed* as a viable option for Puerto Rico. Americans and a growing number of Puerto Ricans, particularly the younger generations, do not support statehood and are beginning to consider sovereignty as the only viable option for Puerto Rico.

While "collective statehood" for Puerto Rico has been consistently denied over and over since 1898 by the U.S. Congress, "personal statehood" is an option that has always been available to statehooders. To put it bluntly, if you want to be a first-class American, vote for the President, pay federal and state income taxes, and have access to all the federal funds within your reach, why not *move* to the United States where there are fifty states and thousands of towns to choose from? Any statehooder in Puerto Rico can enjoy statehood today with a $60 one-way airline ticket, yet many insist on staying in Puerto Rico. Why?

Remember that most statehood supporters are poor, do not speak English, and wish to enjoy the benefits and much-lauded welfare funds of statehood without having to deal and coexist with English-speaking Americans as neighbors. Essentially, they want the supposed monetary benefits of statehood, but without the bothersome English-speaking Anglo and African-Americans, and others that come along with the package. Americans need to know this.

U.S. colonial rule in Puerto Rico has been a blatant failure, and only **sovereignty, freedom, and democracy** can help Puerto Rico to not only protect its national culture, identity, and Spanish language, but to support its own economic development in a globalized world economy. Some form of Puerto Rican sovereignty is inevitable. Whether total independence or a modality of sovereign free association via a compact or treaty, Puerto Rico *will* be free, and Puerto Ricans will finally be able to rule themselves and advance their political and economic interests in the international community and global economy.

The United States needs to accept its past of horrid colonial policies and realize that it cannot hold Puerto Rico as a colony forever. Over 121 years of colonial slavery and humiliation is enough. Colonialism not only demeans and humiliates Puerto Rico, but also demeans, disgraces, and embarrasses the United States on the world stage as well.

How can the United States be taken seriously regarding "freedom and democracy" around the world if it still maintains Puerto

Rico under direct colonial rule? How can American diplomats lecture other countries about "democratic values" when the world *knows* that the U.S. holds Puerto Rico under a colonial and undemocratic regime?

The United States, the current colonial power in Puerto Rico since 1898, needs to face the fact that Puerto Rican sovereignty is in the best interest of both nations and the time to begin the transition to sovereignty and democracy is now. The colonial, political, and economic debacle of Puerto Rico occurred under the U.S. flag and under the total plenary powers of the U.S. colonial regime, not under any real sovereign Puerto Rican government. As a colonial territory, Puerto Ricans have zero say in the running and future development of their own country.

The time has come for the United States to finally realize and accept the fact that Puerto Rico needs to become a sovereign nation in order to better serve both the U.S. and Puerto Rican interests. Sovereignty would allow Puerto Rico to experience freedom and access to the world economy, just as it would unburden the United States from the expensive political and colonial debacle that is Puerto Rico. Freedom and democracy are always good, and it's about time Puerto Rico finally experienced them.

This book will explain why statehood for Puerto Rico is a terrible idea that will never happen because it goes against American and Puerto Rican interests. I will also explain and showcase various reasons why sovereignty (either free association or independence) is the only viable option for both Puerto Rico and the United States, particularly after the Puerto Rican Summer Revolution of 2019.

SECTION 1

FAQs about Puerto Rico Sovereignty & Free Association

What is Sovereignty?

Sovereignty is the ability of people to decide their own internal and external affairs freely. Colloquially, sovereignty is often called *freedom* and *liberty* for a country to rule itself without being ruled by another country. In a personal context, "*sovereignty*" is the right and ability to be in charge of your own personal affairs in your own home, without any interference from neighbors or anyone else. For example, the United States, Mexico, Ireland, and Peru are sovereign nations because they have their own sovereign governments and rule themselves.

Currently, Puerto Rico is not sovereign because it is occupied by the United States, and a large number of the laws that apply to it are federal laws, and its citizens cannot elect the American politicians that approve of such laws. The current government of Puerto Rico is actually a U.S. colonial regime from 1900 that is called the "Commonwealth of Puerto Rico" since 1952, but a mere colony it remains. Currently, as a U.S. colony, Puerto Rico lacks the sovereignty and authority to manage its own political, economic, and cultural affairs.

Under international law and United Nations resolutions, the only decolonization options based on sovereignty are Independence and Free Association. United States refusal to decolonize Puerto Rico is a direct violation of the United Nations Charter and other UN resolutions that have asked the United States to immediately return Puerto Rico's sovereignty back to the Puerto Rican people. Sadly, since the 1970s, the United States has just ignored over thirty-seven UN resolutions demanding Puerto Rican decolonization and sovereignty.

In addition, Puerto Rico is not free to legislate in accordance with its own interests because most of the fundamental issues and policies that affect Puerto Rico fall under the jurisdiction of the U.S. government and American politicians who do not care about Puerto Ricans and often do not even know where Puerto Rico is located on a world map. As a sovereign nation, Puerto Rico would finally be freed of colonial rule and can establish a truly democratic government and implement economic development policies.

What is "Free Association"?

The status option of **Free Association** is a decolonization option based on the sovereignty of both associated nations and recognized by the United Nations. With Free Association, Puerto Rico and the United States would negotiate a compact or treaty that would effectively decolonize Puerto Rico, on the basis that sovereignty will always rest with the people of Puerto Rico. The United States already has such Free Association relationships with the three Pacific insular nations of Micronesia, the Marshall Islands, and Palau.

With Free Association, the new Republic of Puerto Rico will be recognized by the international community as a sovereign nation associated with the U.S. but not subject to the plenary and absolute powers of the U.S. Congress. With Free Association, a partnership and association are sought based on the sovereignty of two countries. This is predicated on the recognition that although both countries have significant differences in size, population, economic strength, and political power, they share significant interests, values, and social and cultural characteristics.

With Free Association, Puerto Rico would not obtain full independence, because Free Association means that, according to the will of the Puerto Rican people, Puerto Rico could delegate some functions and services to the U.S. government. However, those powers that are not expressly delegated, will remain under the sole jurisdiction and sovereignty of the people of Puerto Rico. Sovereignty and Free Association is advocated and supported in Puerto Rico by various organizations.

As in independence, the United States may provide the Republic of Puerto Rico assistance in the formation of a diplomatic corps and its successful integration into the international community. With Free Association, Puerto Rico will be able to establish and maintain diplomatic relations with other countries and enter into various political and economic agreements.

The Republic of Puerto Rico, in free association, will be a real and dignified political relationship with the United States in which the sovereign powers of Puerto Rico will be recognized, not only by the United States, but also by the entire international community. Under a Treaty of Free Association, Puerto Rico will acquire control of its own national government, economy, and foreign affairs, limited only in those areas and functions delegated to the United States. With a Treaty of Free Association, Puerto Rico would become a major ally and strategic partner of the United States.

What are the characteristics of Free Association?

A Treaty of Free Association would grant Puerto Rico its own sovereignty, inserting it into the international community as a sovereign nation with full political dignity. Under a Treaty of Free Association, Puerto Rico will have its own representation at international organizations, including the United Nations Organization (UN), the World Trade Organization, and any regional organizations that Puerto Rico may show interest in joining. Of course, as a sovereign nation, Puerto Rico would continue to have its own Olympic Committee and participate in other international events under its own name.

Is Puerto Rican Sovereignty and Free Association in the U.S. national interest?

Yes, as you will see, transitioning Puerto Rico from a poor and corrupt colony to a sovereign Republic associated with the United States would greatly enhance U.S. national interests, not to mention Puerto Rican national interests.

As a sovereign nation associated with the United States:

The United States would be promoting decolonization and ending the constant ridicule and humiliation at the United Nations of being called a "colonial power";

The United States would be gaining a new ally and strategic partner in Latin America;

The United States would forever end the constant threat of Puerto Rican statehood that would aim at destabilizing the U.S. political system and attacking American unity;

The United States would still maintain access to the Puerto Rican market;

A sovereign and prosperous Puerto Rico would be in a better economic position to import American products and export products to the United States;

The United States would be able to divert federal funds into actual economic development projects instead of promoting welfare and food stamp dependency in Puerto Rico;

The United States, together with a sovereign Puerto Rico, could establish various joint economic and energy projects that would greatly benefit both American and Puerto Rican companies, entrepreneurs, and investors;

The United States, together with a sovereign Puerto Rico, could promote regional, economic, and security initiatives in the Caribbean;

The Treaty of Free Association, as proposed by pro-sovereignty groups in Puerto Rico, would include which important elements of negotiation?

- The inexorable recognition of **Puerto Rican citizenship** and conservation of **U.S. citizenship**, as at present, for those Puerto Ricans that wish to conserve it;
- **Free traffic of persons, goods, and capital** will be upheld and preserved between the two countries;
- The **laws and federal programs to be continued in Puerto Rico** will be mutually and explicitly agreed to, with Puerto Rico retaining all the powers of government needed to steer its own economic, political and cultural development, in accordance with its own national interests;
- The **federal contributions** for Social Security, veterans benefits, federal retirement, or other rights acquired by labor or services rendered, will continue as at present;
- An agreed upon **transition period** and allocation of block grant federal funds which would allow us to finance alternative and self-sustaining development projects in order to

gradually eliminate our current reliance and dependence on federal funds;

- The United States will continue to have **access to the Puerto Rican market** and will continue to benefit from special economic investment incentives and policies that will be approved by Puerto Rico to attract foreign capital and investments;

- **Maintain the U.S. dollar as the official currency** of the Republic of Puerto Rico. Along with the United States, other countries (such as Ecuador, El Salvador, Zimbabwe, Timor-Leste, Micronesia, Palau, the Marshall Islands, Turks and Caicos, and the British Virgin Islands) also use the U.S. dollar as their official currency.

  Other countries, such as the Bahamas, Barbados, St. Kitts and Nevis, Belize, Costa Rica, Nicaragua, Panama, Myanmar, Cambodia, and Liberia, also use the U.S. dollar alongside their national currencies. Globally, there are over 350 million people using the U.S. dollar as their currency, and the U.S. dollar is involved in over $17 trillion of economic activity[3].

  In Puerto Rico, the statehooders and colonialists like to spread the myth that if Puerto Rico were to become a sovereign country, the United States would *punish* Puerto Rico by not allowing us to use the U.S. dollar as our official currency. Obviously, such people are seriously misinformed and do not understand international relations, currency systems, and economic systems.

  A sovereign Puerto Rico using the U.S. dollar as the official currency would be in the U.S. national interest and facilitate trade between Puerto Rico and the United States;

- An agreed upon **Common Defense Agreement with the United States**, who may retain in Puerto Rico, those military bases and facilities that already exist and are indispensable for American and regional defense. All other federal property and assets would be transferred to the people of Puerto Rico.

Is Free Association considered the "consensus option" regarding Puerto Rican decolonization?

Unlike politics in the United States and most other countries, Puerto Rican politics are not based on the usual Left/Right and Liberal/Conservative political spectrum, but on the century's old status issue.

As a Spanish colony and province, Puerto Rican politics were centered as to whether Puerto Rico should integrate with Spain as a full province or should develop autonomous institutions. Pro-independence groups were banned and persecuted by the Spanish government in Puerto Rico. After the Spanish-American War of 1898, Puerto Rico was occupied and became a U.S. colony.

Under U.S. colonial rule, Puerto Rican politics again were centered on status: whether to become a U.S. state, remain a colonial territory called Commonwealth, or become an independent country. Pro-independence groups were also persecuted by the U.S. colonial regime, and even the Puerto Rican flag and anthem were banned. Today, the Puerto Rican political system is still structured around and based on the old status issue. The U.S. Democratic and Republican parties were never able to establish themselves in Puerto Rico as viable political institutions and options.

Currently, the pro-statehood party has been discredited, with many of its leaders arrested in major corruption scandals, its corrupt and inept governor ousted by a civic revolt, and many people now realize that statehood is not an option for Puerto Rico nor the United States. Of course, diehard statehooders and their "lunatic fringe" are always saying that "statehood is just around the corner."

The pro-Commonwealth party has also been mired in corruption scandals, and its "Commonwealth" status option has been repeatedly attacked and exposed as *colonial* by most Puerto Ricans and the very U.S. government itself via Presidential Reports, congressional actions and policies, and U.S. Supreme Court decisions that reaffirm that Puerto Rico has no sovereignty and is merely just a U.S. property, called a *territory*, of course.

As a colonial territory, the U.S. can even sell or cede Puerto Rico away to a foreign country! The pro-independence party and other pro-sovereignty organizations, although persecuted and criminalized for 121 years, have survived, held firm, and are now beginning to experience a surge in support, particularly by professionals and younger generations in Puerto Rico and the Puerto Rican diaspora.

These political organizations work to block and derail each other at every turn in hopes of advancing their own status option, thus creating a deadlock in Puerto Rico. American politicians use this status deadlock as an excuse to do nothing as regards to Puerto Rican decolonization.

Knowing that statehood is no longer an option and that the much-lauded "autonomous" Commonwealth has ceased to exist theoretically, Puerto Ricans have an opportunity to finally find a consensus and forge the path to decolonization via the status option of Free Association. All Puerto Rican political factions can benefit from sovereignty and Free Association:

Statehooders:

In 121 years, the U.S. Congress has *never* once brought up the issue of Puerto Rico statehood because it is not in the United States' national interest to do so. Recent bills in Congress to admit Puerto Rico as a state are a joke and do not even make it to a public hearing. Also, plebiscite after plebiscite continues to show that the majority of Puerto Ricans do *not* support statehood.

Statehood is *not* a right, but a concession that the U.S. Congress grants to territories it wishes to admit into the American union. Admitting a poor and bankrupt Spanish-speaking Latin American and Caribbean nation with an active, vocal, and strong nationalist and pro-sovereignty movement does not fit into that congressional agenda.

Realizing that the U.S. Congress will never make Puerto Rico a state, the Free Association option would offer statehooders a process of decolonization and the establishment of a serious treaty-based relationship with the United States, where Puerto Rico would be a U.S. ally and strategic partner. Diehard statehooders that wish to pay federal taxes and vote for the U.S. President can always move to one of the fifty states of the United States and enjoy the "American Dream" with their fellow American citizens.

In fact, in a Republic of Puerto Rico in free association with the United States, the ex-statehooders in Puerto Rico could regroup as a new center-right conservative party in Puerto Rico that would promote and defend such political and economic ties and policies with the United States, of course, within the framework of our sovereign national government.

Commonwealth Supporters:

Realizing that the autonomous powers and functions of the colonial Commonwealth have been superseded by the undemocratic and unelected U.S.-imposed Fiscal Control Board (La Junta), the option of Free Association would offer the Commonwealth party supporters (the *Populares* of the Partido Popular Democrático) a decolonization process where Puerto Rico would gain actual power and sovereignty over its own affairs, yet be able to maintain political and economic links with the United States that many

Populares desire. In the 2012 plebiscite, much of the support for the Free Association option came from the very ranks of the Commonwealth party. For many Commonwealth party supporters, Free Association would be welcomed and considered the culmination of the autonomy movement. In fact, in a Republic of Puerto Rico in free association with the United States, the *Populares* could remain or regroup as a new center-left liberal and progressive party in Puerto Rico that would also promote and defend Puerto Rico's ties with the United States.

Independence & Sovereignty Supporters:

Although most pro-independence supporters desire full outright independence from the United States, Free Association (as their second preferred option) would allow them to finally achieve Puerto Rican sovereignty and establish the Republic of Puerto Rico, but under a Treaty of Free Association with the United States. Pro-independence supporters will not get their desired full independence, but they would achieve the Republic, a goal that has been desired by all Puerto Rican patriots since the 1800s.

Within the pro-sovereignty political spectrum, there are those that prefer independence, those that prefer free association, and those that would prefer any of those sovereignty options. In a Republic of Puerto Rico in free association with the United States, the pro-independence and pro-sovereignty organizations could regroup as a new liberal, social democratic, and progressive party or electoral alliance in Puerto Rico that would also defend Puerto Rico's ties with the United States and other nations, particularly nations in Latin America and the Caribbean region.

With Free Association, all Puerto Rican political groups can come together at the negotiating table, secure their most important interests, build a consensus, and leave the table with a victory.

All of them would lose their main zero-sum *demands* (statehood, commonwealth, and full independence), yet all would be able to secure their *interests* (strong political and economic links and a strategic partnership with the United States and Puerto Rican sovereignty) within the comprehensive structures and possibilities of a Treaty of Free Association.

Although Commonwealth was historically touted as *"the best of both worlds"*, Free Association would be *"the best of all worlds"* since it would secure Puerto Rico's important ties with the United States, yet allowing Puerto Rico to become a sovereign nation integrated into the world economy and international politics, thus opening up many opportunities for Puerto Rican entrepreneurs, workers, students, universities, and companies.

All in all, Free Association would help create a powerful consensus between Puerto Rico's political organizations and promote our eventual decolonization and freedom. With sovereignty, Puerto Rico would finally be able to establish a functioning democratic government; be accountable to its own people; ratify its own national constitution; establish and implement various modern economic development policies and projects; and create the prosperous, international, and stable Puerto Rico that we all want and need in order to move forward as a free and democratic nation.

How will a Treaty of Free Association between Puerto Rico and the U.S. be negotiated?

When the people of Puerto Rico opt for the Free Association option, pro-sovereignty groups propose a national dialogue through a Constituent or Peoples' Assembly, duly legislated by the Legislature of Puerto Rico. If the Legislature of Puerto Rico is unable or unwilling to bring forth such an assembly, the people of Puerto Rico can assemble among themselves and establish their own Constituent Assembly.

The purpose of this assembly will be to draft and adopt the Treaty Proposal, which will emerge after an extensive process of public hearings. Drafts of such a treaty proposal already exist. Then, a group of delegates, elected by and from among the delegates of Puerto Rico, will negotiate with representatives of Congress and the President of the United States, in order to agree on the specific terms and policies of the Treaty of Free Association that will govern the political relationship between the two partner countries.

The treaty will enter into force only if approved by Congress and the President of the United States and, by Puerto Rico, if it receives a majority vote of the people in a plebiscite. At the very moment that representatives of the U.S. government sit down to negotiate the elements of, the process, and the terms of the agreement with the representatives of the people of Puerto Rico, Puerto Rico's sovereignty will have been recognized by the United States.

What kind of territory is Puerto Rico?

The United States does not use the term "*colony*" to refer to its territorial possessions. They are merely and euphemistically called *territories*. The U.S. Supreme Court determined that there are two types of territories: the *incorporated* and the *unincorporated*. The incorporated territories are those that Congress has determined that, after a period of transition, will become states. The unincorporated territories will continue as "territories" indefinitely until the U.S. Congress decides to dispose of them (or decolonize). Most Puerto Ricans and the international community routinely classify and consider Puerto Rico a "U.S. colony."

According to the U.S. Supreme Court, Puerto Rico is an unincorporated territory that is under the Territorial Clause of the U.S. Constitution. As such, the U.S. Congress has the power to legislate for Puerto Rico and determine which articles of the Constitution of the United States will apply to it or not. Being held under colonial rule is demeaning, humiliating, and wrong, for both Puerto Rico and the United States.

What are the economic advantages of Sovereignty and Free Association?

The biggest economic advantage for Puerto Rico would be that its economic development strategies and projects would be under the direct control of Puerto Rico and respond to the interests of Puerto Rico, our country, not under the laws or guidelines of the United States. As a sovereign nation in free association with the United States, the new democratic Republic of Puerto Rico:

1.1. Would participate in **international economic institutions**, such as the World Economic Organization;
2. Have **control of customs and the laws regulating airports**, ports, and international borders;
3. Would have **access to the U.S. market** and American companies would continue to have access to the Puerto Rican market;
4. Would **establish trade agreements with the U.S. and other nations** with whom it is in our interests to negotiate with. These trade and investment agreements would be international negotiation processes very similar to those that the U.S. has participated in, such as the Free Trade Agreement between Canada and Mexico (NAFTA) and the Trade Agreement with Central America (CAFTA);
5. Would continue to **use the U.S. dollar as its official currency**.
6. Along with developing trading and economic relationship with other nations, Puerto Rico could also enact **entrance**

and exit fees that would generate billions in revenue for the national government of Puerto Rico.

Under Free Association, how would the federal financial assistance that Puerto Rico currently receives be affected?

Currently, two of every three federal dollars received by Puerto Ricans are acquired rights, which are funds that Puerto Ricans contributed to (Social Security and retirement schemes) or earned via federal or military service (Veterans benefits, etc.). Essentially, most federal "aid" is not free money, but earned contributions and benefits that Puerto Ricans paid into.

Under Free Association, Puerto Ricans would continue to receive federal funds under Social Security, Medicare and Medicaid, veterans' benefits, unemployment benefits, and any other benefits because of work or service, in addition to any national social security system established by the government of the Republic of Puerto Rico.

In addition to receiving the mandatory funds mentioned above, the Republic of Puerto Rico could negotiate to receive discretionary funds from various federal programs like FEMA, Pell Grants, and funds for infrastructure, to name a few, if it were in Puerto Rico's interests to do so. Just like the United States supported the reconstruction of Germany and Japan after World War II, with a Treaty of Free Association with Puerto Rico, the United States should also support the reconstruction and development of the Puerto Rican economy because a poor Puerto Rico is a dangerous and unstable Puerto Rico and such an unstable and poor country cannot properly be a strong ally and strategic partner of the United States.

A strong and economically prosperous Puerto Rico would be a strong ally and can support U.S. regional economic development initiatives in the Caribbean and Latin America.

As a sovereign Republic of Puerto Rico, would U.S. companies be willing to invest in Puerto Rico?

International companies, including American ones, invest overseas looking for markets, safety, and low risk. As a sovereign nation in a free association relationship with the United States, Puerto Rico would be able to offer such investors the markets, the safety, and the low risk they are looking for, not to mention excellent physical infrastructure, world-class and professional human capital, and a pro-business and economic development infrastructure and platforms to promote economic growth and long-term development. American companies operate in most countries worldwide, including Brazil, Mexico, Spain, Argentina, the Dominican Republic, and Canada, among others.

The Republic of Puerto Rico will work to attract and procure not just American investment, but foreign investment, opportunities, and companies from around the world. These new economic opportunities, due in large part to gaining sovereignty, will help Puerto Rico create jobs, energize and increase its workforce, sell its products abroad, and become an engine of economic development in the Caribbean and Latin America.

Why is sovereignty in the best interests of U.S. and Puerto Rico bondholders?

A colonial, stagnant, and poor Puerto Rico, such as today's Commonwealth, will never develop economically to be in a position to pay any portion of Puerto Rico's public debt. A hypothetical *"State of Puerto Rico"* dependent on federal and welfare funds will also not be able to develop a prosperous economy nor pay off any debt due to the lower capacity to generate revenues. Even if a large portion of the debt is declared illegal and written off, Puerto Rico would still be unable to pay off such a large debt without the tools of sovereignty and economic development to actually create a viable and prosperous economy that can pay off the debt.

In short, a colonial and poor Puerto Rico cannot payoff off the public debt. A sovereign and economically prosperous Puerto Rico could actually pay off any legal portions of debt as negotiated between Puerto Rico, the United States, and bondholders.

SECTION 2

The Ten Major Reasons Why Puerto Rico will Never become a U.S. State

Below are the **10 major reasons**, organized in three categories, why the United States will *never* grant Statehood to Puerto Rico. The three categories are:

Nationality, Language & Culture
Economics & Dependency
Domestic & International Politics

The following ten major reasons why statehood would be very detrimental for Puerto Rico and the United States are detailed below.

Nationality, Language & Cultural Reasons

1. *Puerto Ricans have their own National Identity*

Puerto Ricans are a Latin American and Caribbean nation and people who are proud of their unique culture and over 500-year-old history. From the Lares Revolt against Spanish colonial rule in 1868 to the Revolution of 1950 against U.S. colonial rule, Puerto

Ricans will continue to endure and will protect their unique cultural and national identity from further colonial assimilation attempts.

Forged in the 1700s and developed in the 1800s, **Puerto Rico's National Identity** is strong, resilient, and unassimilable. Even under both Spanish and American colonial rule, Puerto Ricans continue to assert their national pride, culture, and love of Puerto Rico. In Puerto Rico, "We the People" means *"We Puerto Ricans"*. Puerto Ricans identify Puerto Rico as a nation and a distinct national society. Latin Americans identify Puerto Rico as a nation. The world identifies Puerto Ricans (historically, culturally, and linguistically) as a nation and being different than "Americans".

Puerto Rico is a nation that, due to U.S. colonial rule and the imposition of U.S. citizenship in 1917, currently lacks political sovereignty, freedom, and democracy, but it remains a nation just the same. Puerto Ricans have their own patriots, revolutionaries, founding fathers and mothers, national history and literature, national culture, philosophers, scientists, world-renowned music genres, and have contributed greatly to world civilization.

Political sovereignty does not determine nationhood; it just determines that you are free and sovereign to develop your nation and advance your national interests in the world. A colonized and enslaved nation like Puerto Rico is not allowed to advance its national interests. Does a human stop being a human just because he or she is enslaved? Of course not.

Colonialism is slavery among nations. The Irish nation existed even under British rule. The Polish nation existed even under German, Austrian, and Russian rule. Did British rule make the Irish into English? Of course not. Did Russian rule turn Poles into Russians? Of course not. The French nation existed even under German rule.

The only ones that constantly deny that Puerto Rico is a nation are the few colonized loyalist Puerto Ricans, the U.S. media, and many American politicians that prefer to call the colony of Puerto Rico a "territory" because they cannot fathom nor accept the fact that the U.S. has colonies. The very nation that celebrates its freedom from colonial rule on the 4th of July with parades and fireworks, maintains and occupies five colonies[4] around the world, Puerto Rico being the oldest, largest, and most populous.

These American politicians, both Democrats and Republicans, are in denial of history and prefer to stick their heads in the sand and ignore the calls for decolonization coming from Puerto Rico, the Puerto Rican diaspora, and the United Nations itself who has called on the United States to free Puerto Rico for over thirty years.

For over thirty years, the United Nation's Committee on Decolonization has consistently passed resolutions calling for the self-determination and independence of Puerto Rico, yet these resolutions are just ignored by the United States and the U.S. media.

Although the "Puerto Rican National Identity" goes against the narratives of the pro-statehood party in Puerto Rico and various members of Congress, Puerto Ricans have and will maintain their own proud **National Identity** and are a Latin American and Caribbean people that have more in common culturally, linguistically and historically with Dominicans, Cubans, Mexicans, Venezuelans, Colombians, and Spaniards than with English-speaking "Americans". No amount of statehooder lobbying and dark money can change that.

It's about time to let Puerto Rico go.

2. *Spanish is Puerto Rico's National Language*

Due to over 400 years of Spanish colonial rule, from which Puerto Rico's National Identity developed, **Spanish is undeniably the national language of Puerto Rico and Puerto Ricans**. English has always been considered an *"imposed language"* only spoken by federal officials and authorities in Puerto Rico. Although statehooders would have you believe that all Puerto Ricans are fully bilingual in English and Spanish, that is not the case. The vast majority of Puerto Ricans in Puerto Rico speak only Spanish in their daily lives.

Although learning English is promoted and mandatory in school, the vast majority of Puerto Ricans do not need to use English when communicating with friends, family, their community, and local and Puerto Rico government. In Puerto Rico, English is mockingly called "*la difícil*", the difficult one. When you visit Puerto Rico, Spanish is everywhere and spoken by farmers, workers, families, professionals, academics, and those in public service. Spanish is not a relegated and unvalued minority language; it is the beloved and cherished national vernacular language of the majority.

Although both Spanish and English are official languages of the colonial Commonwealth government, the fact is that Spanish is the primary language of daily life and government in Puerto Rico. English is only an "official language" of Puerto Rico due to the presence of the U.S. colonial regime and to placate federal officials and other Americans when they visit Puerto Rico.

God forbid that Americans go to an American colonial territory, and there is no English signage. Even today, many Americans are dumbstruck that after 121 years of U.S. colonial rule and thwarted assimilation policies, Puerto Ricans continue to speak their cherished Spanish language on a daily basis. Puerto Rican government agencies operate in Spanish, not English. The Puerto Rico court system operates in Spanish, not English.

If a Puerto Rican started to speak only in English in any Puerto Rican government agency, he/she would be ridiculed and mocked by professional colleagues and others. The educational system operates in Spanish, not English. **Having resisted and defeated various colonial English-Only and assimilation policies throughout the decades of U.S. colonial rule**, Puerto Ricans are very adamant about not wanting to assimilate into the American

English-speaking mainstream. English as a unifying language may work in the United States, but it does not work in Puerto Rico. It's about time to let Puerto Rico go.

3. Puerto Ricans Have Resisted American Assimilation Efforts

Puerto Ricans love and cherish their national identity and culture so much that they even maintain it when they move to and reside in the United States. **In Puerto Rico, efforts at "Americanization" were met with fierce resistance, protest, and outright disgust.** Although such "Americanization" was historically supported by pro-statehood and pro-colonialist politicians (who were looking to position themselves as "good and obedient colonial subjects" for the U.S. colonial regime), the vast majority of Puerto Ricans have resisted and will resist such heavy-handed and harsh English language and American cultural policies.

Here are the six main examples of how Puerto Ricans have resisted assimilation and "Americanization":

Resisted the Outlawing of the Puerto Rican Flag & National Symbols:

Even as the U.S. colonial regime outlawed the Puerto Rican flag and national anthem, Puerto Ricans continued to fly the National Flag and sing *"La Borinqueña"*, despite mass arrests, massacres, death squads, violent statehooder mobs (turbas), and persecutions. For many decades under U.S. colonial rule, the only flag that was allowed in Puerto Rico was the U.S. flag.

The Puerto Rican flag was outlawed, and those caught with Puerto Rican flags (even in their homes) were arrested and sentenced to ten years in prison, particularly under the Gag Law (1948-1957). Colonial repression and persecution by local police and federal agencies of pro-sovereignty and independence groups and supporters led to the **criminalization of the sovereignty movement**. U.S. colonial police even committed massacres in Rio Piedras and Ponce in order to quell the rising tide of Puerto Rican nationalism of the 1930s.

Fear regarding sovereignty and being identified as a *"separatist"* still pervades Puerto Rico's political culture and landscape. Although the Gag Law and other such repressive policies have since been repealed since 1957, there are still many people in Puerto Rico that fear hoisting a Puerto Rican flag on their homes because they do not want their neighbors to claim that they are *"separatists"* and report them to the colonial police which would compile dossiers (carpetas) on anyone suspected of desiring Puerto Rico's freedom. Such outright persecution occurred up to the 1980s.

After 121 years of such repression and criminalization, it's amazing that a large, vibrant, and resilient pro-sovereignty and democracy movement still exists in Puerto Rico. This criminalization and persecution of the pro-sovereignty and independence movements ultimately benefited and enriched the growth of the pro-colonialist and pro-statehood movements in Puerto Rico. Let it be clear, the statehooder and colonialist movements in Puerto Rico grew on fertile ground watered by fear, terror, and the blood of Puerto Rican patriots that were murdered and jailed.

Remember, people are willing to die and sacrifice for freedom; no one ever died or suffered for statehood. No one. The pro-statehood movement is only prominent in Puerto Rico's political landscape not because of its compelling arguments, but because it is standing tall atop the bodies of thousands of dead Puerto Rican patriots.

The pro-colonialist and pro-statehood parties always like to mention that today, sovereignty and independence supporters are a minority at the polls…funny how they never mention the terror, persecution, and criminalization that allowed that to happen.

Why not a plebiscite in 1937 or 1943? Why did the U.S. colonial regime wait until 1967 to allow the first status plebiscite? Well, they needed decades to crush, ban, censure, instill fear, and criminalize the pro-sovereignty movement to the point of becoming an electoral minority. It takes time and resources to terrorize people into colonial fear and submission.

According to the American Civil Liberties Union in a 1939 publication regarding civil liberties in Puerto Rico and other American colonies,

"American prestige in Puerto Rico is now at its lowest. The policies of the present administration have given weight to all the accusations of "Yankee imperialism" that have been made against the United States. Thus, instead of crushing the independence movement, these policies have fanned the flames of hatred and suspicion and intensified the desire to be free of American domination. All over Latin America, Puerto Rico is held up as an example of colonial misrule so obvious as to challenge the good faith of the "good neighbor" policy, while in Puerto Rico itself, disillusionment with American professions of liberty and democracy has grown apace.[5]*"*

As in 1939, today, Puerto Rico and its corrupt and inept colonial government are held up in Latin America and the world as an example of colonial misrule and administration. This urge to resist colonial rule and defend Puerto Rico from the brutal absurdities of colonialism and fear are as alive today as they were for our forefathers and ancestors.

Once Puerto Ricans were sufficiently terrorized about supporting independence and having the pro-independence leadership jailed and tortured, *then* status plebiscites were allowed to occur because the U.S. colonial regime needed to legitimize the newly founded colonial farce called "Commonwealth" in 1952.

Yet, even with all this repression and colonial terror, patriotic Puerto Ricans in Puerto Rico and in the diaspora refused to stop fighting for their freedom and liberty as a free nation.

U.S. Colonial Police confiscating illegal Puerto Rican Flags from the homes of Puerto Rican nationalists and other pro-sovereignty and independence supporters. During the Era of the **Gag Law of 1948** (Ley de la Mordaza), possession of a Puerto Rican flag in Puerto Rico would entail a 10-year prison sentence. These photos are essentially a window to the "democracy" enjoyed by Puerto Ricans under U.S. colonial rule.

Failed American Attempts to Replace & Change National Symbols:

When it comes to denationalizing an occupied nation, the U.S. colonial regime does not hold back…it goes after flags, anthems, symbols, everything. The U.S. colonial regime even tried to **replace Puerto Rico's Coat-of-Arms** with a new U.S.-inspired Coat-of-Arms that was protested, resisted, and called *"el escudo intruso"* (the Intruder's Seal).

After fierce protests from various segments of society, the *"escudo intruso"* was only "official" from 1902 to 1905, when the original Puerto Rican Coat-of-Arms was reestablished. These attempts at imposing American-inspired symbols on the peoples of the colonies were successful in other colonial territories like the U.S. Virgin Islands and others, but utterly failed in Puerto Rico.

Literally speaking, Puerto Ricans took such American colonial symbols and stuffed it into the trash bin of history.

Puerto Rico's Official Coat-of-Arms

The *"Escudo Intruso"* (1902-1905) imposed by the U.S. colonial regime, later rescinded after massive protests by Puerto Ricans.

Imposed English & Assimilation Policies:

Early on under the U.S. colonial regime, the U.S. mandated that English be the only official language of government and enacted assimilation policies that would replace Spanish with English as the language of education. For white American colonialists and supremacists, Spanish was a worthless inferior language that needed to be quickly replaced by American English.

The U.S. colonial regime even went as far as to import white American teachers from New England to educate Puerto Ricans (which were viewed as tropical brown savages) in the English language and "American values".

Puerto Rican children were forced to sing the U.S. National Anthem in schools, even though they had no idea what they were saying in a foreign language. Imagine American children being forced to sing the Chinese National Anthem. According to an American Civil Liberties Union publication titled *Civil Liberties in American Colonies,*

> *"The use of English is justly regarded by Puerto Ricans as an arrogant attempt to uproot their own cultural traditions. Over-zealous Anglicizers have even attempted to teach the Spanish classics in the English language! The compulsory use of English is among the American policies which serves to intensify anti-American feeling and to heighten the desire of Puerto Ricans for political independence.*[6]*"*

Some Puerto Rican children were even shipped off to the Carlisle Indian School in Pennsylvania in order to beat their Puerto Rican identity and culture out of them[7]. After years of cultural repression, suffering, and forced assimilation, the hope was for these children to return to Puerto Rico and serve as agents of Americanization and assimilation policies. Sadly, many of these children were never heard from again or returned to Puerto Rico with severe psychological issues.

Imagine American children being shipped off to Hunan Province to attend Chinese assimilation schools where they would be educated in Mandarin Chinese and taught to think of themselves as "Chinese North Americans". These assimilated "American-Chinese" would then return to the occupied United States to administer the Chinese colonial regime and impose its political, economic, and cultural policies. Puerto Ricans had to suffer and survive this hell under the U.S. colonial regime.

Since the very moment American troops entered Puerto Rico guns blazing, racist American officials and soldiers viewed Puerto Ricans as uneducated brown mixed-race savages and subhuman mongrels that needed to learn about "American civilization" and the English language for their own good. This racist perception of being "subhuman" is very similar to how many federal agents in the U.S. border patrol today view immigrants, particularly brown Spanish-speaking immigrants.

This "American Civilization for the Natives" philosophy was influenced by *The White Man's Burden* and became an official American colonial policy in Puerto Rico. Like Native Americans and Mexicans from California to Texas, Puerto Ricans needed to let go of their inferior subhuman culture and Spanish language and adopt superior American cultural values and the English language. This is the essence of colonial rule and assimilation.

These American officials viewed Puerto Ricans as uncultured catholic barbarians that were "yearning for the blessings of American civilization and assimilation" even though Puerto Rican history and civilization predates "American civilization" by centuries. Such racist and white supremacist notions are prevalent today and are the foundation of the U.S. colonial regime and the main pillars of the colonial mentality that still exists today and pervade the U.S.-Puerto Rico colonial relationship. The colonial mentality will be discussed later.

These assimilation efforts were, of course, met with fierce protest and resistance by Puerto Ricans, which included school strikes, overt protests, ignoring these assimilation policies, and students dropping out of such schools *en masse* and being educated at home or via other channels in Spanish.

In the end, facing such overwhelming protest, disgust, and resistance to assimilation and "Americanization", the U.S. colonial regime dropped the most aggressive assimilation policies and settled for having English being a mandatory subject and having English as co-official with Spanish as languages of government.

The Imposition of U.S. Holidays:

The U.S. colonial regime has imposed all U.S. federal holidays on Puerto Rico, even July 4th Independence Day. The irony of celebrating American independence and the struggle against British colonial rule in a U.S. colony where those that struggle for Puerto

Rican independence are jailed, persecuted, and criminalized is quite astonishing and totally awkward. It would be like a slave master who was a former slave celebrating the day he became free in the house of his own slave. Yes, this happens in Puerto Rico.

Puerto Rican colonial loyalists persecute pro-independence Puerto Ricans, then turn around and celebrate American independence, and the struggle against British colonialism...many of them do this in order to look "patriotic" and loyal in front of their colonial masters. In Puerto Rico, political hypocrisy is layered thick and deep. Puerto Rican holidays are relegated as optional second-tier holidays while federal holidays are never touched by the colonial government.

For example, unlike free nations, there are no official holidays in Puerto Rico celebrating Puerto Rico's attempts at freedom...yet there are holidays celebrating dead American presidents, pilgrims, and other American figures, but of course, no Puerto Ricans. For the exception of some political statehooder and veterans' groups, no one actually celebrates American Independence Day in Puerto Rico as they do in the U.S. with reverence and patriotism.

The colonial government holds an official July 4th event every year, but nobody in Puerto Rico really pays attention to it. In Puerto Rico, the 4th of July and Memorial Day are considered beach days, nothing more. Also, Thanksgiving, another imposed federal holiday that has nothing to do with Puerto Rican history at all, is laughingly and mockingly called *"Zangüivin"* (pronounced SAN-GWUI-VIN) in Puerto Rico by most families.

Imposed Americanization of Place Names & Roads:

The U.S. colonial regime, particularly the military branches and military personnel, began to acquire and expropriate large tracts of land and began to change place names, particularly of roads and major avenues. The town of San Idelfonso on Culebra was unilaterally renamed "*Dewey*" on maps, yet even today, nobody calls Culebra "*Dewey*". A major avenue in San Juan is called F.D. Roosevelt[8] Avenue, among many others with American names that people cannot even pronounce (for example, *la rusvel*).

In San Juan, there's a street called *Calle Brumbaugh* (pronounced *brumbo*), which was named after Martin G. Brumbaugh, the American secretary of colonial education appointed after the U.S. occupied Puerto Rico. Mr. Brumbaugh (who later served as Governor of Pennsylvania) sought to Americanize the Puerto Rican educational system by imposing English, firing Puerto Rican and Spanish educators, and rewriting history books to praise the invading Americans. Even today, this humiliating colonial street name reminds Puerto Ricans of the barbaric monster that sought to destroy Puerto Rican education and imposed the English language on all students.

To illustrate the Americanization of our urban geography, this time by colonial lackeys, on the south side of Puerto Rico's capitol building, there are life-size statues of all the U.S. presidents (from Roosevelt to Obama) who have ever set foot in Puerto Rico...yes, statues, all paid for with misused public funds.

These statues at the *Paseo de los Presidentes* were installed by statehooder and colonialist administrations in a sad and trivial attempt to show Americans how pro-U.S.A. and patriotic Puerto Ricans supposedly are for 'Merica. At this spectacle of colonial submission and groveling, brave Puerto Ricans who are disgusted by these statutes have defaced and painted these statues of the foreign leaders that ruled Puerto Rico from afar as a colony.

The defacing of these statues is comparable to the defacing and painting of Red Army and Soviet statues of Stalin and Lenin in ex-Soviet and other East European nations. There are many Puerto Ricans that yearn for the day these statues can be removed, smelted, and replaced with statues of Puerto Rican patriots, heroes, heroines, and other great national leaders.

If that wasn't enough, the U.S. Congress even went as far as to change Puerto Rico's name to "*Porto Rico*" to make it more palatable and anglicized for American ears. Eventually, after years of protests and resistance, the U.S. Congress and the U.S. colonial regime relented and reestablished the name "Puerto Rico" as the official name of the colony.

Regarding Mr. Brumbaugh and his failed assimilationist and educational policies, I think it's historical justice that today there are many Puerto Rican communities in Pennsylvania, speaking Spanish and being proud to be Boricua.

The Rise & Empowerment of Assimilationists & Colonial Lackeys:

With every colonial regime, there always arise certain natives and locals that want to assimilate and be ruled from another country due to their colonial mentality, economic self-interests, and inferior self-worth. The Thirteen Colonies had the Loyalists and Tories, the French had their Vichy French collaborators in WWII, and in Puerto Rico, we have Statehooders and Colonialists, the Puerto Rican collaborators of the U.S. colonial regime.

Americans should know that in Puerto Rican political culture, we have a whole typology and categorization for those that are loyal to the U.S. colonial regime and its ever-present assimilation tendencies. If Americans think they have a complicated political culture with Democrats, Republicans, and other parties going at it, you will not begin to believe Puerto Rico's colonial political culture which is centered, not between Right versus Left, but centered on Puerto Rico's status options.

Americans should also be aware that in Puerto Rico, both the pro-statehood party and the pro-Commonwealth party support and promote the idea of "**generational party loyalty**" where voters vote not based on the quality or platform of a particular candidate, but based on the political party supported by the family, usually the father.

There is an inherent belief that if you vote for a different party or candidate not supported by your family, you are disloyal to your family or memory of a deceased father or mother. By avoiding critical thinking, these parties promote this idea because it assures them of guaranteed electoral support, the so-called "party base" of loyal fanatical voters.

For example, there are many voters in Puerto Rico who vote for the Statehood or Commonwealth parties (and their corrupt candidates), not because they believe in that status option, but because they believe it would please and bring happiness to their deceased party loyalist parents smiling down from heaven into the voting booth. They believe that if they vote contrary to what their deceased father would have voted, their deceased loved one would be sad, ashamed, and disappointed in heaven. After realizing this, now one begins to see why the two traditional parties, particularly the statehood party, develop relationships with various fundamentalist Christian churches.

This notion of "generational party loyalty" is a symptom of a colonial and uneducated electorate and needs to end because one cannot base current political ideas and the future of the country on the supposed political opinions of deceased people in order to benefit political organizations. Such notions can be eradicated via more civic and electoral education, the development of more critical thinking skills, and the depoliticization of the ballot (where only candidates are listed, not political parties nor political logos), among other ideas.

All Americans, whether Democrat or Republican, cherish their independence and freedom as a nation, and would never put up with the antics of the colonial assimilationists. Imagine, for a moment, that a new political party appeared in the United States called the "*British American Unionist Party*" that sought to bring the United States back under British colonial rule by votes, violence and the outright persecution of Democrats and Republicans. If such an American political party emerged, it would be declared illegal and its supporters and leaders ostracized and arrested for treason.

Puerto Ricans have fought and struggled against these empowered assimilationists and their policies since the advent of U.S. colonial rule in 1898. Let's be clear from the outset: colonialist assimilationists in Puerto Rico are mere tools, a means to an end, which are used to entrench and legitimize the U.S. colonial regime. The day the U.S. has no need of these individuals, it will just throw them in the dustbin of history.

Due to the impact that these statehooders and colonialists have had in Puerto Rican politics, Puerto Ricans have coined very creative terms for such individuals. Of course, although the statehooders and colonialists would never tell Americans about these political terms and categorizations related to such assimilationists, here they are for educational purposes:

a. Colonialist (*colonialista*): one who supports the current colonial regime under the name "Commonwealth" (Estado Libre Asociado), accepts Puerto Rico's inferior and subordinate colonial status, yet does not support full statehood since even most colonialists wish to safeguard and protect Puerto Rican culture and the Spanish language.

Such colonialists, although they reject full cultural assimilation, are content with and promote Puerto Rico's colonial and political subordination as a U.S. colony, but prefer to use more euphemistic terms like *territory* or *commonwealth* in order not to offend federal officials and other Americans with the term "*colony*".

Unlike the British, French, Spanish, Portuguese, and Belgians who were upfront about having colonies, the United States seems to want to rule over colonies like Puerto Rico without having to call them "*colonies*" (the C-word) since admitting that the United States has colonies would place the United States and American politicians in an awkward position of trying to defend the indefensible concept of colonialism, especially for a country that fought a war for independence against British colonialism.

Others have colonies, but the U.S. has "*territories*". In Puerto Rico, the colonialists (also called *autonomistas*) are primarily represented by the conservative Commonwealth faction within the Popular Democratic Party.

b. Statehooder (*estadista*): one who supports the annexation of Puerto Rico into the United States as a state of the union. Although statehooders say they support and are proud of their Puerto Rican culture and the Spanish language, they wish to become essentially a cultural and ethnic minority in an English-speaking country instead of being their own masters in their own country. Who in their right mind would willingly want to become an ethnic minority in another country by having their country annexed?

Americans, are these the kind of people you want as "*your fellow citizens*"? Statehooders claim that statehood is a civil rights issue and that as American citizens, Puerto Ricans deserve the same equality afforded to other American citizens, but what they really desire is equality in federal funds and transfers and the ability to influence federal elections while remaining Puerto Ricans.

Today, statehooders are represented by the New Progressive Party, which is also called the Statehood Party. In fact, the New "Progressive" Party was initially a splinter group from the *Partido Estadista Republicano* (Republican Statehood Party). Be forewarned liberals; although the statehood party uses the term "progressive" in its name, it is the farthest thing from progressive since it is made up primarily by fundamentalist Christian extremists, assimilationist loyalists, generational welfare recipients, and rich and corrupt politicians. More on this issue later.

c. **Cipayo** (pronounced SEE-*PA*-YO): one who supports the colonial government and the assimilation policies of another country in your country, yet a cipayo may be a colonialist, but is usually a statehooder. Cipayos can also be called *"lacayos"* which means roughly "colonial lackey", the Puerto Rican "yes-men" for the U.S. colonial regime.

Cipayos are present in both colonial parties and are virulently pro-colonial regime and staunch economic opportunists that believe that their loyalty should be compensated by the colonial political parties via contracts and corruption. While the cipayos support such colonial policies and statehood for economic self-interest, they do know and realize that they are Puerto Ricans and only pretend to be "Americans" when convenient and when they are speaking to Americans.

The cipayos are important to the U.S. government because these are the *loyal natives* that can be bought and paid for and help legitimize and administer the colonial regime that subordinates Puerto Rico. The pitiyankis (coming up next), on the other hand actually *believe* that they are "Americans of Puerto Rican descent". If offered the right amount of money, a cipayo will say that they are *any* nationality and support *any* ideology, as long as they are paid.

If France occupies Puerto Rico, these cipayos would be the first to meet with the new French colonial authorities and pledge their allegiance to France, of course, if the money is right. One may say that they are *political prostitutes* who will sell their loyalty to the highest bidder. My apologies to actual prostitutes if my comparing them to cipayos offended anyone.

d. **Pitiyankis** (from the French *petit yankee*: small and/or fake yankee): considered the highest form of cipayo and colonialist loyalist, a pitiyanki is a Puerto Rican who is so colonized and indoctrinated with the colonial mentality, wishes to assimilate to the extreme, and believes that he/she is an American, yet, according to Puerto Ricans, a pitiyanki will never be a real Yankee (a real American).

Laughingly, it would be like a Puerto Rican named José Pérez *believe* himself to be Chinese just to politically placate Chinese officials in a Chinese-occupied Puerto Rico. These statehooders will say *anything* to placate current and new occupiers. The term *pitiyanki* is believed to have been coined by Luis Llorens Torres, one of Puerto Rico's preeminent poets, after overhearing a conversation between an American and a confused assimilated Puerto Rican who thought he was "American", thus a *petit yankee*.

In Puerto Rican political culture, a pitiyanki is the image of an assimilated Puerto Rican dressed in an Uncle Sam outfit that denies his/her own culture and national identity, is embarrassed about his/her family and culture, tries to only speak English (usually broken and unintelligible), believes that their nation is the U.S.A. and not Puerto Rico, and tries to have an air of superiority when in view of another Puerto Rican.

Pitiyankis are known to equate the *love* of Puerto Rico with the *love* of eating Puerto Rican foods like mofongo, pasteles, alcapurrias, etc. Pitiyankis dislike being called out as "pitiyankis" and think of themselves as "Puerto Rican-Americans" because they eat Puerto Rican food and value their U.S. citizenship. I have seen pitiyankis question other peoples' loyalties to Puerto Rico, a person's Puerto Rican identity, and support for sovereignty, based on whether they eat mofongo or other Puerto Rican foods. Yes, this ridiculousness actually happens.

For a pitiyanki, Puerto Rico is not a nation, but a "territory where American citizens reside". Pitiyankis are experts in *denationalizing* Puerto Rico in order to make it seem to Americans that Puerto Rico is just an island, a rock in the Caribbean where American citizens live, thus negating the fact that we are Puerto Ricans and have our own distinct National Identity.

In Puerto Rico, both cipayos and pitiyankis are considered *traitors*, yet those who are considered pitiyankis today are thought of as clowns, sellouts (*vendepatrias*), corrupt, and are not taken seriously and are not representative of the Puerto Rican people.

Puerto Rico's political class is made up primarily of such corrupt cipayos and pitiyankis because these are the only groups that are loyal to the U.S. colonial regime and allowed to help administer the colony. In an actual democratic, participatory, and fiscally responsible sovereign government, these sellouts would definitely have no place in the new Puerto Rico.

Also, if the U.S. colonial regime establishment feels that Puerto Ricans are getting too patriotic, uppity, and restless with colonial rule, the colonial regime calls on the "*turbas*" to act. The "turbas" are violent and thuggish pro-statehooder and pro-U.S. colonial regime mobs that assemble to terrorize the Puerto Rican people with fear and violence back into submission.

In the past, the turba street thugs would burn down buildings, attack newspapers, and beat people who did not support U.S. colonial rule, but today's turbas will break windows, threaten people with violence, pull down Puerto Rican flags, and hoist American flags on private and public property, all while being protected by the police.

The turbas march through the streets with American flags and have historically operated with impunity since their mission is to terrorize and pressure Puerto Ricans into being subordinate to the U.S. colonial regime. The turbas are usually led and manned by the most ultra-loyalist pitiyankis in the ranks of the statehood party.

Americans, are these statehooders the kinds of people you want having a say on your democracy? The Thirteen Colonies had many Benedict Arnolds, but Puerto Ricans have these retrograde and violent assimilationist pitiyankis and cipayos to deal with, who are denying our right to exist as a free nation.

These are just a few examples of the assimilationists and the assimilation policies that were imposed on Puerto Rico and the complex political culture that has been shaped by such colonial rule. Believe me, a lot of assimilationist pro-statehood supporters are going to be very angry that I am telling Americans and others about the inner workings of Puerto Rico's colonial political culture and landscape. In essence, I'm showing the world Puerto Rico's colonial dirty laundry.

For informational purposes, below is a chart summarizing important current political terms in order to better understand and appreciate Puerto Rico's political culture and colonial party system:

Terms	Definition
Colonialista	One who supports U.S. colonial rule and the territorial Commonwealth government.
Autonomista	One who supports the territorial Commonwealth government, yet would also support more autonomy and freedoms, but within the U.S. Territorial Clause.
Estadista (Statehooder)	One who supports the annexation of Puerto Rico into the United States as a state of the union. In modern Puerto Rico, a statehooder usually supports the pro-statehood New Progressive Party.

Terms	Definition
Cipayo (Colonial Lackey)	One who supports the colonial government and the assimilation policies of the United States in Puerto Rico. As the Puerto Rican "yes-men" for the U.S. colonial regime, cipayos are present in both colonial parties and are virulently pro-colonial regime and staunch economic opportunists. Cipayos realize that they are Puerto Ricans yet pretend to be "Americans" when the need arises or convenient.
Pitiyanki (Fake/ Small Yankee)	One who not only supports the colonial government and the assimilation policies of the United States in Puerto Rico, but also believes that they are "Americans" and the United States is their country. Pitiyankis are ridiculed colonial loyalists who do not believe that Puerto Rico is a nation and almost exclusively support statehood.
Popular	One who supports the pro-Commonwealth Popular Democratic Party. This party is currently divided into a conservative Autonomista faction and a liberal pro-sovereignty faction supporting Free Association.

Terms	Definition
Independentista (*pro-Independence supporter*)	One who supports the sovereignty and independence of Puerto Rico from both Spain and the United States. Although many independentistas support the Puerto Rican Independence Party, many also boycott colonial elections and support other pro-independence organizations such as MINH or the Nationalist Party.
Soberanista (*pro-Sovereignty supporter*)	One who supports the sovereignty of Puerto Rico from the United States via free association or independence. Although many soberanistas support the Popular Democratic Party's pro-sovereignty faction and leaders, many also support other pro-sovereignty organizations such as CONABO, MAP, Alianza Patria, MUS, and others.
	As of the Puerto Rican status referendum of 2012, free association is the option with the largest growth margin among all other status options, experiencing a hundredfold (4,536 to 454,768) expansion in only 14 years[9].

Terms	Definition
Reunificacionista (*Reunificationist*)	One who supports the reunification of Puerto Rico with Spain so that Puerto Rico would attain the status of a Spanish Autonomous Community. This new political movement has various organizations, such as Adelante and MRE, but has yet to create a political party or be represented in any status plebiscites. Most Reunificationists are virulently against any sort of American cultural assimilation and believe that as a Spanish province, Puerto Rico would be better able to protect its Spanish language and culture and develop an economy linked to the European Union.
Nacionalista (*Nationalist*)	One who supports the sovereignty and total independence of Puerto Rico from the United States and supports the Puerto Rican Nationalist Party. The Nationalist Party does not participate in colonial elections and has a long history of struggle and resistance dating back to the 1930s.

In the United States, Puerto Ricans continue to consider themselves Puerto Ricans (Boricuas) and not some kind of Spanish-surnamed American. Although many stateside Puerto Ricans are bilingual or only speak English, the majority still considers themselves Puerto Rican. It's time to let Puerto Rico go.

4. Most Puerto Rico Statehood Leaders Do Not Even Speak English

Although this may be hard for Americans to believe, **most Statehood leaders in Puerto Rico do not speak English** or speak it very badly. How could this be? How can you be taken seriously as a pro-Statehood and pro-U.S.A. movement, and your leaders not even be able to speak the language of the country you want Puerto Rico to be a part of?

Sadly, most statehood leaders and politicians (those who aspire one day to be Puerto Rico's Congressional Delegation) cannot even give a speech in English, let alone address the House of Representatives or the Senate. In Puerto Rico, these statehood politicians do not need to speak English to their Spanish-speaking electorate.

Many of these Statehood politicians and leaders do not even know the basics of U.S. history, civics, and American culture, yet are experts at how to obtain food stamps and other federal assistance and convince some Puerto Ricans that they can get more food stamps if Puerto Rico becomes a state (this is their bread and butter narrative).

Also, to the amazement of Americans, these corrupt and inept statehood leaders go by ridiculous nicknames like El Tiburón (the shark), Tata, Quiquito, JGo, and other such silly monikers. Could you imagine *El Tiburón* or a *Tata* being called to speak on the floor of Congress?

I have witnessed statehood events where pro-statehood supporters (all grown adults) had to phonetically read off the Star-Spangled Banner (*O sei kan yu si, bai de stars erli lait...*) in Spanish because they did not know it from memory nor could read it in proper English. This is a common occurrence at many statehooder events and rallies, especially when any visiting American federal official is present so that this American can take home the fantasy that "Puerto Ricans sang the Star-Spangled Banner".

Ironically, it is generally considered to be true in Puerto Rico that the pro-Sovereignty (independence and free association) leadership is overwhelmingly bilingual (and multilingual) and speaks better English than the pro-statehood leadership, which generally speaks no or little English.

In Puerto Rico, the more professional, educated, well-traveled, multilingual, historically aware, patriotic, and cosmopolitan you are, the more likely you are of being a pro-sovereignty Puerto Rican. The more uneducated, colonized, ignorant about Puerto Rico and the world, corrupt, religious fundamentalist, party loyalist, and less traveled you are in Puerto Rico, the more likely you are of being a pro-statehood and pro-colonial Puerto Rican.

There are exceptions, but in Puerto Rico, these assertions generally hold true. I can already imagine statehooders claiming that these assertions are not true, but seriously, most Puerto Ricans would agree with me on this issue.

Astonishingly, many of these American flag-waving statehood leaders do not even know how to sing the U.S. National Anthem. In fact, many of them are not even ashamed about it; it's a joke to them. For all their justifications for statehood about *"Puerto Ricans have been U.S. citizens since 1917"* and that *"Puerto Ricans have served in the U.S. Armed Forces"*, you would think these "leaders" would at least learn the U.S. National Anthem. Wrong.

If these are the best and brightest of the Puerto Rico Statehood movement, please realize that statehood for Puerto Rico will never happen.

To see Puerto Rican Statehood leaders trying to sing the U.S. National Anthem, please check out the YouTube video at www.PrexitBook.com or via the link below:

https://www.youtube.com/watch?v=FrGJNEFGXTM

After watching this video, please ask yourself:

As Americans, do you think singing the National Anthem is a funny joke, especially for people always talking about Puerto Ricans serving in the U.S. military? Well, the statehooder leadership sure thinks so.

For the two statehooders on the video who recited a few lines, did you notice they were reading it? Yes, they were reading it because they do not know it by memory.

As Americans, after watching the video, do you feel that these Puerto Rican statehooders actually love and cherish "America"? It's about time to let Puerto Rico go.

5. *Creole Statehood & Estadidad Jíbara?*

In Puerto Rico, the statehood movement obtains votes and electoral support due to the **version of statehood** that they sell and peddle out to misinformed Puerto Rican voters, mind you, voters who have been colonized for over 121 years and made to believe that freedom is evil and statehood would be a panacea of federal benefits and free money from U.S. tax payers.

Wait, versions of statehood? Isn't there only one kind of statehood? As Americans, have you ever heard anything as ludicrous as "versions of statehood"? Of course not. Does the U.S. Constitution elaborate on "different types of statehood"? No.

The version of statehood that the Statehood movement in Puerto Rico promotes to poor communities by corrupt politicians in Puerto Rico, called **Creole Statehood** (*"Estadidad Jíbara"* in Spanish), is a *Puerto Rican-centered kind of statehood* where Puerto Rico would supposedly receive **$10 billion** in more federal welfare aid and transfers (free money from U.S. tax payers as statehooders like to claim), yet would be able to maintain its national culture, Spanish language, not have to assimilate into American culture, and also have the freedom to participate in the Olympics and other international events under its own national banner. Americans, does any of this make sense to you?

When lobbying for statehood in Washington, DC, and speaking to American media outlets, the statehood movement's carefully selected narrative centers on two main appeals (which will be studied in another section) in trying to attract Americans towards supporting Puerto Rico statehood:

The Emotional-Military Appeal: "*the Puerto Ricans who have given their lives in the U.S. military in defending our freedoms*".

The Equality/Civil Rights Appeal: "*we Puerto Ricans are American citizens and want equal civil and political rights like all the other American citizens in the fifty states*".

In Puerto Rico, the statehooders primarily peddle the "Creole Statehood" narrative constantly to their supporters, although they do also mention the above appeals at speeches and publications. Americans, please try not to laugh too much at the following summary of "*Creole Statehood*". Sadly, there are many statehooders in Puerto Rico (many of them good people) who believe that the "Creole Statehood" fantasy is possible.

After reading this section on "*Creole Statehood*", you will then understand why there is no chance in hell that Puerto Rico could ever become a U.S. state. To really invalidate this "*Creole Statehood*" fantasy, American politicians need to tell the Puerto Rican people and the statehooder leadership that "*Creole Statehood*" is ridiculous, laughable, and will never be recognized by the United States or the American people.

If the United States government and the American people seriously consider admitting Puerto Rico (a Latin American and

Caribbean nation) into the union as a state, full-disclosure is required, and the following five issues and problems will have to be dealt with and considered by the U.S. government and the American people.

Summary of the 5 Major Problems with "Creole Statehood"

1. Puerto Rico Rejects American Assimilation Policies

Puerto Rico would be a U.S. state that would aim to celebrate, protect, and develop Puerto Rican culture and the Spanish language, relegating American culture, values, and traditions as second tier in that such American cultural concepts and traditions are considered "foreign" to most Puerto Ricans.

Acculturation in the United States is fine (learning to adapt to a new culture and society), but full cultural assimilation, never. Even today, American cultural concepts such as Pilgrims, Cowboys, the Frontier, the West, Paul Bunyan, the South, the Civil War, New England culture, Yankees, Rednecks, Jim Crow, white supremacy, assimilation, the Founding Fathers, the Melting Pot, race relations with African-Americans and Native Americans, are considered "foreign" and "not Puerto Rican" by the Puerto Rican people.

Even after over 121 years of U.S. colonial rule, experiencing racism and discrimination, and having to learn about these American cultural concepts in school and movies, Puerto Ricans still consider American culture and traditions to be "foreign", just like Americans consider Puerto Rican culture and traditions to be "foreign" and "not American".

Let's be real, trying to say that Puerto Ricans are Americans is like trying to say that Puerto Ricans can also be British, Chinese, Russian, Burmese, and Turkish if they were occupied by these countries.

Remember, *citizenship does not equal nationality*. Just because the U.S. Congress imposed (forced upon) U.S. citizenship in 1917 on all Puerto Ricans without their consent and against the wishes of the Puerto Rican House of Delegates at the time (just in time for the WWI draft), does not make all Puerto Ricans into *"Americans"*. An occupying foreign country can impose citizenship on you, but they cannot impose or legislate a nationality on you because your nationality comes from your ancestors and your nation's history, heritage, and culture.

For example, if China occupies the United States and passes a law in Beijing imposing (they would say "granting") Chinese citizenship on their new American subjects without their consent, would that make Americans into loyal overseas Chinese citizens yearning for equality and civil rights with all the other Chinese citizens back in China? Of course not. Consider these questions:

- As an American, how would you feel towards an American neighbor who is happy and ecstatic about colonial Chinese rule and his/her new Chinese citizenship and passport?
- As an American, how would you feel towards an American neighbor who is eager to work for Chinese law enforcement or military to hunt down remaining pro-freedom Americans (rebels) and help impose Chinese assimilation policies on other Americans?
- As an American, how would you feel towards an American neighbor if he/she started to learn Chinese Mandarin in order to accommodate himself/herself with the new Chinese colonial government?
- As an American, how would you feel if Chinese leaders began to refer to Americans, not as *"Americans"*, but as *"our fellow Chinese citizens in North America"*?

In Puerto Rico, Puerto Ricans live this colonial ridiculousness every day due to U.S. colonial rule. Again, just because Puerto

Ricans hold U.S. citizenship and must travel the world on U.S. passports by Congressional decree does not mean they are actually "Americans" or part of the "American Family", they remain Puerto Ricans, the last Latin American country under colonial rule.

The Insular Cases...*not part of, yet belongs to*...

Legally speaking, from the U.S. Supreme Court's Insular Cases (1901), Puerto Rico is *not* part of the United States; it *belongs* to the United States, like a *property*. The United States *owns* Puerto Rico like a person owns a 2-acre tract. Again, I repeat, under U.S. law, **Puerto Rico is *not* part of the United States...it is merely a Caribbean property of the federal government.**

Statehooders and colonialists in Puerto Rico do not like to acknowledge this legal fact because, understandably, it hurts their feelings and makes them feel as mere property and not part of the "American Family" they so desperately want to be a part of. It's like the house slave that desperately wishes to be part of the master's family, yet is simply just another slave, a property owned by the master.

Puerto Rico and the other colonies (euphemistically called *territories*) are considered *property*, and that is why all issues relating to Puerto Rico in the Congress are dealt with by the **Committee on Natural Resources** as if Puerto Rico were some kind of Caribbean federal nature preserve with Puerto Ricans relegated to the status of local fauna.

From an autonomous Spanish province with sovereignty to rule itself and engage in international relations with other nations in 1897 to a federal and colonial nature preserve in the Caribbean with no autonomy or democracy whatsoever ...Puerto Rico really has advanced a lot under the democratic *tutelage* of the United States.

In fact, U.S. colonial rule has delayed and castrated any political, economic, and democratic development in Puerto Rico. In

2019, Puerto Rico is still administered by a foreign colonial regime that was imposed on the country in 1901 by the Foraker Act...a law Puerto Ricans had no say in. You can imagine how bad and antiquated Puerto Rico's current colonial government is when the Puerto Ricans of 1897 had more rights, freedoms, democracy, and autonomy than the Puerto Ricans of 2019 under U.S. colonial rule.

U.S. Government actions recognizing colonial rule...

Recent U.S. Supreme Court decisions (*The People v. Sánchez-Valle/2016*), Executive branch (Presidential Task Force Reports), and Congressional actions (PROMESA) have further proved and established that Puerto Rico has no sovereignty and is nothing more than a *colonial asset property* that can be retained or disposed of due to the United States having total power and sovereignty over Puerto Rico and Puerto Ricans based on Article IV, Section III, Clause II of the U.S. Constitution, also called the Territorial Clause[10].

As a colony (now called Commonwealth since 1952), Puerto Rico's Constitution is nothing more than a *Regulation Guide on Governing the Colony of Puerto Rico*, nothing more, since any law in Congress can override anything in Puerto Rico's "constitution".

In fact, the Congress can abolish Puerto Rico's "constitution", the Commonwealth government, and override any Puerto Rico law without even asking or notifying the Puerto Rican government. Yes, this is called "colonial rule", the very colonial rule "enjoyed" by Puerto Ricans under the American flag.

The ability to sell and cede off Puerto Rico...

To further illustrate the colonial nature of the U.S.-Puerto Rico "relationship" that some politicians deny or ignore, according to two executive-level Presidential Taskforce Reports on Puerto Rico (under G.W. Bush in 2007 and B. Obama in 2011), the U.S. can **sell or cede** Puerto Rico to another country, like *property*. Just like a slave is not part of the master's family, the slave *belongs* to and can be *sold* by the master, yet the slave remains a human being.

In 2019, President Trump has even considered exchanging Puerto Rico for Greenland, because for the U.S. government and under U.S. law, Puerto Rico (and all Puerto Ricans) is a mere property that can be sold, exchanged, or traded off[11]. Puerto Rico, an enslaved, occupied, and colonized country remains a nation, no matter who is occupying it by force. I believe, like many other Puerto Ricans, that Puerto Rico should belong to no other country but to Puerto Rico.

Puerto Ricans are *not* Americans…

The U.S. Congress, although it holds absolute colonial plenary power over Puerto Rico due to the 1898 invasion and occupation (and subsequent abolition of Puerto Rico's democratic and autonomous institutions by U.S. authorities), cannot legislate Puerto Rico's culture and nationality.

Believe me, the U.S. colonial regime has tried to legislate away Puerto Rico's culture, nationality, flag, national anthem, emblem, and other national symbols, but has failed miserably. **Puerto Ricans are *not* Americans; they are Puerto Ricans.**

By saying that *Puerto Ricans are Americans*, the media and the U.S. government attempt to invisibilize and deny Puerto Rico's status as a *nation* and "*distinct society*" because to actually state that Puerto Rico is a "nation" is to confront the ugly fact that the U.S. occupies and colonizes a *nation*, and not just some *territory full of American citizens* as statehooders and the U.S. political establishment like to say.

Puerto Ricans existed before the United States, and they will continue to exist after the end of U.S. colonial rule. Yes, Puerto Ricans are U.S. citizens by congressional fiat, but they are still Puerto Ricans. In Puerto Rico, any Puerto Rican that would actively promote and urge full assimilation would be viewed as ridiculous, buffoonish, shameful, and discredited in public opinion, even by conservative Puerto Rico standards. Puerto Ricans usually mock and ridicule such assimilationists in jokes and parodies.

I doubt that Americans know or realize that in Puerto Rico:

1. The American flag is informally and mockingly called "*la pecosa*" (freckles, in reference to the fifty stars) by many Puerto Ricans,
2. American politicians (from either party) are called "*cangrimanes*"[12],
3. Americans are routinely called "*gringos*" in regular conversations,
4. Federal officials and agents are mockingly called "*federicos*",
5. The United States itself is routinely referred to as "*Gringolandia*" and Washington, DC is mockingly and purposely mispronounced as "*Guáchinton*",
6. In Puerto Rican literature and many traditional folk songs, the United States is portrayed as a foreign occupying intruder,
7. In the song *Preciosa* (considered by many as Puerto Rico's second national anthem), the *tirano* (tyrant) mentioned in the song is in reference to the United States.

Statehooders would never admit this to Americans because it refutes the statehooder narrative that Puerto Ricans are proud and loyal American citizens. Realizing and accepting this difference and "foreignness" of our cultures, one can better accept and embrace the fact that the United States and Puerto Rico are two different nations, two different set of people with their separate national histories and cultures, even after 121 years of U.S. colonial rule.

Even today, the statehood party tells Puerto Ricans that as a state, Puerto Ricans **do not *need* to assimilate into the American culture and adopt American traditions**. Americans need to understand that statehooders reject assimilation into the culture of the country they want to be a part of, the United States. Again, are these the people you want coming into your union and having a say over your country?

2. Puerto Rico's Representation at the Miss Universe Competition and other International Events

Puerto Rico would be a U.S. state that will continue to have its Miss Universe representation, well, at least that's what the statehooders say in Puerto Rico. Although Kansas and Alabama are not allowed to participate in such international events, Puerto Rican statehooders seem to believe that they are "special" and will be the exception.

Statehooders supposedly seek statehood for reasons of "equality", but their notion of "equality" only extends to receiving an "equal" amount of welfare and federal assistance funds that other states receive. Again, for the statehooders, it's all about the money.

3. A State where Spanish will be the Language of Government and Education

Puerto Rico would be a U.S. state that will continue to have Spanish as the principal language of government and the educational system, well, it would at least insist on this. Statehooders envision a "State of Puerto Rico" where Spanish would be the main language of government, government services, schools, and the courts.

I would imagine that a "State of Puerto Rico" would be officially bilingual on paper (like today's Commonwealth), but in practice, it will remain a Spanish-speaking administration and educational system because that is what the statehooders envision.

Also, patriotic and nationalistic Puerto Ricans would never allow the English language to take root in Puerto Rico's government agencies and schools to supplant Spanish. They defeated such English-Only policies in the past and will defeat them in the future.

Puerto Ricans are battled-tested when it comes to fighting against English-Only policies and other such assimilation plans since the advent of U.S. colonial rule. Even bilingual and multilingual Puerto Ricans (usually professionals and pro-sovereignty supporters) would fight against any attempt to impose English-Only policies or the use of English as the language of instruction in schools and government.

Any notions of English as the national unifying language of the United States will die with Puerto Rico. Puerto Rico would be the graveyard of the English-Only and English-First movements.

4. The United States as a "National State" or a "Multinational State"

If the United States admits a new state into the union that comes with its own proud, unassimilable, and unique national culture, history, and language, a "State of Puerto Rico" would essentially turn the United States into a "multinational state", two nations (the American nation and the Puerto Rican nation) under one federal government, at least, that's how Puerto Ricans will view this merge.

Just as Québec insists on being a "distinct society" and "nation" within Canada, is the United States ready to accommodate the Puerto Rican nation on an equal footing with the American nation? Is the U.S. ready, willing, and able to become a "multinational state"?

With Puerto Rico as a state, would the United States declare English and Spanish as the two official languages of the federal government, embrace hispanization, and amend the U.S. Constitution so that Puerto Rico's culture and nationality are protected and recognized within the union?

The statehood movement does not believe that Puerto Ricans should nor need to assimilate into U.S. culture, while the nationalists, independentistas, Commonwealth party activists, anti-statehood activists, and other pro-sovereignty Puerto Ricans (the majority) will actively resist and struggle against such assimilation because for them, Puerto Rico is a nation and the Puerto Rican nation needs to be protected and defended at all costs.

Nothing unifies most Puerto Ricans as the will to *not* assimilate and to remain Puerto Ricans. Americans, is this acceptable to you? Do you really want to annex a proud Latin American nation into the union, thus making the United States a de facto multinational state?

Unlike New Mexico, California, and Hawai'i, when Americans settle in Puerto Rico and become part of Puerto Rican society, they are a minority, and their descendants will mostly likely identify as Puerto Ricans. Puerto Rico has the cultural strength and resiliency to assimilate, in one to two generations, Americans and other foreigners into Puerto Ricans (unless, of course, they live isolated on military bases).

The United States may have the Melting Pot or the Salad Bowl, but in Puerto Rico, we have the Boricua Cultural Stew (*el Sancocho Cultural Boricua*) that non-aggressively assimilates foreigners into Puerto Ricans. Seriously, would Americans really want to make Puerto Rico a state knowing full well the cultural and political consequences? Does the U.S. really want to walk down the path of multinational cultural and political strife that plagued Yugoslavia, the Soviet Union, and other multinational states?

Some naïve American politicians from both parties (duped by the statehooder narrative of equality and civil rights) believe that statehood will bring diversity and more loyal Hispanic-Americans into the union, but what they will really get is a Caribbean Northern Ireland, a tropical Québec, and a Boricua Kosovo that would provoke cultural tensions across the American political and cultural landscape, if Puerto Rico's history of fighting against assimilation and colonialism is any guide at all.

In 1950, Puerto Ricans revolted against the U.S. colonial regime and declared the "*República de Puerto Rico*" in Jayuya before the U.S. colonial regime's air force dropped bombs on the nationalists that were fighting for freedom across the island. In 1954, Puerto Rican nationalists attacked the U.S. Congress under the banner of "*Viva Puerto Rico Libre*" in order to tell the world that Puerto Rico was still a U.S. colony even under the new 1952 Commonwealth status, a reality that the United States accepts today as true.

As you can imagine, these instances of Puerto Rican revolt against the U.S. colonial regime never make it to U.S. history textbooks. In high school, I used to be reprimanded for even bringing this up in my American history class in New Jersey.

In the 1970s, Puerto Rican nationalists managed to take control of the Statue of Liberty's head and crown and placed a huge Puerto Rican flag on the statue's face calling for Puerto Rico's liberty.

Puerto Rican Nationalists protest at the Statue of Liberty, demanding Puerto Rico's liberty from U.S. Colonial rule.

After the defeat of the 1950 Revolution and the fall of the Republic of Puerto Rico in Jayuya, the U.S.-controlled Puerto Rico National Guard rounds up thousands of nationalists and suspected pro-independence supporters and intern them in various concentration camps across Puerto Rico.

In the 1980s, armed Puerto Rican pro-independence groups, among other attacks and bombings, managed to blow up all the planes of the U.S. controlled Puerto Rico National Guard in a single attack. In 2000, Puerto Rican civil resisters and civil society groups, using the tools and tactics of non-violent civil resistance, expelled the U.S. Navy from its Vieques military base and bombing range. Yes, these events actually happened.

Most Americans do not know about all of these historical instances of Puerto Rican resistance because they are not *supposed to know*...the U.S. colonial regime wants Americans and the world to view Puerto Ricans as a submissive and passive people, content with their place under U.S. colonial rule and tutelage. From reading about our history of resistance, one can see that submissive we are not.

Plebiscite after plebiscite shows that statehood is *not* favored by the majority of the Puerto Rican people, even when statehooders try to skew the results and electoral statistics. Statehooders are infamous for manipulating such electoral statistics and referendum status definitions in order to get the results they want.

In 2019, the statehood party even tried to change Puerto Rico's electoral law in order to influence the November 2020 elections. Puerto Ricans love, cherish, and value their national culture and identity. Are Americans sure this is the poor, foreign, enslaved, colonized, and unassimilable country you want to merge into your union? The U.S. federal government is meant for one nation, the American nation, not two.

5. *Puerto Rico's Representation at the Olympic Games*

According to the statehooders, Puerto Rico would be a U.S. state that maintains its national Olympic Team. Puerto Rico, which currently has "sports sovereignty", can participate in international events and sports competitions as itself. Puerto Rico has fielded an Olympic team since the 1948 London Games. Does Florida, New Jersey or Wyoming have an Olympic team? No, of course not.

There's a U.S. federal law (the Amateur Sports Act of 1978) against states participating in such events, but that does not stop the statehooders from telling people otherwise. Americans, please understand this: Puerto Rican statehooders believe that as a state, Puerto Rico would and should continue to have its own national Olympic Team.

If the statehood movement admitted that Puerto Rico, as a state, would permanently lose its Olympic team, many statehooders would abandon the movement because they were sold a *"creole statehood"* package, and that package included a Puerto Rico Olympic team, Miss Universe representation and a Spanish language state government. Even for many statehooders, **Puerto Rico's culture, language, and Olympic representation are non-negotiable.**

Puerto Ricans love and cherish the Puerto Rico Olympic Team (*Comité Olimpico de Puerto Rico*) and its great history, cheer for Puerto Ricans, and wave Puerto Rican flags around the world at such international sporting events. To show the world that Puerto Rico has its own "sports sovereignty" and cannot be controlled by the United States, the Puerto Rico Olympic Team ignored the U.S.-led boycott of the 1980 Olympic Games in Moscow and sent a few athletes to compete, angering the U.S. government and Puerto Rico's pro-statehood governor at the time.

Also, in the 1979 Pan-American Games held in Puerto Rico, a Puerto Rican swimmer named Jesse Vassallo went to the games under Team U.S.A. When Vassallo won gold, and the U.S. National Anthem began to play, the Puerto Ricans in the crowd began to sing *La Borinqueña*, Puerto Rico's National Anthem, drowning out the U.S. National Anthem. Then on the podium, Vassallo even held up a small Puerto Rican flag, inciting the patriotic roar of the Puerto Rican crowds. This act of national pride and defiance is still celebrated and remembered in Puerto Rico. You can watch the video at www.PrexitBook.com.

At the 2004 Summer Olympic Games in Athens, the Puerto Rican National Basketball Team led by Carlos Arroyo defeated the U.S.A. Dream Team. The Puerto Ricans in the crowd and even the Greeks were cheering and celebrating for Puerto Rico (the underdog) having delivered the first defeat to the U.S.A. Dream Team. In Puerto Rico, this victory was celebrated in the streets for weeks.

Also, during the 2016 Summer Olympic Games in Rio de Janeiro, Puerto Rico won its first gold medal at an Olympics for tennis thanks to Monica Puig. Puerto Ricans celebrated her victory for days, and the patriotism and national pride was everywhere. There are even whole YouTube video compilations of Puerto Ricans reacting over joyously to her victory.

For Puerto Ricans, the Olympic Games and other such international sporting events are a way to demonstrate national pride and tell the world that *"Puerto Rico is still here"*. This is why the statehooders tell Puerto Ricans that even as a state, Puerto Rico would continue to have an Olympic team (ignoring the existence of the Amateur Sports Act of 1978). If they admitted that Puerto Ricans could only compete at the Olympics under Team U.S.A., the statehood movement would lose considerable electoral and financial support.

Puerto Ricans are very proud of their Olympic Team. As a U.S. state, Puerto Rico would no longer be permitted to have its own National Olympic Team. As a colony, the U.S. Congress can rescind Puerto Rico's sports sovereignty at any time. In order to guarantee and safeguard Puerto Rico's sports sovereignty forever, Puerto Rico needs sovereignty. Americans, it's time to let Puerto Rico go.

Economics & Dependency Reasons

6. Is Statehood really "for the Poor"?

Although Statehooders would never explain or expose this to Americans, many people in Puerto Rico support Statehood because they believe that **Statehood will bring in an additional $10 billion or more in welfare, food stamps, etc.** This extra $10 billion in federal funds would be paid for by American tax payers, further exacerbating the fiscal and economic black hole that Puerto Rico would become for the United States. The Statehood movement in Puerto Rico encourages people to not work but depend on receiving more and more federal aid and funds.

Their reasoning: the more people go on welfare and use federal assistance programs, the more likely they will become dependent on those funds, and thus, more likely to support statehood since, according to the statehood movement, statehood for Puerto Rico would bring in billions in additional welfare funds.

On March 4th, 2014, the **General Accountability Office** of the U.S. Congress published a report on the high cost of statehood for Puerto Rico. The report detailed how the economic and fiscal costs of statehood for Puerto Rico would represent a massive economic problem not just for the U.S. government and American corporations in Puerto Rico, but also for Puerto Ricans and Puerto Rican businesses.

In essence, statehood would not only negatively affect Puerto Rico's economy and U.S. business interests, but would also decimate thousands of jobs, reduce the government's operating budget, and increase the tax burden on all Puerto Ricans by $5 billion[13].

This $5 billion in increased federal taxes would also increase Puerto Rico's massive dependency on federal funds[14]. Without mentioning the political and cultural consequences of statehood, the economic consequences of statehood are just too great to risk regarding the future of Puerto Rico, and the fiscal and economic health of the United States.

Even with the GAO Report's findings on the high cost of statehood, the statehood party ignored it and has actually planned out how people can remain at a certain level of poverty so that one would qualify for all the federal food stamps and welfare programs (free money from U.S. taxpayers) and tax credits, but not be required to pay any federal taxes (or a small amount) to contribute to the union. They have convinced their followers that they can continue to live in Puerto Rico on free money from U.S. taxpayers and yet not contribute anything to the "nation".

With statehood, the Statehood Party will be ushering in the perfect colonial dependent freeloader state that does not really produce anything but consumes imports. Once you are living in this colonial dependent system, what incentive do you have to succeed in life and start a business, earn more income, etc.? If you work to earn more income, you will lose out on these federal welfare funds, food stamps, and benefits, thus there's an incentive for one not to generate more income.

As a state, Puerto Rico would become an eternal poor ghetto-state where people would not be incentivized to progress and earn more income to overcome poverty, lest they lose the federal welfare benefits (free money from U.S. taxpayers).

The statehooder leadership believes that the worse Puerto Rico becomes economically, the more people will support statehood as a way for the federal government to rescue and bail out Puerto Rico by making it a state. **Statehooders block and attack all initiatives that are aimed at making Puerto Rico more economically stable, secure, and self-sufficient**.

When Puerto Ricans try to create community and entrepreneurial platforms and projects to promote and strengthen Puerto Rico's self-sufficiency, the statehooder and colonialist politicians jump into action to destroy and block such initiatives.

Why don't the statehooders want a stable and self-sufficient Puerto Rico? A stable and economically developed Puerto Rico is a threat to the statehood and colonialist movements because such Puerto Rico-based development would prove that Puerto Rico does *not* need to become a state or remain a colony at all.

Puerto Rican self-sufficiency and resiliency would prove to many people that Puerto Rico can make it on its own as a free country. With welfare dependency, the statehooders hope to link as many Puerto Ricans as possible into dependency and thus supportive of "statehood" and its promised more billions in welfare benefits.

In Puerto Rico, the statehood movement gains support due to this promise of free American taxpayer's money. Americans would be horrified at how statehooders regard the average U.S. taxpayer. **The statehooders believe that poverty is their ally, and they are entitled to more federal funds.** Many statehood supporters have no idea how the U.S. political system works nor have any notion of American history and political culture, thus mainly depend on the Statehood movement and the colonial media/press for all information related to the United States and their quest for statehood.

When the statehooders try to explain American Federalism to their supporters, they use the phrase "a Republic of many republics" (*una república de repúblicas*), ignoring the historical fact of increased federalization in American politics and federal-state relations. Do Americans call their states "*republics*"? Of course not. Growing up in the United States, I have never heard an American call the United States a "*republic of republics.*"

These statehooders pretty much believe that the United States functions today as if it were still under the Articles of Confederation of 1781 and not the U.S. Constitution of 1789. The banner of ignorance is held high and proud by the Statehood movement. Again, I ask, are these the ignorant people you want having influence over the American political system?

The statehooders know that as a poor state, Puerto Rico would receive more in U.S. taxpayer and treasury funds than Puerto Ricans (due to poverty) can contribute back to the U.S. via federal income taxes. The statehooders aim at creating a "**state of beggardom**" whereby billions and billions of more American taxpayer money will be sent to subsidize the maintenance of colonial poverty.

Ironically, the U.S. Senate also knows this and has continuously blocked any attempt to make Puerto Rico a state. Historically, any bill in Congress that *may* lead to statehood for Puerto Rico gets shelved and dies. One can say that the Congress, although it condones colonial rule and might entertain sovereignty, avoids statehood like the plague.

Also, **statehooders do not seem to notice that the United States is in a major financial and economic crisis.** As the Congress and the President debate over tax revenues and spending cuts, Puerto Rico statehooders seem oblivious to this and somehow think that the Congress will be willing to spend billions and billions more to not just rebuild Puerto Rico after the 2017 hurricanes, but to admit a 51st state where the majority live in poverty, do not speak English as their first language, have their own national identity, and has its own nationalists and pro-sovereignty movements.

This policy of dependence and poverty was the last nail in the statehood coffin. Why would the United States admit Puerto Rico as a state when, due to its poverty and chronic colonial dependence and corruption, Puerto Rico would become a major economic and financial burden for the United States? In theory, wouldn't you want to build a strong and prosperous Puerto Rico so that Puerto Rico could contribute economically to the United States?

In trying to create a poor and dependent Puerto Rico that would want to become a state for more federal funds, a poor and dependent Puerto Rico is the main reason *not* to admit it as a state. If the statehooders have their way, Puerto Rico would actually suck the U.S. Treasury dry.

In fact, the statehood manifesto, written by a former statehood governor, is titled "**Statehood is for the Poor**". For statehooders in Puerto Rico, Statehood is not about "becoming American", it's about getting more free money from Americans. Americans need to understand this. As Americans, when you look past the shallow statehooder narratives, appeals, and justifications, you will see a Statehood Party led by corrupt colonial loyalists that want to live off a welfare dependent Puerto Rico and U.S. taxpayer funds.

It's about time to let Puerto Rico go.

Domestic & International Political Reasons

7. *Congressional Representation for the 51st State?*

If Puerto Rico were to become a state, Puerto Rico would receive two senators and six to seven representatives (due to Puerto Rico's population, which is higher than 21 states).

To keep the 435 balance in the House of Representatives, where are those new congressional seats for Puerto Rico going to come from? Those new congressional seats will come from the least populated U.S. states, but which ones? Considering that Puerto

Rico's 2018 population is estimated to be 3,195,153, Puerto Rico has a higher population Utah, Iowa, Nevada, Arkansas, Mississippi, Kansas, New Mexico, Nebraska, West Virginia, Idaho, Hawai'i, New Hampshire, Maine, Montana, Rhode Island, Delaware, North Dakota, South Dakota, Alaska, Vermont, and Wyoming, along with the District of Columbia and all other U.S. territories[15].

Many Americans and Puerto Ricans seriously doubt those states would allow Puerto Rico to become a state when that would entail their loss of various representatives, thus influence in Washington, DC, to promote their political and economic interests. All the Representatives and Senators from these states would work to derail and shelve any possible legislation that could possibly lead to statehood for Puerto Rico. Could you blame these Congressmen and Congresswomen? After all, they would only be looking after their state's interests.

These majority white American and English-speaking states would lose congressional power and representation to one majority Hispanic and Spanish-speaking Puerto Rico. In Puerto Rico, the statehooders even talk about and welcome such a disenfranchisement of those "white" states by Puerto Rico. Believe me, Americans in the Midwestern states are not going to let statehood happen for Puerto Rico, nor should they.

What about the fact that Puerto Ricans have been U.S. citizens since 1917 and have fought for the U.S. in various wars? Sadly, for the statehooders, these narratives and appeals mean nothing to these Representatives and Senators from those states that would lose power in Washington, DC. At the end of the day, every Representative and Senator needs to protect and uphold his/her state's interests.

Are the citizens of Kansas, Nebraska, Iowa, and Wyoming going to depend on Puerto Ricans in San Juan, Ponce, and Mayagüez to care about and lobby on their behalf on major regional and economic issues such as cattle, corn, soybeans, and wheat? No, of course not.

If you are an American who believes that "American culture and traditions need to be protected", annexing Puerto Rico as a Hispanic Spanish-speaking state with aspirations of hispanization would be tantamount to dropping a "political-cultural bomb" on the U.S. political system and to the notion that the United States is an English-speaking nation of immigrants that adheres to American culture and values. Remember, with Puerto Rico as a state; the U.S. will effectively become a multinational country; two nations, one federal government.

The new de facto motto of the United States would be:

E Pluribus Duo (Out of many, Two)

Also, in Puerto Rico, statehooders preach about the great benefits of being able to have **congressional representation** and be able to **vote for the President**. Let's now consider this from Puerto Rico's perspective. As a state, Puerto Rico would have six or seven Representatives and two Senators to represent its interests in Congress. Now, let's say that the Congress wishes to pass legislation that would detrimentally impact Puerto Rico's economy and cultural affairs, such as the new federal ban on cockfighting in the U.S. and all the "territories", including Puerto Rico.

In Puerto Rico, the cockfighting industry contributes approximately $80 million to the Puerto Rican economy and is considered cultural patrimony by many. With six or seven Representatives, Puerto Rico would still not have the power to stop such overreaching legislation.

Other Representatives see cockfighting as barbaric, so they have the votes to impose such laws on Puerto Rico. Can Puerto Rico retaliate back with a bill to ban deer, bear, and quail hunting (which most Puerto Ricans would consider barbaric) in the United States? No, because it would not have the votes to push that bill through and against the wishes of American hunters and the thousands of companies in the hunting industry.

Also, there's no guarantee that Puerto Ricans would elect loyalist pitiyanki statehooders to Congress; what would happen if Puerto Ricans send nationalists and pro-independence Congresspersons to Congress? Would Americans put up with Puerto Rican nationalists co-sponsoring bills for secession and singing Puerto Rico's National Anthem, *La Borinqueña*, in Congress?

Even with six or seven Representatives, the Congress would still be able to impose unjust and unwanted laws in Puerto Rico that would severely impact the economy and Puerto Rico's cultural affairs. Congress can even impose the death penalty on certain federal crimes, even though most Puerto Ricans do not believe in the death penalty.

In terms of voting for the President, Puerto Rico's Electoral College votes would be so negligible as to be insignificant, essentially, no impact whatsoever in a Presidential election. Candidates would go to Puerto Rico, take pictures with piña coladas, receive donations, say *"Buenos días"* to the crowds, secure a portion of the "Latino" vote, and then leave, never to remember or consider Puerto Rico during their whole term, just like today under colonial rule. Would a proud Puerto Rican ever have an actual chance of becoming President of the United States? Probably not.

For Puerto Ricans, regarding congressional representation, statehood would just be a crueler and more aggressive continuation of colonialism. Puerto Rico would have a seat at the Congressional table but would always be ignored and drowned out over the wishes and "American" priorities of the other 50 states. Statehood would be like a Puerto Rican living in a white American family's basement, eating scraps, and always being reminded that you are not "family, just a "visitor" or a "ward" that will never actually be "American". With sovereignty, Puerto Ricans would finally have their own house they can be masters in. It's time to let Puerto Rico go.

8. International Outrage & Condemnation

If Puerto Rico were ever annexed and became a U.S. state, it would cause an uproar at the United Nations and a major rift between the United States and Latin America. **Both the United Nations and all Latin American countries regard Puerto Rico as a nation, with its own national identity and language that is currently held under U.S. colonial rule.**

Although ignored by the U.S. mainstream media, since the 1970s, the U.N. Decolonization Committee passes an annual resolution calling for Puerto Rico's decolonization and independence.

In the eyes of the world, particularly Latin America, statehood for Puerto Rico would be seen as an American attempt to politically and culturally absorb and assimilate a Latin American and Caribbean people and nation into its Anglo-American society and political union. For many in Puerto Rico, Latin America, and the world, it will be regarded as a political and cultural attack on Puerto Rico and Puerto Ricans as a distinct and national people.

As a state, many believe that Puerto Rico will suffer the same fate as Hawai'i, where non-Hawaiians (Asians and Whites) are currently the majority of the population. With statehood, Hawaiians are now about 9% of the population of Hawai'i and the majority of these live in extreme poverty. With U.S. occupation and statehood, Hawaiians have gone from masters to squatters in their own country.

Hawaiian culture and language have been genocidally impacted, now reduced to a few marginalized communities. Puerto Ricans do not want to become a minority in their own country and have our Spanish language reduced to a high school elective as it is in the fifty states.

Also, as a state like Hawai'i, Puerto Rico would still be under the retrograde and repressive Jones Act of 1920 that forces Puerto Rico to use and subsidize the U.S. Merchant Marine ships and companies that enforce a virtual colonial shipping monopoly on Puerto Rico and increase the price of all imported goods. With statehood, the Jones Act of 1920 would still be choking Puerto Rico's economy. It's time to let Puerto Rico go.

9. *Puerto Rico's Historical and Active Sovereignty & Nationalist Movement*

Although statehooders would have Americans believe that all Puerto Ricans are "loyal and proud American citizens resident in Puerto Rico", nothing could be further from the truth.

Puerto Ricans have been struggling since the 1500s for their freedom and sovereignty, first from Spanish colonial rule and now from U.S. colonial rule.

In 1511, the native Tainos of Borikén, led by Chief Agüeybaná II, declared a "**Guazábara**" (war) and rebelled against Spanish rule and the Spanish conquistadores that enslaved and murdered them.

Although the Guazábara was defeated, the **Taino Resistance** lasted for decades via raids on Spanish settlements and the establishment of native communities in the remote interior areas of Puerto Rico.

In 1809, residents and prominent leaders of San Germán, in southwestern Puerto Rico, prepared and were organizing an insurrection against Spanish rule in the **San Germán Conspiracy**.

In 1838, under the leadership of Andres Vizcarrondo, Puerto Ricans first revolted against Spain in the **Trujillo Bajo Revolt**[16].

In 1868, Puerto Ricans again revolted against Spanish rule in the "**Grito de Lares**". At Lares, the patriots and revolutionaries established the short-lived *"República de Puerto Rico"*. This first *República de Puerto Rico*, led by President Francisco Ramirez, organized its own provisional government, had its own national flag, and enacted the first Puerto Rican Constitution, before being defeated by Spanish colonial troops.

The Lares flag was designed by Dr. Ramón E. Betances, first sewn by Mariana Bracetti, and was the flag of the first Republic of Puerto Rico proclaimed at the Grito de Lares of 1868.

In 1873, Puerto Ricans revolted against Spanish rule in the "**Estrellada de Camuy**" (The Camuy Revolt).

In 1897, Puerto Ricans once again revolted against Spanish rule in the town of Yauco (**Intentona de Yauco**). At this revolt, it was the first time the modern Puerto Rican flag debuted in Puerto Rico and used by the Puerto Rican resistance movement.

On August 13, 1898, during the U.S. invasion of Puerto Rico, about 400 Puerto Rican rebels from Ciales and Villalba attacked and defeated the Spanish forces in **Ciales**, captured the town, and declared the short-lived *"República de Puerto Rico"*.

In 1838, under the leadership of Andres Vizcarrondo, Puerto Ricans first revolted against Spain in the Trujillo Bajo Revolt in what is modern Carolina.

"*El Grito de Lares*" by Leonardo Rivera

El Grito de Lares was the independence revolt on September 23rd, 1868, that established the first Republic of Puerto Rico with a Constitution, a provisional government, and a small liberation army of the Republic.

During the Revolution of 1950 against U.S. colonial rule, the Puerto Rican Nationalists proclaimed the Republic of Puerto Rico on October 30th, 1950. In this photo, a U.S. colonial soldier removes the banned Puerto Rican flag in Jayuya.

In 1898, Puerto Rico was invaded and occupied by the United States. Although statehooders will say that the "Americans were invited by the Puerto Ricans", it is hard for them to explain the joint Spanish-Puerto Rican resistance that sprang up around Puerto Rico. The Spanish and Puerto Rican militias even defeated the U.S. troops in the *Battle of Asomante* in the mountains of Aibonito.

Yet, for all the resistance, Spain surrendered, and Puerto Rico was ceded to the United States as its new colonial property and war prize.

During the Treaty of Paris negotiations, no Puerto Rican was allowed to participate nor represent Puerto Rico. For the United States, Puerto Ricans were not regarded and treated as leaders and authorities, but rather like local subhuman fauna that came along with their new postwar land acquisition.

Thus, Puerto Rico and all Puerto Ricans were transferred from one owner to another with the stroke of a pen. The United States quickly installed a military dictatorship, abolished Puerto Rico's democratic autonomous government and peso currency, and established the formal U.S. colonial regime via the Foraker Act of 1900.

From 1898 onward, Puerto Ricans have revolted and protested U.S. colonial rule and assimilation policies. Regarded as a threat to U.S. colonial rule, Puerto Rican nationalism and patriotism were persecuted and banned. The Puerto Rican flag and the national anthem, *La Borinqueña*, were also banned. Pro-sovereignty and independence supporters were routinely persecuted, arrested or killed. U.S. colonial police even massacred Puerto Rican nationalists and routinely jailed anyone suspected of being a nationalist.

With the colonial **Gag Law (Ley de la Mordaza)** of 1948, supported by Luis Muñoz Marín, the colonial regime further clamped down on nationalism, free speech, and democratic rights. The **culture of fear** that this law and the violent pro-colonial turbas created can still be felt and witnessed today throughout Puerto Rico.

On October 30, 1950, under the leadership of Dr. Pedro Albizu Campos, **the Nationalists led a revolution that almost destabilized the local colonial regime**. Nationalists attacked the colonial regime in the towns of Mayagüez, Arecibo, Utuado, Jayuya,

Peñuelas, Ponce, Naranjito, Santurce, and La Fortaleza itself in San Juan. In Jayuya, the patriots and revolutionaries, led by Blanca Canales, took over the town and hoisted the banned Puerto Rican flag atop a building and proclaimed the second short-lived "*República de Puerto Rico*".

Dr. Pedro Albizu Campos was the President of the Puerto Rican Nationalist Party, which sought independence from the United States. Today, Albizu Campos is considered a symbol of Puerto Rican nationalism, patriotism, resistance, and revolution.

If it were not for the U.S. aerial bombardment of nationalist towns and strongholds (especially the mountain towns of Utuado and Jayuya), the nationalist revolution against U.S. colonial rule could have succeeded.

After the Revolution of 1950 was defeated, the colonial regime of Luis Muñoz Marín began mass arrests of any suspected Puerto Rican Nationalists or those supporting independence, leading to thousands of people being held in colonial concentration camps. At the time, the U.S. mainstream press called the Revolution of 1950 "an incident among Puerto Ricans" in order to minimize the revolt against colonial rule.

In Puerto Rican schools today, the Revolution of 1950 is not really mentioned, and if it is, it's merely called an "incident" in order to devalue and invisibilize this very important historical event. This topic is very politicized because the colonial regime's education department, particularly when led by statehooders, does not want to teach young Puerto Rican students that Puerto Ricans in 1950 actually rebelled against U.S. colonial rule and that Puerto Rico had to be aerial bombed back into colonial submission.

Also, ironically, not since the U.S. Civil War were U.S. citizens bombed and attacked by the U.S. government for rebelling against U.S. rule.

This map of Puerto Rico details the municipalities and areas where Nationalists engaged and fought the colonial regime during the Revolution of 1950.

In Jayuya, the Nationalists defeated the local colonial police and proclaimed the *"República de Puerto Rico"*. With U.S. military support, the colonial Puerto Rico National Guard eventually defeated the Nationalists, some of whom formed guerrilla groups and continued to fight from the mountains.

Naranjito was the last Nationalist stronghold to fall back to the colonial regime after Nationalist leader José Antonio Negrón (a

World War II veteran) was captured and arrested on November 10th, 1950.

When the town of Jayuya was finally captured by the U.S.-controlled Puerto Rico National Guard after being held for three days by Nationalist forces, a colonial soldier removed the banned Puerto Rican flag that was hoisted by Blanca Canales.

This particular Puerto Rican flag, a major item of historical importance, was "disappeared" by the colonial regime and its whereabouts are still unknown. It was either burned, thrown into a lost evidence box, or discarded in the garbage by the colonial regime. Today, if that flag was ever recovered, it would be honored, preserved, and displayed in a museum.

While this Puerto Rican revolution was being put down in Puerto Rico, **Puerto Rican nationalists attempted to assassinate President Truman at Blair House** in Washington, DC. Also, on March 1, 1954, in order to call the world's attention to Puerto Rico's colonial problem and the Commonwealth farce, another **group of nationalists,** led by Ms. Lolita Lebrón, penetrated the U.S. House of Representatives, shouted *"Viva Puerto Rico Libre"* from the gallery, and shot at congressmen on the floor, wounding some and creating a pandemonium of screaming and stampeding Americans running for their lives.

This Puerto Rican attack on Congress was significant because not since the War of 1812 between the United States and Great Britain, had the U.S. Capitol been attacked and fired upon. The four nationalists (Lolita Lebrón, Rafael Cancel Miranda, Andres Figueroa Cordero, and Irvin Flores Rodríguez) were arrested and later pardoned in the 1970s. There have been various other times when Puerto Ricans have resisted colonial rule, colonial policies, and all efforts at "Americanization".

Today, pro-sovereignty and nationalist sentiment is alive and well in Puerto Rico. Even many stateside Puerto Ricans in New York, Florida, and throughout the United States support the struggle for Puerto Rico's sovereignty (similarly to how many Irish-Americans supported the struggle for Ireland's sovereignty and independence from British colonial rule).

Although the U.S. allows American citizens (of any political party) residing, working, traveling, or studying overseas to vote in federal and state elections as absentee voters, in Puerto Rico, the colonial Commonwealth government forbids stateside Puerto Ricans (the diaspora) from voting in Puerto Rican elections because it is believed (unofficially) that many of them would support the sovereignty options of Free Association or Independence, and not statehood. This is unacceptable to Puerto Rico's colonial pro-statehood lackeys.

Having been raised in the U.S., many stateside Puerto Ricans (such as myself) are taught in American schools to respect and admire freedom and independence and despise colonialism, ideals that are considered "criminal" and "separatist" by the colonial regime in Puerto Rico.

Essentially, stateside Puerto Ricans are considered politically dangerous to the colonial regime because many of them were raised in the U.S., admire freedom, have experienced racism, and do not have a colonial mentality that facilitates Puerto Rican cooperation with their own colonial subjugation, although there are some that are colonized because they may have been educated in Puerto Rico or military schools.

Also, stateside Puerto Ricans cannot be controlled and manipulated by the pro-Commonwealth and pro-statehood party machines since these Puerto Ricans are beyond their reach of political and colonial indoctrination and intimidation. The pro-statehood and pro-Commonwealth neighborhood party bosses, lackeys, and political thugs (called *presidentes de barrios*) can intimidate Puerto Ricans in Puerto Rico, but not Puerto Ricans in Florida or New Jersey.

I remember an incident in 2006 at the U.S. Post Office in Isabela, Puerto Rico, where my wife and I experienced the political thugs at work. My wife and I were trying to mail a package and witnessed a statehooder political thug giving a pro-statehood speech and decrying the evils of independence in the very lobby of the U.S. Post Office.

Customers waiting in line and postal employees were nervous and scared to confront him and ask him to leave in fear of this thug's political influence or retaliation. Even though this thug was violating postal regulations regarding disturbances and public assembly (*Rules & Regulations Governing Conduct on Postal Service Property*), the entire post office staff did nothing. Other customers in line told me that even the postal employees feared retaliation from the statehooder political machine since they also lived in the area.

This is the kind of "democracy" Puerto Ricans enjoy in Puerto Rico. These statehooder thugs can get away with such intimidating behavior in Puerto Rico, but not in the United States. If anyone tried such a stunt in a post office lobby in the United States, that individual would be dragged out and arrested.

Many stateside Puerto Ricans are actively pro-sovereignty, advocate against assimilation, and are very proud of their Puerto Rican culture and national identity. Is the United States ready to admit a new state to the union that has such a long history of resistance and revolt to American rule and Americanization? Like I said before, is the United States interested in gaining its own Caribbean Québec or Boricua Northern Ireland? We highly doubt it.

As a U.S. colony, Puerto Rico is a "nobody" in the eyes of the United States. When the United States engages Caribbean nations in dialogue and regional economic initiatives, Puerto Rico is never invited nor considered an entity worth engaging with…why should it? It's a colony with no power or sovereign representation whatsoever.

It's like considering the opinion of a slave in a meeting of masters. As a colony or a U.S. state, Puerto Rico and Puerto Ricans would be invisible, voiceless, and irrelevant not only in U.S. affairs but in Latin American and Caribbean affairs as well.

As pro-sovereignty supporters in Puerto Rico and the U.S. continually state, the United States will only engage with and respect Puerto Rico as an equal partner in international affairs when Puerto Rico has political sovereignty, freedom, democracy, and full authority over its own government. Remember, no country, especially the "administrating power", respects a colony.

If the United States decides to take the political and cultural cyanide pill that would be the unilateral annexation of Puerto Rico as a state (against the wishes of Puerto Ricans), if history is a guide, there would surely be political violence, massive anti-colonial and anti-statehood protests, and constant patriotic civil resistance campaigns to fight against such an usurpation of Puerto Rico and show the world the ugly face of U.S. colonial policies in Puerto Rico.

With today's social media platforms and video sharing sites like YouTube and Vimeo, it is a lot harder to hide colonial abuses, terror, and repression like in the days of the Winship colonial dictatorship. Puerto Rico has an active, strong, and historical pro-independence movement that will not just sit by idly and allow the annexation of Puerto Rico. Guam may be "Where America's Day Begins", but Puerto Rico will be "Where Colonial Rule Goes to Die".

The majority of Puerto Ricans reject statehood and will *not* allow that to happen, particularly when white supremacy and racist anti-Hispanic attacks increase in the United States. Puerto Ricans may be U.S. citizens, but they are surely not welcomed in the U.S. nor considered *Americans* by many other U.S. citizens. Americans, is this the political and cultural headache and turmoil that you want when annexing a foreign nation into your union?

Once Americans understand the legacy of U.S. colonial history in Puerto Rico, you will see that the pro-sovereignty movement is actually doing the United States a favor by trying to help the U.S. avoid the political and cultural chaos that will ensue with the annexation of Puerto Rico. It's time to let Puerto Rico go.

10. *The Puerto Rican Statehooder "Lunatic Fringe"*

According to many analysts, the Statehood movement has been the biggest obstacle to Puerto Rican Statehood. Pro-statehood governments, particularly from 1993 to 2019, are extremely corrupt, thuggish, and violent. Many statehooder politicians and government appointees are now in federal prison for stealing federal funds and committing fraud against the U.S. government. One of them, the ex-Secretary of Education, was found with thousands of dollars in federal funds in his freezer, while another statehooder politician stole federal funds that were supposed to go to AIDS clinics.

There are literally so many other instances of corruption, that whole books can be written about statehooders fleecing the federal government. Remember, these corrupt politicians are the people that supposedly love "America" very much and want Puerto Rico to become a state.

As of 2019, the pro-statehooder Rosselló colonial administration has been involved in countless corruption scandals and investigations by the federal government, particularly the FBI. From the handling of the hurricane reconstruction to the recent uncovering of the "institutional mafia" that pervades the statehooder administration, any government led by such corrupt, unscrupulous, inept, and morally bankrupt colonial lackeys is doomed to failure because their aim in government is not to support and advance Puerto Rico's economic development and society, but to rob and steal their way to more government contracts and public funds.

The Statehood movement, along with its "Lunatic Fringe", can trace their origins to the aftermath of the Spanish-American War of 1898 and the establishment of the new American colonial regime in Puerto Rico. Today, this "lunatic fringe" is mainly made up of ultra-loyalist pitiyankis. Under Spanish rule, the ultra-conservative **"Incondicionales"** were pro-Spain, pro-Spanish monarchy, and anti-Republican (democratic-republican government).

These Incondicionales wanted Puerto Rico to be a full Spanish province, with little autonomy in Puerto Rico. These Incondicionales were the "statehooders" of their time. Essentially, these Puerto Ricans liked being ruled by Madrid and Spanish officials, as long as they could participate too. During the Spanish-American War of 1898, these Incondicionales were vehemently anti-American and supported Spain.

Quite amazingly, after Puerto Rico was ceded to the United States, many of these pro-monarchy Incondicionales (realizing the new colonial reality) switched allegiances and, overnight, became pro-America, pro-Americanization, flag-waving Republicans.

My own great-grandfather, Eusebio Hernández, went from being a pro-Spanish monarchist and militia supporter to a pro-U.S. Republican at the conclusion of the 1898 war. Why Republicans? The old Incondicionales became Republicans because that party, they believed, most represented power, loyalty to the United States, "Americanism", and "Americanization".

As Republicans, the old Incondicionales could assure the new U.S. colonial regime of their allegiance, loyalty, and obedience to American colonial rule thus were born the *cipayos* and the *pitiyankis*. Becoming pro-U.S. colonial regime pretty much guaranteed their survival because as a *Republicano*, you would not be labeled "nationalist" or "separatist" by the U.S. colonial regime.

From wanting to become a Spanish province, now the new "*Republicanos*" wanted Puerto Rico to become a U.S. state. With the advent of U.S. colonial rule (military and colonial institutions) and the support of the violent turba mobs (to terrorize the Puerto Rican people into submission), hence, the official and organized Statehood movement was born.

Statehooders, like their *Incondicionales* predecessors, are only loyal to whoever has power. If the U.S. were to sell or cede Puerto Rico to France, these same statehood leaders would quickly drop the American flag, pledge allegiance to the French flag, and shout "*Vive la France*" that very night.

In August 2019, when President Trump made comments about exchanging Puerto Rico for Greenland with Denmark, some statehooders on social media actually made statements about how much better Puerto Ricans would be treated under Danish colonial rule. At the drop of a hat, these "pro-U.S.A. statehooders" would drop the U.S. flag and pledge allegiance to the Danish flag in order to secure their standing and local power in the new colonial regime. From demanding to be the 51st State of the United States, the statehooders would now demand to become the 6th Danish

Region. While their allegiances flow like the wind, the majority of Puerto Ricans will always remain loyal to Puerto Rico.

The Lunatic Fringe that affects Puerto Rico's political landscape today can trace its beginnings to the **pro-American Republican "Turbas"** (violent mobs and thugs) that terrorized Puerto Rico during the early 1900s until the present era. As mentioned before, these turbas are violent, armed, and terrorized any opposition to U.S. colonial rule, the old Republican Statehood Party, and today's Statehood movement. Founded and led by the infamous and violent gangster José Mauleón, the pro-American turbas attacked and beat up political opposition politicians, harassed citizens, shot at opposition homes, and burned down newspaper publishing houses, all in the name of "America" and "American Democracy".

Due to their support of the U.S. colonial regime, **the turbas operate with impunity**. Committing felonies, vandalism, and beatings of citizens were tolerated and observed by the colonial police because the turbas marched with American flags, the symbol of colonial impunity in Puerto Rico. Many times, the turba mobs would assemble in front of the home or office of a politician or citizen they considered "un-American" or "too patriotic for Puerto Rico". The turba mobs, in their true thuggish spirit, would begin by issuing threats and later try to force their way in to destroy the place, usually with police officials standing by watching.

If you believe that the turba mobs and their terroristic violence and fear-mongering are a thing of the distant past, I'd advise you to think again. The Statehood movement can always count on colonial government impunity and their *lunatic fringe* to call up turba attacks at any time if they believe the situation calls for it.

In 2002, a **modern-day pro-statehood turba mob turned its fury on the Office of Women's Affairs**, in San Juan. The pro-statehood turba mob attacked and, led by its gubernatorial candidate who was lagging in the polls, forced and punched their way into the building with an American flag. As is common with such turba attacks, the statehood leadership sincerely believes that they are more "American" than George Washington and that they are fighting and leading the charge for "America" and their U.S. citizenship against the *evil forces* of independence. Yes, they actually believe this.

At this turba attack, people were beaten, hit, and punched as the gubernatorial candidate and his violent statehooder entourage pushed people down and broke windows and assaulted public employees who feared for their lives.

Due to the videos and photos of the attack, these statehood leaders were arrested, but (of course), later released even after having vandalized a public building and physically assaulted people on camera. If you or I did that, would we be released by the police? Of course not. The colonial regime in Puerto Rico protects its own.

Why such a thuggish attack on the Office of Women's Affairs? The director of that office, as stipulated by local guidelines, **only had the Puerto Rican flag present in the visitor's area, without the American flag.**

That "act of defiance" against the U.S. colonial regime was enough to justify a turba mob attack on the office by pitiyanki loyalists that, ironically, is supposed to help and support women that are victims of domestic violence.

Did CNN, Fox News, and the U.S. mainstream media cover this outrageous event? Of course not. Americans are supposed to think that everything in Puerto Rico is "just fine".

If you want to see the 2002 pro-statehooder turba attack in San Juan for yourself, please access the following YouTube video (4.48 minutes) at www.PrexitBook.com or via the link below:

https://www.youtube.com/watch?v=PoEJCiihBSQ

If you are unable to click through the link, follow these steps: Go to YouTube; Type *"Motin en la Procuraduria de la Mujer"*, it's the first video at the top. Americans, to fully understand the statehood movement and see them as they really are, need to see this video.

Obviously, the statehooder establishment does not want anyone, particularly Americans, to see this video.

After watching this video, please ask yourself:

1. Are these the violent "statehooder lunatic fringe" people you want having influence in U.S. politics and democracy?
2. If this mob had been pro-independence supporters or striking university students trying to push and punch their way into a government building, would the police stand by and observe like they did in the video?
3. At any point in the video, did the police pull out their batons to stop the turba attack? You have just witnessed statehooder impunity in action.
4. As an American, what did you feel watching the statehooder leaders and thugs holding American flags as they threatened and beat people in the name of "America"?
5. Would you say that these violent statehooder thugs represent American values and democratic ideals?

Americans, it's time to let Puerto Rico go.

SECTION 3

List of Colonial Atrocities, Repression, and Policies Committed on Puerto Rico by U.S. Colonial Rule

To better understand the colonial legacy and detrimental impact of U.S. colonial rule in Puerto Rico, one needs to know about certain historical events, atrocities, and policies that have been imposed on Puerto Rico…details that usually do not make it to the pages of U.S. and Puerto Rico history books or the media.

These are the events the statehooders and colonialists *don't want you to know about*. For many statehooders, the mere act of *knowing* these facts and historical events would mark you as a dangerous "separatist" in the U.S. colony of Puerto Rico. I ask you to read on and not be intimidated by the statehooders. Puerto Ricans and Americans need to know this information in order to fully understand and appreciate the true colonial nature of the U.S.-Puerto Rico political and economic relationship.

These are stories, facts, and details that many Puerto Ricans sadly do not know about since many received a colonial education that expressly does not mention or advocate dissemination of these facts. Yes, the mere act of disseminating these historical facts in Puerto Rico and elsewhere will have me labeled a "separatist" by the colonial government and the pro-statehooder groups that do not want this information made public since it would destroy their carefully curated narratives of "obedient Puerto Ricans." Thomas Jefferson and Simon Bolivar were also labeled "separatists" by colonial governments, so that puts us in good company.

Many of the atrocities and policies mentioned below are shocking, disgusting, depraved, and have had a direct and indirect impact on Puerto Rico's political, economic, and social development. This list of atrocities and colonial policies was inspired by the 2012 article "*8 Atrocities Committed Against Puerto Rico by the U.S.*" by José L. Vega Santiago[17]. I have expanded this list from 8 to 26 major atrocities, acts of repression, and historical events that exemplify and represent U.S. colonial rule in Puerto Rico. Let's begin.

1. *Abolition of Puerto Rico's Democratic Institutions*

After the U.S. invasion and occupation of 1898, the U.S. military abolished by decree Puerto Rico's democratic institutions and its autonomous government and parliament, setting Puerto Rico back decades in democratic development. After all, what could these *brown mixed-race mongrels* know about democracy and enlightened civilization if not for the superior white Americans to show them…by force? Of course, these enlightened colonialists just ignored the fact that Puerto Rico had elections during the Spanish Period and had recently elected their new autonomous government a year prior.

The elected Puerto Rican ministers of government of the Puerto Rican Autonomous Government (1898) that was established by the Charter of Autonomy of 1897, yet later abolished by U.S. military decree.

By 1898, Puerto Rico even had various parliamentary representatives (*diputados*) in Madrid with full voting rights in the Spanish Parliament. A Puerto Rican, Ramón Power y Giralt, was even the Vice-President of the Spanish Parliament and helped draft the Spanish Constitution of 1812.

After 121 years of U.S. colonial rule and experience of watching American democracy at work, Puerto Ricans only have one inconsequential non-voting Resident Commissioner (like all U.S. colonies) sitting in a corner on Capitol Hill to represent Puerto Rico's interests in the U.S. Congress.

Representationally and democratically speaking, Puerto Rico was better off with monarchical Spain than with the "democratic" United States". One would think that being occupied by the country that professes to be the "Land of the Free, Home of the Brave" and the "City on the Hill", it would have ushered in an era of democracy and freedom in Puerto Rico. As we've seen, that was not the case and *never* will be the case. No one is holding their breath on that.

After Spain ratified the Charter of Autonomy (*Carta Autonómica*) in 1897, Puerto Rico had its own democratically elected government, parliament, and more self-government, autonomy, freedom, civil rights, and insular sovereignty over its external relations with foreign nations than at any time under the U.S. flag, even today. With the Charter of Autonomy, Puerto Rico could even establish treaties with foreign nations.

Spain was very far from perfect, but without a doubt, the Puerto Rico of 1897 had more rights, freedoms, and self-government than today's colonial "Commonwealth" government.

After three years of a strict and harsh U.S. military dictatorship after the 1898 invasion and occupation, the U.S. imposed the Foraker Act of 1900, which created the new U.S. colonial government in Puerto Rico, which is the same U.S. colonial regime in existence today. In the 21st century, Puerto Rico is still saddled with the humiliating distinction of having an imposed foreign colonial regime from 1900 as its current model of government.

It may have changed its internal structure and name to "Commonwealth", but it is still the same colonial government established by the Foraker Act of 1900 and rearranged with U.S. Public Law 600 (the law that established the colonial Commonwealth government). How far we have advanced politically, democratically, and economically with the Americans at the helm.

2. *Devaluation & Abolition of Puerto Rico's Currency*

Exemplar of the Puerto Rican Peso. At the time of the U.S. invasion, the Puerto Rican Peso was equal in value to the U.S. dollar.

The U.S. colonial regime, in order to destroy Puerto Rico's capitalist landowning class and debilitate the economy, decreed the devaluation of the Puerto Rican peso (at the time, equal in value to the U.S. dollar) by 40%. Yes, Puerto Rico *had* its own currency. Overnight, Puerto Ricans lost 40% of their wealth due to this U.S. colonial decree, which plunged many out of business and into poverty. This decree destroyed farms and impoverished thousands of Puerto Rican families.

Later, the U.S. colonial regime totally abolished, by decree again, the entire peso currency and imposed the U.S. dollar as the official currency of the colony. Today, most Puerto Ricans may not even know that Puerto Rico once had its own currency. This devaluation and subsequent abolition of the Puerto Rican peso destroyed the economy, plunged thousands into poverty and bankruptcy, and made it ripe for attack by absentee U.S. landowners and business interests. Let the Era of American Sugar Barons begin!

3. *Impact of U.S. Colonial Rule & Political Limbo*

Since the U.S. began to rule Puerto Rico in 1898, the United States has not just occupied and colonized the country but has also kept Puerto Rico in political limbo for over 121 years. Colonialism, as you have seen, has had nefarious and devastating impacts on Puerto Rico's political, social, democratic, cultural, economic, and international development and progress.

Colonialism has impacted *every* aspect of life in Puerto Rico. These colonial policies and constant indifference and interference from the U.S. Congress have resulted in the political, social, and economic disaster and stagnation that is today's Puerto Rico. Remember, nothing happens in Puerto Rico without the express consent and will of the United States.

Since the U.S. Congress holds all sovereign authority and plenary powers over Puerto Rico, all major decisions and policies in Puerto Rico are made and legitimized by such U.S. sovereignty. Everything that the colonial Puerto Rico government does, happens because the U.S. wills it so. Colonies do not have sovereignty; colonial administrating powers do.

In Puerto Rico, governors and politicians are nothing but mere *colonial upper management*, the ruler is and has always been, since 1898, the United States. Today, Puerto Rico is a poor colonial laughingstock on the world stage because the limitations and ineptitudes of U.S. colonial rule do not permit Puerto Rico to be anything else but a colony. The enlightened Americans make the decisions and the profits, and the Puerto Ricans live in poverty with the political and economic consequences of U.S. colonial failures.

The U.S. Supreme Court, in the Insular Cases (1901), declared that Puerto Rico was an *"unincorporated territory"*, basically, an American legal jargon for *colony*. Calling a colony an "unincorporated territory" is like calling a slave a "permanent outdoor unpaid employee". The difference between *incorporated territories* and *unincorporated territories* was that incorporated territories such as Alaska and other continental territories (Wisconsin, the Dakotas, Wyoming, etc.) were going to become U.S. states at some point, of course, once white Americans became a majority of the population via demographic displacement and had established political and economic dominance in the territory.

On the other hand, as Puerto Rico was invaded, occupied, and acquired as war booty in the Spanish-American War of 1898 and with a majority Catholic Puerto Rican Hispanic mixed-race and black population who spoke Spanish and had their own national identity and culture, it was never destined to become a state. Unlike in the continental U.S., white American settlement (Anglo demographic displacement) never happened and would have been resisted aggressively by Puerto Ricans.

The Insular Cases allowed the United States to hold on to these new "unincorporated territories" (colonies) indefinitely without the obligation or promise of transitioning them towards statehood or to any other status for that matter. The U.S. Constitution's Territorial Clause (Article IV, Section III, Clause II) even justified and legitimized the holding of said territories (colonies) until the U.S. Congress deems fit to dispose of them.

Is the United States waiting for a consensus in Puerto Rico?

Ever since 1898, the United States government has *never* promised to make Puerto Rico a state. For 121 years, a bill regarding statehood has *never* been ratified by the U.S. Congress. Since the advent of the United States in Puerto Rico, the U.S. government has kept Puerto Rico in a political limbo where talk of Puerto Rico's future and final status is avoided like the plague.

While American politicians say *"we are waiting for Puerto Ricans to come to a consensus"*, the colonial regime and its colonial lackeys continue to divide Puerto Ricans into political partisan tribes that pretty much guarantees that such a consensus is never going to be reached and the colonial regime can continue to exist.

Now, is the United States *really* committed to Puerto Rico reaching a consensus regarding status? As detailed by Juan Gonzalez in *Harvest of Empire*, the Puerto Rico House of Delegates in 1914, led by the famous pro-independence legislator and patriot, José De Diego, **unanimously voted in favor of independence from the United States**, yet, as expected, this "will of the Puerto Rican people" was rejected by the U.S. Congress as "unconstitutional" and in violation of the colonial Foraker Act of 1900 that established the first civil American colonial government in Puerto Rico[18].

The only time the U.S. Congress considered and drafted a bill to grant Puerto Rico its independence resulted from the anti-colonialist and nationalist disturbances in the 1930s and 1940s. In 1943, U.S. Senator Millard Tydings, a Democrat from Maryland, drafted a **legislative proposal to grant independence to Puerto Rico**.

Senator Tydings was also responsible for the Philippine Independence Act of 1934, which established the process to transition the Philippines from a U.S. colony to an independent country. The proposal to grant independence was welcomed by *every* political party in Puerto Rico (political consensus), including Senator Luis Muñoz Marín's Liberal Party.

Yet, even with unanimous political consensus for independence, Senator Muñoz Marín, who considered himself the self-proclaimed representative of all Puerto Ricans, *opposed* the proposal for independence. How would Americans feel if Benedict Arnold had considered himself the representative of all Americans in the Thirteen Colonies, went to London on his own accord to discuss the future status of the Thirteen Colonies, and then opposed independence in favor of continued British rule…in the name of all Americans? Would his opinion and interests go over the wishes of all the other Americans? Of course not.

Another example of the U.S. colonial regime and American politicians ignoring their own *"we are waiting for Puerto Ricans to come to a consensus"* narrative occurred in 1946. In that year, Puerto Rico's colonial legislature (led by the Partido Popular Democrático) **approved a legislative bill for a plebiscite** between the options of independence, statehood, and some sort of autonomous dominion status.

The unelected and appointed Anglo-American governor of the time, Rexford G. Tugwell, vetoed the bill since having Puerto Ricans decide their own fate and future went against U.S. colonial interests. The vetoed bill returned to the Puerto Rican colonial legislature (as expected) and was approved again by a majority, overturning Tugwell's veto, which was considered an act of defiance.

At this point, the upheld bill for a plebiscite went to the desk of President Truman, who unilaterally vetoed it again and squashed that attempt to resolve Puerto Rico's status. President Truman did not support any changes in Puerto Rico's colonial status (ignoring the will of Puerto Rico), and he would only consider cosmetic reforms regarding colonial governance because no matter what the Puerto Ricans wanted, the U.S. colonial regime and its plenary control must remain. One can now understand why the Puerto Rican nationalists sought him out. Here's a quick summary of the three times the U.S. has ignored and rejected Puerto Rican consensus on independence in order to continue its colonial rule:

Year	How Puerto Rican Consensus was Rejected by the United States *(although American politicians are always waiting for Puerto Rican consensus)*
1914	The **Puerto Rico House of Delegates** unanimously voted in favor of independence from the United States, yet this Puerto Rican consensus was rejected and ignored by the U.S. Congress.
1943	**U.S. Senator Millard Tydings** drafted a legislative proposal to grant independence to Puerto Rico. This proposal to grant independence was welcomed by every political party in Puerto Rico. Even with unanimous political consensus for independence, the proposed bill was blocked and defeated by Senator Muñoz Marín, a compromised U.S. puppet.
1946	Puerto Rico's colonial legislature approved a legislation for a **plebiscite** between the options of independence, statehood, and some sort of dominion status. Rexford G. Tugwell vetoed the bill. The vetoed bill returned to the Puerto Rican colonial legislature and overturned Tugwell's veto. The upheld bill for a plebiscite went to the desk of President Truman, who unilaterally vetoed it again and squashed that attempt to resolve Puerto Rico's status.

Anyone who says that the U.S. is just waiting for the Puerto Ricans to come together in consensus in order to act is either lying or ignorant of such historical facts. All three times Puerto Ricans have come together in political consensus to support decolonization and independence in 1914, 1943, and 1946, they have only been ignored and rejected by the U.S. Congress, the very entity that complains that it cannot act without Puerto Rican consensus.

Senator Luis Muñoz Marín (as a true colonial lackey and opium addict[19] that was being blackmailed by federal agencies in Puerto Rico), now believed that independence would hurt Puerto Rico's economy and sought a colonial option that offered more autonomy in purely local affairs, yet keep Puerto Rico under colonial rule: thus, was born the concept of the *Commonwealth* (Estado Libre Asociado de Puerto Rico). In essence, it gave the Puerto Ricans a few crumbs of local autonomy without changing the colonial relationship at all.

It's like promoting a field slave to become a house slave with fancy new clothes, but a slave he still remains. If a master allows the slave the freedom to pick the color of window curtains or the number of forks in his slave quarters, has that slave now experienced freedom? Of course not. As admitted to by the U.S. Supreme Court, the U.S. Congress, and various executive branch memos and reports (all three branches of the U.S. government), the "Commonwealth of Puerto Rico" has no shred of sovereignty whatsoever…in plain English, it's a colony.

Even fellow prominent party members, like Vicente Geigel Polanco, who realized early in the 1950s that the Commonwealth did not change the colonial nature of the U.S.-Puerto Rico relationship, were ousted from the party and marginalized. Muñoz Marín even expelled all *independentistas* from the party, and they regrouped as the modern Puerto Rican Independence Party (PIP), which of course, was later persecuted and criminalized by the colonial regime. Almost like a political and lexical Lord Voldemort, the word "*colony*" became "*the word that shall not be said*" in public nor official Puerto Rico government circles.

Even today, Puerto Rico and U.S. officials do not like to use the word "*colony*" since it creates an awkward and embarrassing situation for American politicians that prefer to think of themselves as the brave descendants of anti-colonial revolutionaries like George Washington and Thomas Jefferson. For many Americans, the notion that the United States has *colonies* is one to be avoided, ignored, and mocked since the very acceptance of this fact would shatter their fragile sensibilities and notions of democratic grandeur and national exceptionalism.

With the colonial Commonwealth of Puerto Rico firmly in place, the United States even strong-armed the United Nations in 1953 to take Puerto Rico off the list of non-Self-Governing Territories [20] (I prefer to call it the List of Occupied & Enslaved Nations). Luis Muñoz Marín was a colonial slave that was offered freedom, yet chose to embrace and dance to the sound and clattering of his own chains.

He will surely go down in Puerto Rican history as one of our nation's most despised and pathetic traitors and colonialists. His *personal* decision to oppose and reject the proposal for independence offered by Senator Tydings and the U.S. Congress in 1943 set Puerto Rico back decades in its struggle for freedom and democracy. And to think that Puerto Rico's principal international airport and various schools and roads are named after this despised traitor. The colonial regime surely does celebrate its champion!

Luis Muñoz Marín

Due to his sole opposition (ignoring the wishes of all the political parties in Puerto Rico to support the Tydings independence bill and turning his back on this once in a lifetime opportunity), Puerto Rico did not receive its freedom and political independence from the United States in 1943. With the advent of the Commonwealth in 1952, Muñoz Marín became the first elected Puerto Rican colonial governor of Puerto Rico and his new colonialist Commonwealth party, the *Partido Popular Democrático (PPD)*, dominated Puerto Rico's politics for decades.

As an opioid addict that did not want his secret made public by the Feds (who mentioned this in his declassified police dossier), he was the perfect colonial puppet governor that could legitimize and administer the new Commonwealth government.

During his decades of "strongman" Stalin-like rule (diehard party followers and loyalists would have portraits of him in their homes), Governor Muñoz Marín:

1. persecuted and jailed independence leaders and sympathizers;
2. labeled his political opponents "communists" just to get them persecuted, blacklisted or arrested by federal authorities;

3. enjoyed a personality cult where he was called *"El Vate"* (pronounced EL VA-TEY) and his strict loyal followers were called *muñocistas*;
4. created the perception that he was like a "father" that brought progress and stability to Puerto Rico;
5. sought to create the perception that U.S. colonial rule was not just needed and beneficial, but actually protection and tutelage;
6. promoted the belief that he was the *only* political leader that knows what is best for Puerto Rico;
7. further consolidated the colonial system and colonial mentality in Puerto Rico by supporting the Gag Law and promoted the idea that Puerto Rico could not survive without U.S. control and tutelage;
8. supported the U.S. Navy expropriations in Vieques and Culebra;
9. denationalized Puerto Rico's flag and national symbols;
10. claimed that Puerto Rico was not a colony after 1952 in order to legitimize his "Commonwealth";
11. fortified the colonial economic dependency model and began an industrialization program (Operation Bootstrap) based not on production, self-sufficiency, and long-term economic development, but on federal funds, foreign investments, tax incentives to U.S. companies, and the emigration of masses of Puerto Ricans to the United States as low-skilled workers for textile and agricultural companies.

This 1950s colonial dependent economic model is still in use today. Muñoz Marín's industrialization did eventually create jobs and led to the birth of a small middle-class due to U.S. investments and U.S. companies that took advantage of federal and local tax haven policies, but all that came at the expense of violating civil and human rights, destroying the agricultural sector, promoting a mass exodus of rural Puerto Ricans and dissidents to the United States, and consolidating U.S. colonial rule over Puerto Rico.

Also, by entrenching the colonial mentality in future generations, Muñoz Marín inadvertently supported and created the political and economic conditions that would later create poorer and more dependent statehooders – people who strive for more welfare and food stamps, not personal economic progress.

In 1943, the U.S. Congress finally had the consensus it was always asking for regarding Puerto Rico's independence, but chose to ignore this consensus and only listened to the opinion of a colonial lackey in regard to the future of Puerto Rico. In 1946, they ignored the consensus and vetoed twice Puerto Rico's attempt to have a plebiscite. It would not be until 1967 that status plebiscites and referendums were *allowed* by the U.S. in order to validate the Commonwealth at the polls, thus having Puerto Rican voters *consent* to their own colonial bondage.

The 1951 Referendum for Public Law 81-600 (to establish the Commonwealth) was opposed by 66% of voters who voted against it and who abstained due to the pro-independence call for an electoral boycott. By ignoring the mass electoral boycott abstentions, the U.S. colonial regime was able to claim that the Puerto Ricans approved the referendum on Law 81-600 by 76.5%.

Then, in 1952, the final referendum to approve and validate the new colonial Commonwealth constitution and government was only supported by 32% amid a massive electoral boycott where only 39% of the entire electorate voted[21].

Of course, the U.S. colonial regime ignored the majority that abstained and only recognized the votes in support of the new colonial Commonwealth, thus being able to claim that the Puerto Ricans approved the new colonial Commonwealth by 81.9%. Yes, statistics can be manipulated. After being approved by the U.S.

Congress and signed by President Truman, the new colonial Commonwealth constitution came into effect on July 25th, 1952,[22] with much fanfare and festivities along with the official hoisting of the denationalized Puerto Rican flag as the flag of the Commonwealth of Puerto Rico.

Puerto Rican nationalists and other pro-independence and sovereignty advocates did not support this referendum because it did not offer any real options, just colonial Commonwealth: Yes or No. Independence was not offered as an option; thus, the referendum was regarded as a sham and an undemocratic farce by Puerto Rican nationalists and other pro-sovereignty supporters.

Ironically, in 1980, the U.S. Supreme Court, in *Harris v. Rosario*, established and recognized that the 1952 referendum did not change Puerto Rico's actual territorial status[23], as had been stated by nationalists for decades. In essence, Puerto Rico was still a colony that did not actually enjoy any measure of self-rule.

And yet, in 1952, the United States could now claim that the Puerto Ricans democratically approved the colonial Commonwealth. It's actually quite genius on the part of the U.S. colonial regime. It's like having a slave consent to their position by voting on either to become a house slave or a field slave. At the end of the day, he/she is still a slave, although they would have them believe they had participated in actual decision-making. If a slave votes to remain a slave, is he/she still a slave? Should a slave's decision to remain in slavery be disregarded or upheld? If a slave *believes* he/she is free, are they free? According to Muñoz Marín and his colonialist followers, if a colony votes to remain under colonial rule, they are not a colony anymore; they are now a *Commonwealth*.

After the establishment of the Commonwealth in 1952, has the United States ever seriously considered decolonizing and changing Puerto Rico's status? According to documents studied, analyzed, and later published by noted Prof. Jaime L. Rodríguez Cancel, in the 1970s, President Jimmy Carter began a process to explore decolonization options for Puerto Rico, particularly after pressure and specific United Nations resolutions calling for Puerto Rico's self-determination and independence.

In 1977, Robert Pastor, head of Latin American Affairs at the National Security Council (NSC), informed Zbigniew Brzezinski, the National Security Advisor, that the United States is facing major problems at the United Nation's Committee on Decolonization, particularly by various Puerto Rican representatives publicly calling Puerto Rico a "colony".

As one could imagine, American calls for democratization and freedom in other countries, especially those under communist governments, were continually undermined when various countries at the United Nations brought up the issue of Puerto Rico and its struggle against U.S. colonial rule. It would be like an abolitionist preaching to others about the evils of slavery, yet having a slave chained in his basement. Due to changing geopolitical conditions, some in Washington, DC, thought that the time had come to reformulate Puerto Rico's relationship with the United States.

In July 1978, Robert Pastor and Henry Richardson drafted a document where the United States government would reaffirm its commitment to Puerto Rico's self-determination. This draft document supported the idea of a plebiscite in 1981 between the three UN-approved decolonization options of Independence, Free Association, and Integration (statehood). Soon afterward, the NSC established a committee to review and study the various Puerto Rico status options, particularly how they would affect U.S. national interests and security. From this study, recommendations would be sent to Brzezinski in December 1978.

According to this NSC study and its findings, it stated that **independence** was the best political status option for Puerto Rico and that the United States should begin preparing and taking all the necessary steps to prepare the Puerto Rican people for these changes. This study was not made by a group of leftists or Puerto Rican Nationalists, but by American national security analysts and professionals concerned with defending and advancing U.S. interests and national security.

In December 1980, these NSC recommendations regarding Puerto Rican self-determination and independence were sent to President-Elect Ronald Reagan's Transition Committee, which subsequently canceled the proposed 1980 plebiscite and shelved the entire study and ignored the recommendations[24].

Now, why would President Reagan shelve and ignore these NSC recommendations and abort a process of decolonization and independence for Puerto Rico? Well, it was no secret that President Reagan's presidential campaign received large donations and support from Puerto Rican statehooders and colonialists affiliated to the Republican Party. Sadly, for President Reagan, large donations from statehooders trumped national security recommendations.

With so many donations to his campaign, the statehooders even managed to get President Reagan to endorse statehood on a promo video, even though the Republicans, like Democrats, have never actually advanced the statehood agenda in Congress. The statehooders and colonialists did a great job in stopping the decolonization process in 1980 and ensured that Puerto Rico remained a pathetic and powerless U.S. colony for decades to come just to placate their own political and economic reasons.

In 1989, the Congress actually held hearings and meetings regarding Puerto Rican self-determination with the three principal Puerto Rican political parties, but this process was eventually derailed and ended by Congress when the statehooders insisted that Puerto Rican voters, in a binding referendum, could *force* Puerto Rico statehood on the United States. Again, understanding that statehood is not in the U.S. national interest, the Congress just ended the negotiations and moved on to other issues, leaving Puerto Rico just as it left it, a pathetic and powerless U.S. colony. There's a joke in Puerto Rico that goes: How do you get the United States quickly out of a room? Bring up statehood.

Today, the United States is still facing major problems at the United Nation's Committee on Decolonization, particularly by the endless stream of Puerto Rican representatives from all sectors of society publicly calling Puerto Rico a "colony", with the majority demanding a transition to sovereignty. The U.S. Mission to the United Nations (USUN) also continues to not only ignore calls for Puerto Rican decolonization, but its diplomats do not even attend meetings and panels discussing issues related to Puerto Rico. Of course, the U.S. mainstream media does not provide televised coverage nor news stories about these hearings to the American public.

In essence, these American diplomats and other U.S. Foreign Service officials do not care nor think about Puerto Rico in any way. I'm sure many of them, if asked, could not even locate Puerto Rico on a world map. At the annual meetings of the UN Committee on Decolonization, year after year, Puerto Ricans photograph the empty U.S. seat and post it on social media so that Puerto Ricans and the world can actually see how much American diplomats could care less about Puerto Ricans and decolonization. Puerto Ricans, I ask you, are these the concerned "diplomats" you want representing us as Puerto Ricans at the United Nations?

As a colony or U.S. state, Puerto Ricans are stuck with these ignorant and indifferent Americans representing them on the world stage. With sovereignty, Puerto Rico would have its own Diplomatic Service to properly represent Puerto Ricans and Puerto Rican interests at the United Nations and around the world.

Photos taken during two UN Committee on Decolonization hearings where U.S. diplomats refuse to participate and listen to Puerto Ricans explain the effects of U.S. colonial policies and demand sovereignty for Puerto Rico.

The Congress, just like the USUN, keeps ignoring Puerto Rico and insists on kicking the Puerto Rican "status can" down the road, until one day the can is going to hit a rock and bounce back and smack them in the face. Puerto Ricans need to *be* that rock. Today, the only bill in the U.S. Congress that would recognize Puerto Rico's sovereignty and support a referendum between the two sovereignty options of Independence and Free Association is H.R. 900, introduced by former Illinois Democratic Congressman Luis Gutierrez.

Since the United States has *never* brought up the topic of statehood to the Puerto Rican people in 121 years, it is obvious that the U.S. *never* intends to make Puerto Rico a state, yet it seems very amenable to have Puerto Rico remain a colony and captive market indefinitely, an option that is rejected by Puerto Ricans. One does not have to be a political genius or Washington political insider to realize that the United States has never been interested in Puerto Rico statehood. In fact, the United States invented the term "*unincorporated territory*" in the Insular Cases (1900) in order to never be in a position where Puerto Rico could actually aspire to statehood.

Forcing an occupied nation to live in political limbo, colonial purgatory, and uncertainty regarding its future is a political and democratic atrocity of major proportions. For the majority of Puerto Ricans, remaining a U.S. colony indefinitely is out of the question.

4. *The Imposition of English & Assimilation Policies*

The main goal of such assimilation policies instituted by the U.S. colonial regime were to break down and relegate Puerto Rico's culture, national identity, and any cultural and linguistic links and ties with Spain and Latin America so that Puerto Ricans could become, at some point, some sort of Spanish-surnamed Americans, a model colonial Puerto Rican[25].

Regarding such blatant and despised assimilationist efforts imposed on Puerto Ricans by the U.S. colonial regime, the American Civil Liberties Union states:

"The fact that these possessions were inhabited by non-English speaking peoples of diverse background was an obstacle to incorporating them as states or territories of the Union. The record made by forty years of administration is not a commendable one. The promise to prepare these peoples for independent, democratic self-government has remained largely unfulfilled. Conflict between the American rulers and the black, brown or white native peoples arises from an attitude of superiority. No better evidence of it can be cited than the imposition of the English language on children in the schools, the employment of American teachers particularly in the higher grades, and the adoption of the traditional American school education, regardless of students' practical needs.[26]"

The main assimilationist policies imposed on and fought against by Puerto Ricans were:

    a. **LANGUAGE:** the imposition of English to replace Spanish in government and education.

b. **CULTURE:** the teaching of American history and cultural norms while denigrating and relegating Puerto Rican history and culture.

c. **NATIONAL SYMBOLS:** the banning of the Puerto Rican flag and National Anthem (*La Borinqueña*) and promoting only the U.S. flag, the U.S. Pledge of Allegiance, and the Star-Spangled Banner in government and schools.

d. **RELIGION:** the opening of Puerto Rico to various evangelizing American Protestant sects to reduce the control and influence of the Catholic Church, which was also considered a bastion of Puerto Rican culture and identity and a link to the world outside of colonial rule.

5. *The Attacks on the Catholic Church and the Imposition of American Protestant Evangelization Policies*

In 1899, Protestant groups that supported the U.S. colonial regime and efforts to weaken the Catholic Church in Puerto Rico even went as far as to divide Puerto Rico up into sections on a map where different Protestant sects would be designated to evangelize the "uncultured" Catholic Puerto Ricans. From Presbyterians and Methodists to Baptists and Congregationalists, all these sects initially came to Puerto Rico as agents of U.S. colonialism to displace Catholics and disseminate their "gospel" of American values and assimilation.

Today, although Protestants in Puerto Rico make up approximately 15% of the population, there is no religious conflict nor animosity between Puerto Ricans of different Christian faiths as occurred in Ireland and other countries under colonial rule. Here's the map of Protestant evangelization of Puerto Rico as decided by Protestant groups in 1899:

*Samuel Silva Gotay, Protestantismo y Política En Puerto Rico: 1898-1930, pg. 113

Along with the Protestant evangelization policy, the Catholic Church was directly attacked by the U.S. colonial regime. Many churches and church properties were confiscated by the colonial regime and the military. From being the official religion of state in Spanish Puerto Rico since 1511 to a disempowered religious sect under siege by American colonial policies, the Catholic Church in Puerto Rico had to react.

The Catholic Church went from official conservatism to outright subversive militancy to defend the faith and Puerto Rico's Hispanic Catholic identity. Like Irish and Polish cultural identity, the Puerto Rican culture is greatly rooted in Catholic traditions, values, and is seen by many as a core aspect of Puerto Rican identity.

In response to these colonial attacks to the Church, two devout Catholic Puerto Ricans, José de los Santos Morales y José Rodríguez Medina, with the support of the Catholic community, established a rebel Catholic organization called *San Juan Evangelista* (later called *Los Hermanos Cheo / The Cheo Brothers*)[27] to fight against these anti-Catholic and anti-Puerto Rican policies.

Los Hermanos Cheo went to various towns and cities to discuss the attacks on the Church and Puerto Rico's culture and rally the rural jíbaros (farmers). They began to build up a following and were soon targeted by the Insular Police as "subversives", which resulted in riots in Ponce and other towns.

Los Hermanos Cheo were the first group in that era after the U.S. occupation that vocally advocated for Puerto Ricans to resist and fight against assimilation and Americanization and to struggle to defend Puerto Rico's national identity and culture. When Los Hermanos Cheo began to draw crowds in the thousands coming from all parts of Puerto Rico, attacks on the Insular Police and U.S. military were more frequent.

In order to stop a potential rebellion across Puerto Rico, the colonial court eventually ruled in favor of the Catholic Church and ordered the U.S. military to return all confiscated church properties back to the Catholic Church. Catholic Puerto Rican militancy had won.

The Vatican (The Holy See) came to the aid of Catholic Puerto Ricans as well. Up until that time, the Diocese of Puerto Rico was affiliated to the Diocese of Cuba. It was feared by the Vatican and Catholic Puerto Ricans that the U.S. would unilaterally disaffiliate the Diocese of Puerto Rico from Cuba and affiliate it with an American diocese (possibly New York or Boston), thus facilitating the process of Americanization. In Puerto Rico, Americanization means the total destruction of the Puerto Rican nation, culture, and national identity.

On February 20th, 1903, to counter this religious and cultural threat to Puerto Rico and Puerto Rico's Hispanic Catholic identity, Pope Leo XIII, in an unprecedented ecclesiastical-diplomatic move from Rome, enacted an Apostolic Proclamation unilaterally disaffiliating the Diocese of Puerto Rico from Cuba and affiliating it *directly* under the authority, protection, and sole jurisdiction of the Vatican itself.

Under this new arrangement, only the Pope himself, not the U.S. President or any colonial official in Puerto Rico, would have any authority over the affairs of the Diocese of Puerto Rico. This move angered U.S. colonial officials, but who would go against the Pope? No one. Today, the overwhelming majority of Puerto Ricans (70%-85%) are Catholic and adhere to the Catholic Church's Hispanic-American Liturgical Calendar and customs, which are observed by all Catholic dioceses and parishes throughout Latin America.

Today, Puerto Rico constitutes one ecclesiastical province comprising an archdiocese in San Juan and five dioceses (Arecibo, Fajardo-Humacao, Caguas, Mayagüez, and Ponce), which together form the Puerto Rican Episcopal Conference (*Conferencia Episcopal Puertorriqueña*), which continues to remain separate and independent from the United States Conference of Catholic Bishops. The courage of Los Hermanos Cheo and the decision by Pope Leo XIII to protect the Diocese of Puerto Rico from Americanization and cultural assimilation is still recognized and celebrated by Catholic Puerto Ricans today.

Overall, these assimilation policies aimed to destroy and displace Puerto Rico's language, history, culture, and spirituality. The mere existence of a Puerto Rican Nation was a threat to the U.S. colonial regime's legitimacy and assimilationist plans, and that had to be attacked from day one.

Like policies used on Native Americans, the American narrative of wanting to "*Kill the Puerto Rican, Save the Man*". American colonial officials believed that if such assimilation policies could work in Texas, New Mexico, and California on such Hispanic subjects, it would surely work in Puerto Rico. As we know, they were gravely mistaken.

Puerto Ricans had to suffer decades, not only of inept, corrupt, and racist appointed American governors and officials (particularly the buffoonish governor Montgomery Reilly), but also of official English language policies in government and education until those policies were finally rescinded due to massive disgust and protests. As we already know, through legal and cultural battles and protests, all those cultural and linguistic assimilation policies were ultimately defeated and sent to the colonial garbage heap.

6. Outlawing & Coopting Puerto Rico's National Symbols

The U.S. colonial regime banned the Puerto Rican flag and Puerto Rico's National Anthem for decades. Even patriotic songs and poems deemed "*seditious*" were banned by the U.S. colonial authorities. Puerto Rican nationalists were routinely jailed and tortured by local police simply for having an illegal Puerto Rican flag in Puerto Rico, particularly under the Gag Law of 1948. The Puerto Rican flag only became "legal" after the establishment of the colonial "Commonwealth" in 1952.

In order to make the new colonial Commonwealth regime more palatable to Puerto Ricans, Muñoz Marín coopted Puerto Rican national symbols (once considered illegal by himself and the colonial regime) in order to help legitimize his new Commonwealth in the eyes of Puerto Ricans and the world.

Here's how he did it:

Muñoz Marín **adopted the Puerto Rican flag** (the national symbol of a Free Puerto Rico) and made it the official flag of the colonial Commonwealth. In order to help denationalize it, the Commonwealth government changed the flag's sky-blue color to a dark navy-blue color to more closely resemble the navy-blue color of the U.S. flag.

This would be tantamount to co-opting the flag of a Free Ireland and making it the official flag of the British-Irish colonial government. The adoption of the Puerto Rican flag by the colonial Commonwealth government did not sit well with the Nationalists and other patriotic Puerto Ricans since they had suffered jail and torture for defending the Puerto Rican flag from that very colonial government.

The original Puerto Rican Flag, created by Antonio Vélez Alvarado and later adopted by the Puerto Rican Revolutionary Committee on December 22, 1895.

Flag of the Commonwealth of Puerto Rico (1952)

Muñoz Marín also **changed the meanings of the Puerto Rican flag** to better represent colonial, not national Puerto Rican values. The white star went from representing the Puerto Rican Nation to representing the colonial government. The three red stripes went from representing the blood of Puerto Rico's patriots and martyrs to representing the three branches of the colonial government. George Orwell would have been astonished.

Muñoz Marín's new Commonwealth government even **coopted La Borinqueña** as the new official anthem of the colonial regime, but not without changing its lyrics. *La Borinqueña's* patriotic and revolutionary lyrics, written by Lola Rodríguez de Tió, were deemed too dangerous, patriotic, and seditious for Puerto Ricans so they were replaced by lyrics, from a poem, that just focused on Christopher Columbus and Puerto Rico's beaches and natural beauty so as not to inspire nationalism and national pride. Today, this colonial version of *La Borinqueña* is the one still taught to children at schools across Puerto Rico. Suffice it to say that today, pro-independence and pro-sovereignty advocates only recognize, honor, and sing the original patriotic and historic lyrics of *La Borinqueña*.

7. Using Violence & Terror to Subjugate Puerto Ricans

To quell the rising nationalist tide in the 1930s, the United States sent **Colonel Elisha Francis Riggs** as the Police Chief and American **Governor Blanton Winship** to attack the nationalists and further clamp down and secure colonial rule. The Puerto Ricans were getting restless at the blatant political, democratic, and economic failures of U.S. colonial rule and needed to be put back in their place by "tough" and "no-nonsense" Americans that the U.S. could trust…such as two white supremacist military officers that hated Puerto Ricans and sought to destroy all resistance to U.S. colonial rule via fear, violence, and terror.

These two colonial American officials were responsible for the **Rio Piedras Massacre** and the **Ponce Massacre,** where many Puerto Ricans were killed. After the Rio Piedras Massacre of 1935, which killed four Nationalists at the University of Puerto Rico, Colonel Riggs was shot and killed in 1936 in retaliation by two other Nationalists, Hiram Rosado and Elias Beauchamp. These two Nationalists were arrested and executed at the police precinct[28]. As one might expect, no police executioners were arrested.

Regarding Winship's hellish tenure as American colonial governor of Puerto Rico, the American Civil Liberties Union states,

"Under his administration freedom of speech and assembly have repeatedly been denied, teachers have been summarily discharged or disciplined for their views, violence by the militarized police has resulted in deaths and in injuries running into the hundreds. Courts of law have been used as instruments to support American colonial rule. Suppression has aroused violence by extremist youths among the Nationalists, who have attempted acts of assassination and in two instances killed an American official.[29]*"*

Hiram Rosado & Elias Beauchamp

Blanton Winship

Colonial U.S. Governor of Puerto Rico

Governor Blanton Winship was a racist Southern military man that set out upon his arrival to destroy Puerto Rican Nationalism, squash anti-colonial defiance, and consolidate U.S. colonial rule and hegemony in Puerto Rico by violence and brute force. He quickly militarized the Insular Police, established Tommy Gun squads, and began to arrest Nationalists and other independence sympathizers.

On March 21, 1937, Governor Winship ordered his militarized police force to stop a lawful peaceful protest march by unarmed Nationalists in Ponce. The Insular Police surrounded the marchers, fired hundreds of bullets, and killed 21 and wounded 235 people, including passersby and innocent women and children. The Insular Police even killed two of their own in the police crossfire.

Ponce Massacre of March 21, 1937

Due to the outcry, the American Civil Liberties Union (ACLU) became involved and after an investigation, determined that a *massacre* had occurred in Ponce. The commission that investigated the Ponce Massacre stated:

"*Civil liberties have been repeatedly denied during the last nine months by order of Governor Blanton Winship. He has failed to recognize the right of free speech and assemblage. Force has been threatened toward those who would exercise these rights.*[30]"

Of course, as the appointed American governor, nothing happened to Governor Winship, no investigations, no federal probes, nothing. No one under Governor Winship's chain of command was investigated or prosecuted. Even police officers who admitted to the massacre were not arrested, prosecuted, punished, or reprimanded. Again, American colonial officials, particularly the appointed governor, operate in the colony with impunity.

Nationalist Angel Estebán Antongiorgi, shot and being taken by the colonial police after attempting to assassinate American Governor Blanton Winship in 1938.

In 1938, a year after the Ponce Massacre, Governor Winship decided it would be a great idea and show of American strength in the colony to have a U.S. military parade in Ponce, the very city still reeling from the traumatic aftereffects of the massacre. Of course, at the parade, Governor Winship, in full military regalia, was shot at by a young Nationalist, Angel Esteban Antongiorgi.

Although Antongiorgi was killed, he died defending Puerto Rico's honor, and he *did* put a stop to the governor's grand U.S. military parade in Ponce, which ended in utter chaos and pandemonium. Antongiorgi's corpse was taken by police and never recovered.

Governor Winship survived the attack and continued to abuse, arrest, and terrorize more Puerto Ricans during his tenure. After this attack, Governor Winship arrested many more nationalists across the island, even ones that were not involved in the U.S. military parade attack.

Under Winship's colonial dictatorship and the brutal suppression of civil rights and liberties, the American Civil Liberties Union also noted that,

"Nationalists and their sympathizers were denied permits to hold meetings and parades. In one instance, troops surrounded a church and denied entrance to thousands of Puerto Ricans who had come to attend mass in celebration of a patriotic holiday. Where permits for meetings were granted, speakers were told in advance what they might and might not say.[31]"

Although appointed by democratic President Franklyn D. Roosevelt (FDR) in 1934 to subdue Puerto Rico and curb the rise of Puerto Rican nationalism by violence and force, the pressure and criticism from some members of Congress eventually led FDR to remove Winship as governor in 1939. Even Democratic U.S. Congressman Vito Marcantonio, a supporter of Puerto Rican independence, called Governor Winship a "tyrant" in a congressional speech.

Although he behaved like a murderous Nazi in Puerto Rico, during WWII, Winship was ironically rewarded and chosen to participate in military tribunals that tried Nazi saboteurs, a clear moment of the pot calling the kettle black. In Puerto Rican history, Winship will be remembered as the "Heinrich Himmler" of U.S. rule in Puerto Rico.

Along with the violence and terror of U.S. colonial rule, Puerto Ricans under the U.S. flag suffered from a selective utilization of civil liberties. Puerto Ricans were free to advocate for continued U.S. rule, Americanization, statehood, and carry the U.S. flag, but they were not free to advocate for independence, patriotic causes, nor carry the banned Puerto Rican flag. Regarding blatant violations of civil liberties in Puerto Rico in the 1930s, the American Civil Liberties Union states,

"In 1931, the Unionist Party was barred from the ballot by the Puerto Rican Supreme Court, and strong reasons support the charge that it was due to the party's campaign for independence. In the same year, the

late Senator Antonio Barcelo, leader of the Unionists, was refused use of the radio in New York City to broadcast a pro-independence speech, and in San Juan the Radio Corporation refused to carry the speeches of Unionists and Nationalists. At the University of Puerto Rico students were expelled for signing a manifesto calling for Puerto Rican independence.[32]"

This ladies and gentlemen, is a highlight of Puerto Ricans enjoying U.S. civil liberties in Puerto Rico.

8. Using Violence, Terror & Torture on Pro-Independence Supporters

The U.S. colonial regime not only arrested and tortured nationalists but also subjected them, like nationalist leader Pedro Albizu Campos, to radioactive experimentation that burned his whole body. Puerto Rican nationalists were routinely beaten and placed in bedbug-infested cells in order to punish them, drive them crazy, and try to break their spirits for daring to defy colonial rule and believing that Puerto Ricans have a right to freedom.

Imagine being placed in a small dark cell with millions of starving bedbugs biting you over and over, day after day, in order to break your will. Regarding Albizu Campos' claim of radiation torture, the U.S. colonial regime simply dismissed him as insane, even when photographic and medical evidence proved otherwise.

In 1994, the U.S. Department of Energy[33] revealed that human radiation experiments had, in fact been conducted without consent on prisoners in Puerto Rico during the 1950s and 1970s. Pedro Albizu Campos and the nationalists were no doubt victims of this cruel, barbaric, and inhumane colonial policy.

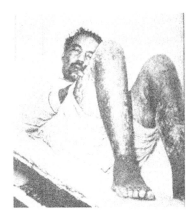 

Pedro Albizu Campos showing his radiation burns

Julio Pinto Gandía

Some nationalist leaders, like prominent nationalist lawyer Julio Pinto Gandía, were arrested in 1976 and never seen again. His physical remains have never been found. Like I mentioned before, the fear of being arrested or targeted by the colonial regime for being pro-independence or pro-sovereignty is still present and pervasive in today's Puerto Rico.

In Puerto Rico, being a pro-independence supporter was dangerous, and if you wanted to survive and not be persecuted, you had better support colonial rule or statehood. This very fear is alive today and is what fuels the colonialist and statehood movements in Puerto Rico...yes, the very movements that try to convince Americans that Puerto Ricans desire statehood and U.S. rule.

According to declassified documents and oral accounts in the seminal book *"War Against All Puerto Ricans"*, by author Nelson Denis, many Puerto Ricans in the aftermath of the Revolution of 1950 were also taken to a U.S. interrogation and torture facility known as the *"Academy of Truth"* where they were physically and mentally tortured for days and weeks by U.S. military personnel and assisted by loyalist Puerto Ricans.

Puerto Ricans, both men, and women suspected of being nationalists, were beaten, starved, and electrocuted while surrounded by laughing and sadistic American soldiers. If you can imagine a tropical Abu Ghraib prison, this would be it.

In this nightmare, some Puerto Ricans would be electrocuted until they yelled "*Que viva los Estados Unidos*" (Long-live the United States), yet the abuse and torture would not stop. Let's reflect on the fact that these were Americans (U.S. citizens) beating, starving, electrocuting, and killing scores of Puerto Ricans (U.S. citizens) for rebelling against the United States in Puerto Rico.

I can only imagine the screams, the sexual assaults, human rights violations, and sadistic immorality that these Puerto Ricans had to endure at this factory of terror by their "fellow U.S. citizens". These sadistic and brutal horrors probably made the movie *Saw* look like a Christmas romantic comedy.

In my opinion, the most depraved and infuriating oral account told by survivors about the tortures at the "Academy of Truth" involved a Puerto Rican father who was starved for two weeks and then given a plate of cooked meat, which he ate. After eating the meat, American soldiers came into his cell with his son's severed head and told the father that he had just eaten his cooked son. The father vomited his son out, fell into shock, and died of a heart attack[34].

This father and son were never identified and became two of the many people that disappeared into the ugly black hole of despair, depravity, and terror that is U.S. colonial rule in Puerto Rico. The family of this father and son that disappeared in 1950 are probably still wondering whatever happened to them. They never returned home, and families were destroyed forever. No records, no closure, and no accountability. Who cares? They're just Puerto Ricans.

For these American soldiers, the Puerto Ricans were simply subhuman *spics* that no one would care about. Some people eventually survived and made it out with physical and mental scars, but many others never made it out alive. This is the terrorized colonial Puerto Rico that never makes it to the tourist magazines, congressional reports, nor academic articles and reports of American agencies and think-tanks.

Hopefully, one day, there will be a full-scale investigation regarding these acts of torture and a memorial site erected for the victims of the terror and torture at the "Academy of Truth". I'm sure a sovereign Puerto Rico would make such an investigation and memorial site a reality.

The current colonial government of Puerto Rico does *not* dare ask the United States about these events or actions for fear of angering some federal or military officials. Quite understandably, as occurs in colonies, these events and actions during the Revolution of 1950 were suppressed and did not make it to the pages of Puerto Rican history books for students to learn about.

Even today, these events and acts of state-sanctioned torture, barbarism, and terrorism are largely unknown by most Puerto Ricans. This book aims to rectify this situation. Puerto Ricans *need* to know this.

9. *The Imposition of U.S. Citizenship & Military Draft on all Puerto Ricans by Decree*

In 1917, President Woodrow Wilson signed the Jones-Shafroth Act that reconfigured the colonial government and imposed U.S. citizenship on all Puerto Ricans even though it was unanimously rejected by Puerto Rico's House of Delegates. As U.S. citizens, Puerto Rican males were now subjected to the military draft, and more than 20,000 Puerto Ricans were sent to serve and die in foreign wars fighting for freedom and democracy that they themselves did not enjoy in Puerto Rico.

All colonial powers use colonial natives to supplant and reinforce their colonial and military adventures and policies. The

British used Africans, Indians, and Malays as colonial troops. The French used Africans, Caribbean Blacks, Arabs, and Pacific islanders as colonial troops in WWI and WWII. Imagine this, Africans fighting in France to preserve France's independence, yet when they return to Africa, they would be arrested if they wanted independence for their countries.

The United States used and continues to use Puerto Ricans, Guamanians, Samoans, and Northern Mariana islanders as colonial troops.

Economic and professional opportunities are so dire and bleak in U.S. colonies that many youths see the U.S. military as their only way out of poverty. Thus, one can see how maintaining the colonies in utter poverty creates a supply of fresh recruits for the U.S. military. Sadly, many of these very Puerto Rican, Samoan, and Chamorro U.S. soldiers will be yelled at to "Speak English" by their "fellow Americans".

Remember, just because some natives (Puerto Ricans) served and fought bravely as colonial troops in U.S. wars, does not mean that the U.S. now must make Puerto Rico a state (as statehooders claim).

- Did Kenyan troops serving in the British Army obligate Great Britain to retain Kenya and make it a British realm in Africa? No.
- Did Senegalese troops serving in the French Army obligate France to retain Senegal and make it a French overseas region? No.
- Did Angolan troops serving in the Portuguese Army obligate Portugal to retain Angola and make it a Portuguese region or African province? No.

The United States is no different. Even if they fought bravely in various wars, like the *Borinqueneers* of the 65th Infantry Regiment, Puerto Rican troops serving in the U.S. military do not obligate the United States to make Puerto Rico a U.S. state. For the United States' point of view, the imposition of U.S. citizenship in 1917 on all Puerto Ricans was merely a way to secure more soldiers for the military draft, the front lines, and future wars and a way to tell the world that Puerto Ricans were now "Property of the U.S.A.", like a legalistic slave branding.

After decades with U.S. citizenship, many Puerto Ricans see U.S. citizenship as important in their lives since it allows one to travel unrestricted to the United States, reside and work in the United States, and receive federal social welfare benefits. The statehooder and colonialist movements have done a great job in making Puerto Ricans believe and feel that without U.S. citizenship, they are nothing. The statehooders fund and promote whole media campaigns directed at their followers, reminding them to be appreciative of their U.S. citizenship and saying that only with statehood can people guarantee their U.S. citizenship.

This U.S. citizenship issue is very complicated and has been used by both statehooders and colonialists to scare people about the supposed dangers of sovereignty. Since the U.S. cannot deny or take back citizenship to those who already are U.S. citizens, the real issue is whether Puerto Ricans born in the post-colonial era will acquire U.S. citizenship at birth as well. This issue will be further discussed below in the proposal section. Sadly, many Puerto Ricans (mainly pro-independence supporters) that wish to renounce their U.S. citizenship, cannot.

In 1994, a Puerto Rican pro-independence leader, Juan Mari Bras, renounced his U.S. citizenship at an overseas U.S. embassy and demanded to be recognized only as a Puerto Rican citizen[35]. As the U.S. Department of State determined the issue of his renunciation, the Puerto Rico Supreme Court ruled that Puerto Rican citizenship can be recognized under the law and that Juan Mari Bras would be the first Puerto Rican citizen. After another legal ruling, Juan Mari Bras was now able to vote in Puerto Rican elections without having to be a U.S. citizen.

Along with being big news in Puerto Rico, this was also a dangerous precedent in the eyes of statehooders and colonialists because it was considered inconceivable that a Puerto Rican citizen *without U.S. citizenship* would be walking, working, voting, and living in Puerto Rico. Under the statehooder and colonialist worldview, a Puerto Rican cannot exist without also being a U.S. citizen. Any Puerto Rican without U.S. citizenship would be considered a walking threat.

Such a Puerto Rican would be a living symbol of defiance every day, and everywhere he would go. After many more Puerto Ricans began to express interest in renouncing their U.S. citizenship *en masse*, the U.S. government wanted to avoid an embarrassing avalanche of thousands of U.S. citizenship renunciations by Puerto Ricans.

Remember, the official narrative is that Puerto Ricans are happy and loyal U.S. citizens…a sudden avalanche of citizenship renunciations would greatly shatter and destroy that narrative. The U.S. Department of State later rescinded the earlier decision recognizing Juan Mari Bras' renunciation of U.S. citizenship. They had to nip that Boricua defiance in the bud.

Today, due to the Juan Mari Bras court ruling, the Puerto Rican government can issue *Certificates of Puerto Rican Citizenship*. Subsequent statehooder administrations, believing that anything that celebrates and highlights Puerto Rico's national identity is dangerous, have since tried to make it difficult to apply for, refuse to sign the certificates, taken it off the government's website, and have legally watered it down to make it so that any American citizen (even an American from Wyoming or Nebraska) can acquire said Certificate of Puerto Rican Citizenship if they wanted to, almost like some novelty gift ID card. The pettiness of the statehooders is legendary.

Most Puerto Ricans don't even know this *Certificate of Puerto Rican Citizenship* is available to them. Legislative attempts to give Puerto Rican citizenship more governmental and international recognition and stature have been thwarted by pro-statehood politicians who fear that Puerto Rican citizenship could become an option for Puerto Ricans, thus not binding Puerto Ricans only to U.S. citizenship. God forbid that Puerto Ricans start to value and cherish their *own* citizenship and not the citizenship of a foreign country that imposed it on all Puerto Ricans in 1917 by decree. For many colonial politicians, that is a dangerous idea.

Ironically, although the colonial government in Puerto Rico has tried to deny recognition to the *Certificate of Puerto Rican Citizenship*, the Kingdom of Spain has decided that a Puerto Rican in possession of said legal certificate of citizenship would be considered a "national of an Ibero-American country" under Spain's immigration and naturalization laws. Thus, if a Puerto Rican with the *Certificate of Puerto Rican Citizenship* wanted to also acquire Spanish & European Union citizenship, he/she would only have to reside in Spain for two years. A Puerto Rican without such a *Certificate of Puerto Rican Citizenship* would be considered only a U.S. citizen and would have to reside in Spain for ten years if they wanted to naturalize.

As far as the U.S. government is concerned, a Puerto Rican cannot renounce his/her U.S. citizenship if they plan on residing in Puerto Rico. If a Puerto Rican moves to France and renounces his/her U.S. citizenship there, then returns to colonial Puerto Rico, he/she would essentially be a foreigner in his/her own country. This "foreign" Puerto Rican in Puerto Rico, under U.S. immigration laws, would have the status of an immigrant and alien, even though he/she was born in Puerto Rico.

This scenario created a potential dilemma for the U.S. colonial regime: *where do you deport a Puerto Rican who was born in Puerto Rico?* These are the sorts of ridiculous colonial and political situations that occur in Puerto Rico. Thus, even when many Puerto Ricans who live in Puerto Rico *want* to renounce their U.S. citizenship and only be Puerto Rican citizens, under federal and colonial law, they cannot. They are essentially *stuck* being U.S. citizens.

As a sovereign nation, Puerto Rico would most likely recognize dual citizenship as the normal policy of the government. In a sovereign Puerto Rico, Puerto Ricans would be able to have both United States and Puerto Rican citizenships or have the freedom to renounce their U.S. citizenship should they individually desire to live in Puerto Rico simply as Puerto Rican citizens.

10. *Using Puerto Ricans to Subjugate Other Puerto Ricans*

Along with the Insular Police (the precursor to the Puerto Rico Police), the U.S. also created the Puerto Rico National Guard, a paramilitary force made up of Puerto Rican soldiers that would be loyal to the U.S. colonial government and defend Puerto Rico from external attacks. Ironically, the only "enemies" that the Puerto Rico National Guard has had to fight against were, of course, other Puerto Ricans, namely nationalists.

The Puerto Rico National Guard, in attempting to appear as a sacred and historical institution, frequently tries to claim it is the historical heir of Puerto Rico's past Spanish military units, but we all know that they are simply the U.S. military unit made up of Puerto Rican soldiers and weekend-warriors that was created to defend the rule and interests of the U.S. colonial regime in Puerto Rico.

In Puerto Rico, they have only defended Puerto Rico, not against external threats, but against Puerto Ricans. In fact, the Puerto Rico National Guard routinely states in press releases and public announcements that their "nation" is the United States. Remember, the principal role of the Puerto Rico National Guard is to keep Puerto Ricans under U.S. colonial control, even by force if necessary.

During the Puerto Rican Revolution of 1950 and the declaration of the "*República de Puerto Rico*" in Jayuya, it was the Puerto Rico National Guard that fought the Republic, protected the colonial regime, and then killed and interned thousands of Puerto Ricans suspected of being nationalists and independence sympathizers in makeshift concentration camps.

The Puerto Rico National Guard is the perfect colonial security tool, *using natives to subjugate natives*. That way, actual real Americans from Tennessee and Alabama don't have to go to Puerto Rico to squash rebellions...they have loyalist Puerto Rican soldiers to do that for them. Having Americans from South Carolina and Texas go to Puerto Rico to beat anti-colonial Puerto Rican protesters with batons does not look good for the cameras, especially in the era of social media.

During the Vieques protests of the early 2000s, real Americans from the States (U.S. Navy and federal personnel) had to come to Puerto Rico to arrest, beat, and put Puerto Ricans in dog cages in front of U.S. and international media, and we all know how that turned out for the U.S. Navy. It's better if loyalist Puerto Ricans do that dirty work. Even today, the Puerto Rico National Guard stands watch to defend Puerto Rico from the forces of freedom and democracy.

11. *Impunity of American & Colonial Officials in Puerto Rico*

In 1931, Dr. Cornelius Rhoads, an American doctor working in Puerto Rico, admitted to a friend in the United States in a letter that he hated Puerto Ricans and had killed off several by injecting them with cancer. According to Dr. Rhoads' letter:

"The Porto Ricans [sic] are the dirtiest, laziest, most degenerate and thievish race of men ever to inhabit this sphere... I have done my best to further the process of extermination by killing off eight and transplanting cancer into several more... All physicians take delight in the abuse and torture of the unfortunate subjects."

After the letter was uncovered and made public by Dr. Pedro Albizu Campos and the Puerto Rican Nationalist Party, Dr. Rhoads left Puerto Rico to avoid the public fallout. He returned to the United States, where he continued his cancer research and later infected thousands of other individuals in Latin America and Puerto Rican soldiers with other diseases in order to observe the results.

Dr. Rhoads, as an American in a U.S. colony, was never fully investigated nor prosecuted for his crimes against the Puerto Rican people. In Puerto Rican history, Dr. Rhoads will be remembered as the "Joseph Mengele" of U.S. rule in Puerto Rico.

Remember, in a colony, the colonial official has impunity, and the colonial natives are not considered human beings. From 1898 to the 1950s, a white American official could conceivably go to Puerto Rico, shoot and kill a random Puerto Rican on the street, and nothing would happen. He would be taken out of Puerto Rico and never heard from again. As stated by Nelson Denis, "What happened in Puerto Rico, never happened at all"[36].

In the United States, white Americans usually enjoy "white privilege" in relation to law enforcement issues, but in Puerto Rico, Americans (particularly federal officials and agents) enjoy "American privilege" within Puerto Rico's colonial society and political system. Those who enjoy and use their "American privilege" in Puerto Rico are presumed to be superior, correct, intelligent, and powerful (even when they are not). Obviously, such notions are false and are the result of the colonial mentality that chains Puerto Ricans to the colonial regime while claiming many Puerto Rican lives in the process.

12. *The Confiscation of Land & Historic Patrimony by the U.S. Government*

After the invasion and occupation, the U.S. military began to acquire and confiscate properties belonging to the Puerto Rican autonomous government, Spain, and the Catholic Church. Most of these properties and structures are Puerto Rico's cultural and historical patrimony. The U.S. military took control of Puerto Rico's two major fortresses (El Morro and San Cristobal) in Old San Juan.

In the 1950s, they established a golf course and pool on the sacred historic battlegrounds surrounding El Morro[37]. Yes, on the sacred grounds where thousands of Puerto Ricans have died and spilled blood fighting over the centuries to protect Puerto Rico from foreign invasions, the U.S. military thought it would be a great place for military officers to play golf and swim laps. The disrespect and contempt of colonial rule knows no bounds.

Photo of Americans playing golf on the sacred grounds of El Morro (Public domain).

Today, the only evidence of this sacrilegious act is a historical marker and the imprints of golf balls on the walls of El Morro. Also, a historic Spanish lighthouse in Arecibo has been turned into a museum that extolls, not the greatness of Puerto Rican maritime history, but instead celebrates the greatness of the U.S. during the Spanish-American War of 1898 in Puerto Rico. This lighthouse museum even has a replica of the U.S. Constitution, as if that were a part of Puerto Rican history.

In Old San Juan, the historic Spanish Customs House, *La Aduana*, has been converted into the U.S. Coast Guard headquarters in Puerto Rico. The list of such colonial ridiculousness and sacrilege goes on and on. Many ancient indigenous artifacts from the Arawak, Pre-Taino, and Taino Periods have been stolen by U.S. anthropologists and excavators and are now housed in U.S. and European museums and artifact warehouses.

To understand the rage Puerto Ricans feel about this, Americans need to imagine Chinese military officers playing golf on the Washington Mall while hitting golf balls off the Vietnam Memorial, having equestrian competitions on the Gettysburg battlefields, converting the Lincoln Memorial into a Chinese Naval Museum, and then renaming the *Liberty Bell*, the *Bell of Chinese & American Friendship*.

Even today, El Morro and San Cristobal fortresses (which are classified as World Heritage Sites by the United Nations) are under the control of the U.S. National Park Service, not Puerto Rico. The thousands of yearly tourists who pay to visit these historic fortresses are funding the U.S. National Park Service, not Puerto Rico.

For example, in 2013, San Juan National Historic Site (SJNHS) park recreation visitors totaled 1,328,801[38]. If all these visitors paid the $7.00 entrance fee, the SJNHS would have generated $9,301,607 in gross revenues that go directly to the U.S., not Puerto Rico. It would be like China making a profit from yearly visitors to the Statue of Liberty.

13. *Puerto Rico is not allowed to have Foreign Relations*

Due to the Federal Relations Law, Puerto Rico is *prohibited* from developing its own political and economic affairs and relations with other countries. The colony is not allowed to communicate with nor represent itself to the outside world without U.S. approval. As a colony, Puerto Rico's relations with other countries are handled by indifferent and ignorant American officials in Washington, DC, that know nothing about Puerto Rico nor even consider Puerto Rico as a factor in any important political or economic calculations or plans (some even despise Puerto Rico).

As a colony, Puerto Rico is essentially invisible and blockaded from developing political and economic relations with other countries. Puerto Rico had foreign relations in 1897, but not in 2019. During the aftermath of Hurricane Maria[39] in 2017, Puerto Rico was *not allowed* to accept aid and resources (food, water, fuel, electrical poles, medical equipment, etc.) from foreign nations without U.S. approval, thus Puerto Rico could only rely upon the inefficient, inept, indifferent, and contemptuous "aid" from the federal government and its very slow agencies and "profit-seeking" American contractors.

For example, Puerto Rico was not allowed to purchase electrical poles from foreign nations to help rebuild the electrical grid because the United States wanted Puerto Rico to only purchase expensive electrical poles from American companies. The problem is that there was a shortage of such electrical poles in the United States, and Puerto Rico was left waiting and unable to rebuild the electrical grid due to American greediness and profit margins.

Many international ships were not allowed to come to Puerto Rico due to the nefarious Cabotage Laws (Jones Act of 1920)[40]. The world, particularly Spain and Latin America, quickly came to support Puerto Rico, but the federal government said No. Would the federal government at least exempt Puerto Rico for a year from the Jones Act in order to better facilitate the recovery? No…the Jones Act lobbyists made sure of that.

Even though Puerto Rico was devastated, their profit margins from their monopoly on Puerto Rico's trade could not be threatened. Puerto Rico could *only* rely on the help of the United States, and we all know how that turned out...an utter political and logistical disaster that only worsened Puerto Rico's recovery and reconstruction efforts.

Picking up Puerto Rican soldiers to fight in faraway wars, hundreds of military and cargo planes quickly arrive on time, but to come to Puerto Rico's aid...oh, sorry, too much big ocean. Eventually, the United States lifted the Jones Act for a few days after protests and pressure from certain politicians, but the Jones Act restrictions were quickly reestablished.

Many in Puerto Rico realized, finally, that *U.S. citizenship really doesn't mean much since the federal government views Puerto Ricans as expendable liabilities* and must spend money on Puerto Rico, its colonial responsibility.

Imagine this scenario: Puerto Rico is floating adrift at sea after surviving a disaster. Puerto Rico comes upon various life vests and other flotation devices that were made and sent by foreign nations to help Puerto Rico. Yet, just as a relived Puerto Rico reaches for a flotation device to survive, the United States appears in a helicopter and says:

"Hey, Puerto Rico, we did not authorize you to take and use such foreign flotation devices. C'mon, you know better! You are only authorized to use Made in the U.S.A. flotation devices, not foreign ones...but we don't have any available at the moment since they are currently being used in Texas and Florida for actual Americans, so just keep floating and trying to survive on your own in the middle of the ocean. We'll get back to you...some day."

That ladies and gentlemen, was the initial federal response to support Puerto Rico after the 2017 hurricanes. Did the U.S. mainstream media report on the various international cargo ships that were turned away and *not allowed* by U.S. authorities to deliver goods and emergency relief to Puerto Rico? Of course not. This ridiculousness encapsulates how U.S. colonial policies impact life and death issues in Puerto Rico.

Even to survive in an emergency, Puerto Rico is *not allowed* to engage foreign nations to meet its needs and must *only* rely on the benevolence of various inept American lawmakers, officials, and contractors that despise Puerto Ricans, hate going to Puerto Rico, and are tired of talking about Puerto Rico. Puerto Ricans deserve better. Colonial rule isolates Puerto Rico and Puerto Ricans from the world.

Although Puerto Rico is *not allowed* to make its own foreign policies, it can (with American permission), establish representational offices in the U.S. and overseas to promote tourism, cultural affairs, and economic development (of course, under U.S. regulations and laws). These "commercial offices" help attract tourists, businesses, and foreign investments to Puerto Rico and assist Puerto Rican businessmen and women in accessing foreign markets and economic opportunities.

As expected, these commercial offices are a political issue in Puerto Rico due to the statehooder insistence that such offices, particularly the overseas ones, promote the notion that Puerto Rico is a country and not part of the United States (a dangerous idea for statehooders), thus almost every statehooder administration limits, restricts, cuts funding, and even closes such offices because they consider them a threat to their narrative that Puerto Rico cannot and should not forge its own course in the world and the global economy.

Most statehooders have an intense aversion to anything "international" and want Puerto Ricans that wish to access foreign markets to go through U.S. channels like the U.S. Commercial Service (USCS) and Select U.S.A. for export promotion, ignoring the fact that these American entities do not communicate in Spanish, know virtually nothing about Puerto Rican businesses, and hardly care about promoting such Puerto Rican businesses overseas.

The USCS does provide good service and great programs for American businesses, entrepreneurs, and investors, but for Ms.

María López, a Spanish-speaking entrepreneur from Las Marías interested in exporting her goods to Colombia or Peru, the USCS is useless and foreign. That's why the commercial offices were very important and supported by many Puerto Rican entrepreneurs.

Citing fiscal reasons to close these commercial offices in Bogotá, Lima, Panamá, and Madrid demonstrate that the statehooder administration fails to understand that these offices are not businesses, but are tools to promote tourism and economic development. Will the USCS individually meet with and address Puerto Rican entrepreneurs and investors in Spanish and connect them with businesses that wish to import Puerto Rican goods? No. Will the USCS help these Puerto Rican businesses and investors establish a presence in foreign markets? No. The commercial offices used to do all these functions for Puerto Rican businesses and investors.

The statehooder administration used the financial crisis as an excuse to close these offices, yet, of course, made available millions of dollars in contracts to friends, exorbitant salaries for corrupt American and statehooder officials, and associated statehooder businesses. Money "appeared" for expensive high-end luxury colonial government SUV vehicles and for corrupt individuals and groups, but there were no funds to support Puerto Rico's network of commercial offices that worked to attract tourism and investors to Puerto Rico. The only survivors from the statehooder internationalist shutdown were the Santo Domingo and New York City offices.

Right now, Puerto Ricans must hope, trust, and rely that a Mr. Johnson or a Mrs. Andrews at some U.S. diplomatic mission's economic section or USCS unit would consider the needs of Puerto Rican businesses...and of course, as we all know, that does not happen. Remember, these Puerto Rican commercial offices do *not* conduct foreign policy (since Puerto Rico is a colony); they only *promote* Puerto Rico abroad as a tourist and business destination, along with facilitating Puerto Rican businesses' access to foreign markets.

Puerto Ricans, ask yourselves who would do a better job at advancing and promoting Puerto Rico's economic, tourism, and business interests overseas: bilingual and multilingual Puerto Rican professionals with experience and degrees in diplomacy, tourism, and economic development or monolingual Americans from Omaha and Nashville who know nothing about nor care about Puerto Rico? Exactly.

With sovereignty, Puerto Rico would finally be able to:
- establish its own diplomatic service;
- accord treaties and conventions;
- establish embassies, consulates, and various commercial and cultural offices;
- develop bilateral relations with foreign nations and international organizations around the world to advance and protect its national and economic interests...and yes, these Puerto Rican diplomatic missions would be administered and staffed by *Puerto Ricans*.

14. *Puerto Rico is not allowed to join International Organizations*

The United States does *not allow* Puerto Rico to become a full member of regional and international organizations such as CARICOM, the United Nations, and other organizations. As a colony or a state, Puerto Rico would continue to be voiceless in the international community. Currently, as a colony, Puerto Rico cannot establish relations and direct communications with its own neighbors (Dominican Republic, Cuba, Colombia, etc.) without obtaining permission from the U.S. Department of State.

With sovereignty, Puerto Rico would finally not just have a voice in the world, but diplomatic representation in the international community to advance and protect its national and economic interests.

15. *The U.S. does not allow Puerto Rico to Declare Bankruptcy and Resolve its Own Financial Issues*

The United States does not allow Puerto Rico to declare bankruptcy nor have the option to renegotiate its public debts. As a colony, Puerto Rico can *only* use the financial resources and institutions that the United States has decided upon.

When Puerto Rico tried to create its own Puerto Rico Bankruptcy Law (Ley 71 de 2014) to manage the financial crisis, the U.S. Federal District Court in Puerto Rico stepped in and declared that proposed law would be "unconstitutional" because it would infringe upon the U.S. Bankruptcy Code (the very bankruptcy code that does *not* protect Puerto Rico), and the proposed law was shelved.

Again, the U.S. government was stabbing Puerto Rico in the back and *not allowing* Puerto Rico to defend itself by its own laws. So much for the lauded "self-government" of Puerto Rico.

The Puerto Rico Oversight, Management, and Economic Stability Act of 2016 (PROMESA)[41] is just one manifestation of colonial rule that promises, not debt relief and fiscal solvency, but decades of austerity, suffering, and the socio-economic destruction of Puerto Rico.

Let there be no mistake: PROMESA is designed not to help Puerto Rico, but to extract the wealth and economic resources of Puerto Rico and hand it over to bondholders and vulture funds who made bad investments yet demand astronomical returns over the lives of millions of Puerto Ricans, all under the watch, rules, and permission of the United States.

Congressional attempts at making PROMESA more "sensitive" to Puerto Rico is tantamount to using a softer whip instead of a hard whip in abusing Puerto Ricans. As we saw with the PROMESA Law, signed by President Obama, the United States can impose upon Puerto Rico an unelected junta (euphemistically called the *fiscal control board*) with unaccountable American officials to:

- oversee Puerto Rico's finances,
- impose severe austerity measures,
- defund the university and other essential services like health and security,
- ignore economic development,
- make sure bondholders get paid for their irresponsible investments in an illegal and documented debt scheme orchestrated by corrupt politicians, bankers, Wall Street financiers, credit houses, and vulture funds.

The PROMESA Law ensures that Puerto Rico (the occupied country going through a colonialism-induced financial crisis) is the one paying the bills, exorbitant salaries, and expenses of this unelected colonial junta appointed by the U.S. President that controls Puerto Rico's fiscal resources and was imposed by the U.S. Congress.

The colonial PROMESA junta and the colonial regime do not want to audit the debt because it may show who was responsible, where the funds ended up and may reduce the amount owed to bondholders because a large portion of Puerto Rico's debt may be considered illegal debt. Also, the colonial junta, led by an appointed ex-Ukrainian finance minister[42], is a blatant showcase of *conflict of interest issues* and corruption when some of its appointed members are current bondholders and were the very people responsible for the emission of such bad debt knowing there was no source of repayment.

The PROMESA Law is forcing Puerto Rico to pay the expenses and costs of the U.S. colonial regime. The U.S. Congress is obligating Puerto Rico to pay for its own colonial humiliation and the failures of U.S. colonial rule. When it comes to skirting away from one's colonial responsibilities and not wanting to pay for the costs of colonial rule, the U.S. Congress is ahead of the game. Would Americans accept a fiscal control board imposed by a foreign power (China, for example) to make sure the United States pays all its debts, even illegal debts?

Let's consider this: How would Americans react if the Peoples Republic of China, via a *Chinese PROMESA*, forced the United States to host and pay for a Chinese-imposed Fiscal Control Board (债务重组委员会)[43] to restructure and pay off the $22.03 trillion American national debt[43], approve infrastructure projects, and impose austerity measures on its fiscally irresponsible American subjects looking for a Beijing bailout?

With a $22.03 trillion national debt, it makes one wonder about the fiscal health and responsibility of the United States. A good name for the law that would establish this Chinese-imposed Fiscal Control Board would be the *Peoples Republic Oversight, Management, and Economic Stability for Americans Act (PROMESA)*.

Even with PROMESA, the entirety of Puerto Rico's public debt, under international law, is considered illegal, *odious debt* since Puerto Rico, as a non-sovereign entity, does not have sovereignty and authority to emit its own debt. All colonial debts are ultimately the debt of the colonial power, in our case, the United States.

As a sovereign nation, Puerto Rico would have the power to:

- finally audit the entire public debt (something that the colonial junta has been unwilling and unable to accomplish),
- free itself from such illegal colonial *odious debt* since sovereign nations are not responsible for the debts of previous colonial governments,
- and arrest and prosecute those that benefited from and committed financial crimes related to such emission of illegal debt.

As a colony or a state, Puerto Rico cannot seek help from international financial institutions, other countries, and those corrupt officials that allowed such an illegal debt scheme to flourish would escape justice.

16. The U.S. has imposed a Colonial Shipping Monopoly to Control Puerto Rico's trade, customs, and economy

The United States, via the Jones Act of 1920, has imposed a colonial shipping monopoly on Puerto Rico. Under the cabotage laws of the archaic Jones Act of 1920, Puerto Rico can *only* use the U.S. Merchant Marine ships and companies (U.S. flag vessels) to transport goods to Puerto Rico's ports. Since Puerto Rico is an archipelago and does not produce everything it consumes, it must import goods, but those goods must *only* be imported on U.S. Merchant Marine ships due to the Jones Act of 1920.

Puerto Rico is *not* allowed to create its own shipping fleet nor use cheaper and more efficient international shipping companies, which would reduce the cost of production of various Puerto Rican manufactured goods, thus making them competitive with imports.

These American maritime companies, based primarily in Jacksonville, Florida, control and choke Puerto Rico's ports and economy. These American maritime companies that enjoy huge profits on the backs of Puerto Rican consumers and businesses, even have lobbyists and organizations in Washington, DC, and Puerto Rico protecting their colonial shipping monopoly, mainly the American Maritime Partnership.

These Jones Act lobbyists have bought so many congressional Democrats and Republicans; one does not have to wonder why the Jones Act is still enforced, despite the protests from Puerto Rico and the other colonial territories. Under the mantra of "national security" and "protecting American jobs", these lobbyists and organizations make millions of dollars off Puerto Rico's economic and shipping servitude.

Because Puerto Rico is *forced* to use such old, expensive, few, and inefficient U.S. shipping vessels, these companies extort Puerto Rico out of more money than if Puerto Rico had its own shipping fleet or could use cheaper international ships. Since Puerto Rico is a colonial captive market for American shipping and goods, the control of Puerto Rico's trade essentially controls Puerto Rico's economy and hinders economic development. According to author Nelson Denis, "from 1970 through 2010, the Jones Act cost Puerto Rico $29 billion. Projected from 1920 through 2015, this cost becomes $75.8 billion"[44].

Sovereignty and freedom from the reviled Jones Act would allow Puerto Rico to control, develop, and promote its own maritime activities, promote exports, establish maritime trade relations with other countries, establish maritime businesses, and develop a Puerto Rican shipping industry that would generate thousands of jobs in Puerto Rico and across all sectors.

Due to this colonial shipping monopoly and "price protection" racket, Puerto Ricans are forced to pay more for imported food and products, increasing the cost of living for everyone. Consider the following additional facts detailed by author Nelson Denis[45]:

- Due to the Jones Act, prices paid by Puerto Rican consumers are roughly 20% higher than in the United States.
- Annual consumer spending by Puerto Ricans is approximately $35 billion.
- 20% of $35 billion is $7 billion. This $7 billion is the amount of excess prices on goods paid every year by Puerto Rican consumers.
- Approximately 85% of all imports to Puerto Rico comes from the United States.
- 85% of $7 billion is $5.95 billion.

Thus, Puerto Ricans pay approximately $5.95 billion in annual excess profits to U.S. corporations due to the Jones Act (in addition to the original profits). This $5.95 billion *exceeds* the $4.6 billion in federal monies and "benefits" that the U.S. sends to Puerto Rico. The Jones Act is literally the federal codification of a colonial mafia-structured price protection racket that generates billions of dollars for these corrupt American shipping companies, all on the backs of Puerto Ricans. Their new motto could be: *"The U.S. Merchant Marine: Riding the High Seas on the Backs of Puerto Ricans."*

With sovereignty, Puerto Rico would be free of such nefarious cabotage laws and be able to develop its own maritime shipping industry, consequently creating jobs for thousands of Puerto Ricans, and being able to import and export goods that would develop Puerto Rico in the long run.

Every year, Puerto Rico loses approximately $1.5 billion due to higher prices of goods related to these cabotage laws[47]. Other estimates show that "the Jones Act costs Puerto Ricans more than $500 million per year"[48].

The Jones Act is a colonial noose that keeps choking Puerto Rico, the Puerto Rican economy, and any chance of Puerto Rican economic development. The faster Puerto Rico can free itself from these cabotage laws via sovereignty; the faster Puerto Rico can finally take control and develop its own economy. As long as Puerto Rico remains under the Jones Act, it will remain a poor and bankrupt colony that only serves the United States as a "captive market".

Sadly, the same nation that resisted and fought against such restrictive British colonial maritime trade policies like the Navigation Acts of 1651, 1660, and 1663[49], is also the same nation that now imposes restrictive American colonial maritime trade policies like the Jones Act of 1920 on Puerto Rico. Like the detested Navigation Acts on the Thirteen Colonies, the hated Jones Act must be resisted and fought against by Puerto Ricans. If Puerto Rico is to have a future, it *cannot* be under the criminal, burdensome, and detested yoke of the Jones Act that imposes economic and maritime servitude on the Puerto Rican people.

Jones Act lobbyists may have enough dark money to buy off politicians in Congress, but they cannot buy off the math that exposes such colonial economic slavery to the world. Via the Jones

Act, we see that it is not Puerto Rico that depends on the United States, but the United States and U.S. shipping interests that depend on the colony of Puerto Rico, particularly Puerto Rican consumers...pretty similar to how British shipping interests depended on consumers in the Thirteen Colonies.

Once Puerto Ricans realize this fact, they can summon up the anger to begin a robust and multifaceted resistance to this criminal colonial law that denies Puerto Rico the future it deserves.

Also, customs duties on imported goods into Puerto Rico are collected by U.S. Customs & Border Protection (CBP), not a Puerto Rican Customs Authority. Why? As a colony or a state, Puerto Rico is *not allowed* to establish its own customs authority to enforce duties and tariffs on all imported goods, funds that could go to help develop the economy.

Thus, billions of dollars in funds that could go to developing Puerto Rico's economy instead go to subsidize U.S. federal government operations and programs.

17. *The U.S. promotes Dependency, not Self-Sufficiency in Puerto Rico*

As a colonial captive market, the United States does not promote Puerto Rican self-sufficiency, but *dependency*. As a dependent consumer of U.S. goods that arrive on U.S. ships, from U.S. companies, Puerto Rico's role is to consume imported goods, not produce. Puerto Rico's entire economic system is modeled and set up to be dependent, not because Puerto Ricans want that, but because the United States desires that.

Any local Puerto Rican production that starts to compete with American imports will most likely receive a visit from a federal food regulatory official to close them down for some ridiculous reason or price them out of the market, since Puerto Rico is not allowed to implement protective anti-dumping legislation to support and promote Puerto Rican businesses and industries. Why?

Well, since Puerto Rico is a colonial territory under the U.S. Constitution, the Interstate Commerce Clause (Article I, Section 8, Clause 3)[50] forbids such legislation. As a U.S. colony, the federal government selectively determines when, if, and what parts of the U.S. Constitution apply to Puerto Rico.

In short, Puerto Rican businesses and producers cannot compete with cheaper American goods because those goods have a lower cost of production. American companies can source their raw materials from local and regional markets in neighboring counties and states, markets with lower fuel costs, and not burdened with obscene 20% Jones Act cabotage costs. Since Puerto Rico does not control any of its economic factors of production (because of its colonial status), Puerto Rico cannot (aka *is not allowed to*) implement long-term economic development plans, nor compete with cheaper American imports because, as stated, Puerto Rican businesses have to pay the high cost of shipping raw materials on expensive U.S. ships (cabotage laws).

This is not accidental; the Puerto Rican colonial economy is structured this way in order to limit Puerto Rican production and competition and facilitate American imports in a captive economy that is engineered to consume American products. This is not free trade; this is colonial economics and exploitation tactics.

In order to increase imports to Puerto Rico, the U.S. colonial regime even established and promoted campaigns to change the eating habits of Puerto Ricans in order to benefit U.S. businesses. For centuries, Puerto Ricans survived off millions of breadfruit trees and various other tubers like Yucca. Breadfruit (*pana*) was a ubiquitous starchy crop that provided sustenance to thousands of Puerto Rican families throughout Puerto Rico, particularly those in rural communities.

With Puerto Ricans eating breadfruit as a common dish, they were not interested in buying American potatoes. Thus, in an effort to push Puerto Ricans away from breadfruit and towards imported American potatoes, the U.S. colonial regime began a campaign associating breadfruit with diseases and illnesses, advocating that people cut down such trees as a health and sanitary measure (of course, nothing to do with colonial economics).

In a few years, this *breadfruit massacre* helped destroy Puerto Rico's food sovereignty and consolidated Puerto Rico's dependence on imported American potatoes, which many Puerto Ricans considered bland and of poor quality. Although areas of eastern Puerto Rico survived the breadfruit massacre, breadfruit trees became scarce throughout Puerto Rico for decades. Thankfully today, local Puerto Rican breadfruit has been returning to the Puerto Rican market, but more needs to be done to re-establish Puerto Rico's food sovereignty and agricultural sector.

There are many more examples of such policies, but I think the breadfruit massacre best captures the spirit of colonial rule and ruthlessness of colonial economics. Today, planting a breadfruit tree in one's backyard in Puerto Rico can be considered an act of patriotism and defiance.

The United States forbids Puerto Rico from enacting protective measures and major subsidies to protect and develop local Puerto Rican industries. Due to these colonial political and economic limitations, Puerto Rico does not have the power to develop its own economy, the agricultural sector, and other local industries.

Whenever you hear American politicians complain about and lecture Puerto Ricans regarding their poverty and lack of economic development, please remind them about Puerto Rico's lack of control over its own economy and its status as a colonial captive market that subsidizes the expensive U.S. Merchant Marine.

18. *The U.S. promotes Fossil Fuels, not Renewable Energy in Puerto Rico, in order to benefit U.S. energy companies*

Even in the energy sector, the United States does not promote Puerto Rican self-sufficiency, but dependency. For an island nation drenched with solar energy and surrounded by oceanic wave energy, Puerto Rico should be a leader and beacon of renewable energy, yet as a poor and backward U.S. colony, the colonial government and its energy cartels and corporate interests, with congressional support, are still promoting fossil fuel dependency.

After Hurricanes Irma and Maria, Puerto Rico had a chance to rebuild its energy infrastructure using renewable energy sources, primarily the sun and wind. As always happens in Puerto Rico, U.S. corporate interests trump the interests of the Puerto Rican people. Instead of focusing on clean, renewable energy, the U.S. Congress (believing that such renewable energy goals are too lofty) is set to have Puerto Rico dependent on liquified natural gas imported on large cargo ships[51].

Someone must buy the surplus natural gas produced by U.S. fracking companies and who better than Puerto Rico, the colony that will be *forced* to buy such natural gas because it lacks the sovereign power to rule itself and decide its own affairs and policies. With sovereignty, Puerto Rico could have the power to develop its own energy policy and diversified renewable energy infrastructure.

19. *The U.S. promotes social welfare dependency, not Economic Development*

In the 1970s, the United States established various social welfare programs to supposedly help Puerto Ricans in poverty, yet with the aim of creating more consumers and supporting U.S. companies. Through the federal government's Nutritional Assistance Program, many Puerto Ricans qualify for food stamps (called *cupones* in Puerto Rico) for which they can go and shop for food at almost all supermarkets.

The issue is *which* products qualify for the program and can be bought by program recipients, and of course, almost all these food products are cheap imported American boxed and canned products.

With this system, the welfare funds sent to Puerto Rico to alleviate poverty return back to the U.S. economy by supporting the American companies that provide goods for the program. As soon as the federal money arrives in Puerto Rico, it goes back to the U.S. without circulating in the Puerto Rican economy and generating wealth. Since the funds return to the U.S. quickly, wealth is generated there, not in Puerto Rico.

Puerto Ricans in this program pretty much remain in poverty and can buy just enough food to survive until the next payment is supposed to arrive. Due to Puerto Rico's lack of power to grow and develop its own economy and control its factors of production, many Puerto Ricans remain stuck in a generational cycle of poverty and hopelessness that makes them more and more dependent on federal funds, thus more liable to end up supporting the statehood movement since they are the ones constantly saying that with statehood, poor Puerto Ricans would receive $10 billion more in welfare money from U.S. taxpayers.

In essence, the U.S. colonial regime in Puerto Rico creates the poverty (due to lack of economic development) and then also provides poor Puerto Ricans the help (food stamps) to survive such poverty (creating dependency), while making a great profit for U.S. companies. As you can see, statehooders promote dependency, while pro-sovereignty supporters promote production and self-sufficiency in order to escape such colonial dependency.

20. *The Establishment of the Colonial Mentality*

The U.S. colonial regime in Puerto Rico is only able to operate because Puerto Ricans *cooperate* with the regime and allow it to remain. What allows Puerto Ricans to cooperate with an imposed foreign and colonial regime in their country? It's called the *colonial mentality*. Like Puerto Ricans, Filipinos and other colonial people also suffer the consequences of the colonial mentality.

Spanish and American colonialism have fortified and consolidated the colonial mentality in the psyche of the majority of Puerto Ricans. In Puerto Rico, the main pillars of the colonial mentality are:

1. The United States, Americans, and American civilization are superior, while Puerto Rico, Puerto Ricans, and Puerto Rican civilization are inferior.
2. Without the United States, Puerto Ricans would starve and die and thus need to be dependent on the United States for their survival.
3. Because Puerto Ricans are an inferior culture and people, they are incapable of ruling themselves under their own free government, thus need to be ruled as wards by the United States and administered by Americans for their own good.
4. Puerto Ricans should fear supporting independence and freedom for Puerto Rico because it is dangerous and may lead to your arrest, loss of your job, or persecution from the authorities. If you want to survive and play it safe, just support the colonial regime.

According to Dr. Ronald Fernández in a paper titled "*A Joy Ride: U.S. Attitudes Toward Puerto Rico, Its People and Its Culture*", the four attitudes that are a constant in U.S. -Puerto Rico relations are[52]:

- The United States presumed sense of superiority,
- The presumed inferiority of the Puerto Rican people,
- The assertion of plenary or absolute power over Puerto Rico, its people and cultural development,
- The indifference and ignorance of U.S. officials and the American people towards Puerto Ricans

Sadly, many Puerto Ricans experience these attitudes and are taught this colonial mentality and "learned helplessness" in school, from their families, from the media, and from the colonial government itself. The best way to avoid a slave rebellion is to have the slave *doubt* he/she can ever live free. The slave will mentally chain himself to the master.

This, in my opinion, is the worst atrocity one can commit on a nation: convincing them to believe that they are inferior, helpless, and worthless and can only live under the rule of another country.

For the statehooder and colonialist political class that administers the colonial government of Puerto Rico, supporting sovereignty and independence is blasphemy and dangerous. These individuals, infected with the colonial mentality, cannot fathom a Puerto Rico where Puerto Ricans are in charge; they can only fathom a Puerto Rico ruled by foreigners since they actually believe they are inferior.

As an inferior people, the political class really believes that Puerto Ricans cannot rule themselves and can only thrive under the rule and tutelage of a foreign colonial ruler, be it Spain, the United States or any other country.

When confronted by a pro-sovereignty advocate and any pro-sovereignty discourse, the statehooder and colonialist political class view the pro-sovereignty advocate with disdain and a *"how dare you?"* attitude. How dare the pro-sovereignty advocate support freedom? How dare the pro-sovereignty advocate talk about how Puerto Rico can be successful without colonial rule? How dare the pro-sovereignty advocate even suggest that Puerto Ricans can be considered as equals on the world stage and have the capacity to rule their own country? How dare they suggest this?

Pro-sovereignty advocates are dangerous to the colonial regime because they show people that another Puerto Rico is possible. The pro-sovereignty advocate's existence actually proves that not all Puerto Ricans subscribe to the belief that Puerto Ricans are inferior people, thus threatening the entire notion of colonial rule.

This is why the statehooder and colonialist political class have always persecuted and repressed the pro-sovereignty and independence movements in Puerto Rico. Such pro-sovereignty Puerto Ricans, by their mere existence, threaten the legitimacy and acceptance of the colonial mentality that allows and facilitates Puerto Ricans to cooperate with colonial rule. When Puerto Ricans debunk the colonial mentality, they will then be able to debunk the colonial regime and the political class that lives off it.

Some Puerto Ricans, infected by this psychological disease called *colonialism*, actually believe they are inferior and can only be someone special and important if they are considered Americans. Please understand, not all Puerto Ricans subscribe to colonial inferiority and believe that Puerto Ricans, if given the opportunity, can rule themselves in freedom and democracy.

In my experience, the best ways to fight this colonial mentality are:

- to educate oneself about Puerto Rico's history, culture, and patriots;
- realize that such notions of superiority and inferiority are false, subjective, and based on racist theories of Social Darwinism meant to keep Puerto Ricans submissive and controlled;
- realize one's self-worth and importance as a Puerto Rican;
- realize the awesome and overwhelming potential that a free and sovereign Puerto Rico has to advance all Puerto Ricans in their quest for happiness, prosperity, and liberty.

After decades of terror, criminalization, and colonial education, many Puerto Ricans with a colonial mentality believe that if Puerto Rico were to become independent, they would fail and become like Haiti and other developing countries in a matter of weeks. Today, statehooders are more likely to use *socialist Venezuela* as an example of what Puerto Rico would be if it were sovereign.

The fear-mongering and false analogies continue nonstop for the statehooders.

This binary anti-independence narrative and rhetoric (Evil Independence v. Good Colonial Subservience) have been constantly repeated by pro-colonialist and pro-statehood politicians and media since the U.S. troops invaded. Of course, examples of successful and prosperous small nations such as Singapore, Ireland, New Zealand, and Estonia, are never considered as an option in Puerto Rico.

Statehooders hate when Puerto Ricans mention Singapore (a successful small island nation 14x smaller than Puerto Rico) as a model for Puerto Rico because Singapore's political and economic success was only possible because it is *sovereign* and free to decide its own political, cultural, and economic policies. The mere existence of the Singapore model destroys every pillar of the colonial mentality and pro-statehood arguments.

The Singapore model (a free market-based state capitalist and structuralist economic planning model based on state enterprises and investments, business services, transshipment hubs, innovation, foreign investments, industry, and exports) allows Puerto Ricans to see beyond the statehooder *wall of fear and colonial dependency* and envision a viable option and model for a future sovereign Puerto Rico.

This fear of freedom is so ingrained that today, some Puerto Rican statehooders cannot fathom living free and having relations with foreign nations. Statehooders believe they are incapable of making their own decisions and cannot be successful, thus prefer Americans to rule them and make all the important decisions. Pro-sovereignty supporters, on the other hand, have been studying various models of successful sovereign nations (like Singapore, Malta, Israel, and Ireland) and are confident in Puerto Rico's ability to become a successful, democratic, and prosperous country.

In order to succeed as a free and sovereign nation, Puerto Rico's future leaders cannot come from the inept, corrupt, and colonized political class made up of statehooders and colonialists. A new political class is urgently needed that can not only lead Puerto Rico to freedom but also lead the country towards political and economic stability and development.

For many in Puerto Rico, freedom is evil, and sovereignty and independence are equated with communism, socialism, and every other negative "ism" that can be conjured up due to Cold War propaganda scripts that statehooder and colonialist politicians in Puerto Rico still use to fan the flames of fear. Yes, in Puerto Rico, many statehood politicians believe the Soviet Union still exists and see communists behind every tree. For the typical statehooder, if one does not believe in statehood for Puerto Rico, then you must be a socialist, communist, anarchist, anti-American, and must be persecuted.

These statehood politicians and supporters have yet to receive the memo that the Cold War ended in 1989. The colonial mentality constantly tells Puerto Ricans that they cannot do anything without the approval of the United States.

The colonial mentality is not unique to Puerto Ricans, other colonized peoples have also dealt with this mental disease, and many have overcome it. With sovereignty, Puerto Rico will finally be able to address this political and cultural mental health issue called colonialism and the colonial mentality.

21. Puerto Rico is a U.S. corporate tax haven

As a colonial territory, captive market, and tax haven, Puerto Rico generates a lot of profits for U.S. companies, particularly U.S. multinationals (like Microsoft and Pfizer) and American millionaires that seek to evade federal taxes. For these American multinational companies, why pay 21%-35% corporate tax in the United States, when you can legally pay just 4% in the tax haven colony of Puerto Rico? Every year, the U.S. extracts approximately $71.6 billion from Puerto Rico's captive colonial economy[53].

Due to tax rules and tax loopholes in Puerto Rican law, these U.S. companies and millionaires generate a lot of capital that ends up being repatriated back to the U.S. tax-free.

While the U.S. colonial regime sets up this tax haven infrastructure to benefit its companies and millionaires to extract the wealth of Puerto Rico, these same people then turn around and lecture Puerto Ricans on how Puerto Rico lacks wealth and would become a poor country without the tutelage of U.S. colonial rule. It's like a master trying to convince a newly freed former slave that he should just remain on the plantation and work for a meager income because he is too inferior and backward to actually survive in the real world, all the while the master continues to benefit and profit off his former slave's labor.

You see, Puerto Rico *can* create wealth, but only wealth for the U.S. colonial regime, its colonial lackeys, U.S. companies, and American millionaires, *not* for the Puerto Rican people. Without the powers and tools of sovereignty, Puerto Rico *cannot* and is *not allowed* to create an economic system that would benefit the Puerto Rican people. Remember, the whole purpose of a colony is to *exploit* and extract its wealth, not to help the natives develop their economy.

22. *The U.S. forcibly Sterilized Thousands of Puerto Rican Women*

In a U.S.-sponsored population control and sterilization program tied to U.S.-led industrialization (Operation Bootstrap), thousands of Puerto Rican women were sterilized without their consent. Apparently, for the Americans who were running the U.S. colonial regime, most problems in Puerto Rico stemmed from overpopulation[54], thus sterilization was promoted and made very accessible to Puerto Rican women.

For U.S. colonial regime scientists and eugenicists, there were just too many "hyper-fertile" Puerto Ricans in Puerto Rico, and that had to be dealt with via a multifaceted overt and covert population control program. With this policy, thousands of Puerto Ricans were erased from history and families destroyed. The U.S. colonial regime even had its own "eugenics board" that forcibly sterilized 97 Puerto Rican women[55]. According to sources, by 1965, 34% of women between the ages of twenty to forty-nine had been sterilized, making Puerto Rico the country with the highest incidence of sterilization in the world[56]. To learn more about the forced sterilization policy and its effect on Puerto Rican women, please watch the seminal documentary "La Operación": https://www.youtube.com/watch?v=e3RPScdod6E

23. The U.S. forcibly Used Thousands of Puerto Rican Women as Guinea Pigs in Anti-Contraception Experiments

The U.S. colonial regime, in conjunction with U.S. pharmaceutical entities, used thousands of targeted poor and uneducated Puerto Rican women as experimental guinea pigs and lab rats when they were developing **contraception pills**. The lack of anti-birth control laws and the extensive network of government birth control clinics facilitated this process[57].

Many women suffered painful medical issues, and three young women died. To learn more about the use of Puerto Rican women as human guinea pigs to test contraception drugs, please watch the following video:

https://www.youtube.com/watch?v=DICH3-YdVIU

24. The U.S. used Agent Orange in Puerto Rico's El Yunque Rainforest

The U.S. military, before using Agent Orange in Vietnam and Cambodia, tested it out in Puerto Rico's famous and beautiful El Yunque National Forest. According to recently disclosed documents from the Veterans Affairs Administration and U.S. Army

Corps of Engineers, from 1956 to 1968, the U.S. Department of Defense not only sprayed dioxin-powered herbicide Agent Orange in El Yunque Rainforest, but also used similar herbicidal and defoliant chemicals in experiments involving forested areas throughout Puerto Rico in the 1950s and 1960s, particularly in Luquillo, Las Marías, Mayagüez, and Río Grande[58]. These chemicals killed thousands of trees, vegetation, and animals and did indescribable harm to El Yunque, Puerto Rico's largest and most important rainforest.

These previously classified experiments used dangerous chemicals that were found to cause such grave illnesses such as leukemia, diabetes mellitus, heart disease, Parkinson's disease, Alzheimer's disease, and prostate and respiratory cancers[59]. Yes, many Puerto Ricans would die slow deaths over the years and decades due to these military experiments, but who cares, they're just expendable Puerto Ricans. So much for the protection and civil liberties of U.S. citizenship.

25. *The U.S. used Culebra & Vieques as Live-Fire Weapons Ranges and Terrorized the Civilian Population*

The U.S. military used the Puerto Rican island-municipalities of Culebra and Vieques as military weapons storage facilities and live firing ranges. According to sources, the U.S. Navy fired or dropped more than 300,000 bombs, rockets, and other munitions on Vieques from the mid-1940s to 2003, ultimately occupying 77% of the island[60].

After establishing their presence on Vieques in 1941, the U.S. Navy destroyed the local agricultural economy and expropriated over 22,000 acres of prime farmland and homes (two thirds of the island), leaving *viequenses* to survive in the central civilian strip or relocate to the main island of Puerto Rico or relocate like refugees to St. Croix and St. Thomas in the U.S. Virgin Islands. Today, Puerto Rican-Virgin Islander descendants of the Vieques refugees make up about 10.3% of the population of the U.S. Virgin Islands[61].

The U.S. Navy even rented out the firing ranges so that other NATO allies can shoot and bomb Puerto Rico as well, similar to how a master would rent out a slave to work for another master. The millions of bullets and bombs that were dropped and munitions casings left on these two municipalities have greatly damaged the ecosystem, created a health crisis, and left a mountain of military debris and garbage that even today, the U.S. military refuses to clean up and rehabilitate it in its entirety.

Even though the U.S. Navy and other U.S. military units left Vieques in 2003 after a massive civil disobedience campaign to oust them, these lands are now under the control of the U.S. Fish & Wildlife Service and the U.S. Department of the Interior, other federal entities, not Puerto Rico. In short, U.S. colonial rule is still in Vieques; they've just changed their uniforms.

Federal authorities and the colonial regime in Puerto Rico have not allowed Vieques and Culebra to develop economically. This federal and colonial indifference to economic development, particularly in Vieques, has been considered the punishment and petty retribution for having kicked out the U.S. Navy. Whenever Vieques residents and community organizations complain about the lack of economic development and terrible transport services, the response is, *"Ah, those are the consequences..."*.

The decades of U.S. military bombing have poisoned the water, the ground, and the air of these municipalities to the point where many residents have developed cancer and other related serious and deadly diseases.

During the time when the military would practice live fire exercises, residents lived in total fear that a stray bomb would kill them or their families. Also, many U.S. servicemen would be unleashed on these towns like a pack of wild animals where they would become drunk, start street battles and riots, beat up Puerto Rican civilians, and engage in prostitution[62]. Many of these U.S. servicemen would also urinate on the streets[63]. The U.S. Navy would take custody and remove such violent and unruly sailors from Vieques, sparing them from the local justice system.

I have heard of accounts where families would not allow young women into the town by themselves, and fathers would protect their homes with guns and machetes in case a drunk, deranged, or perverted U.S. serviceman tried to enter the house to attack their wives and daughters…or as they would say *"looking for señoritas."*. Yes, this happened, and no amount of *"I'm a U.S. citizen"* was going to save them from this terror. For most Americans, Puerto Ricans are only U.S. citizens just to put them on military cargo planes to fight in U.S. wars, nothing else.

26. The Use of Colonial Education Policies to Consolidate Colonial Rule and Destroy National Pride and Identity

The U.S. colonial regime's education policies in Puerto Rico aim at creating workers, not entrepreneurs (resumés, not business plans), and work to invisibilize Puerto Ricans from history. In the 1900s, Puerto Rican schools, led by imported racist Martin G. Brumbaugh and others, were forced to use a Puerto Rico history book written by Paul G. Miller[64] which reduced Puerto Ricans to savages with no great history to speak of until the great Americans arrived in 1898 to bring them the "blessings of civilization". It would seem that the colonial education department's pedagogical philosophy helped inspire the book "1984".

Many Puerto Ricans who went through the Puerto Rican school system lack even basic knowledge of Puerto Rican history. Any Puerto Rican that knew a bit too much about Puerto Rico's past, patriots, and struggles against colonialism was in danger of being labeled a "separatist" which could mean exile, persecution, arrest, or loss of their job. Many Puerto Ricans do not even know the names of great patriots and revolutionaries that fought for Puerto Rico's freedom or of Puerto Ricans that contributed to world civilization.

There are taxi drivers in Cuba that know about Ramon E. Betances and rural Dominicans that know of Eugenio M. De Hostos, but these Puerto Rican patriots are virtually unknown in Puerto Rico, particularly by students. Children are supposed to think that Puerto Rico is worthless, has nothing of value, and that Puerto Ricans need the United States or a U.S.A. flag patch on their arm in order to be someone important.

The colonial education department even used to mockingly call Puerto Rico's patriots *"los barbudos"* (the bearded ones) in order to negate their contributions, and any reverence people may have of them. Puerto Rican patriots, like Pedro Albizu Campos, are classified as "separatists", while colonial lackeys and traitors, like Luis Muñoz Marín, are classified as "advocates of democracy" and "statesmen". The post-1952 colonial regime was now called "Commonwealth", although Puerto Rico was still the same U.S. colony that it was prior to 1952.

A technique used by the colonial education department was to mention certain important Puerto Ricans, but never as pro-independence patriots. Ramon E. Betances, the doctor; Jose De Diego, the poet, and legislator; Eugenio M. De Hostos, the educator; Agustín Stahl, the great scientist, although all of them were primarily known as pro-independence patriots and activists.

Puerto Ricans are not supposed to learn that these great historical figures were also pro-independence patriots (since that goes against the colonial narrative that pro-independence activists are criminals not to be emulated).

Female patriots like Maria Mercedes, Mariana Bracetti, Lolita Lebrón, and Blanca Canales, are not even mentioned. Would Americans be pleased if George Washington was mentioned in U.S. history classes and books, not as the *Father of the Nation*, but merely as a rebellious and malcontent Continental British subject that was a Virginia landowner, and a general during the French & Indian War? Of course not.

Another common technique used by the Puerto Rico colonial education department is to minimize great events in Puerto Rican history as mere riots or civil disturbances by a few disgruntled leftists and anti-establishment folks. The Grito de Lares Revolution of 1868 against Spain that established the first Republic of Puerto Rico is often referred to as a mere riot by colonial officials and lackeys.

During the Puerto Rican Revolution of 1950 against the U.S. colonial regime, various towns across the island revolted, the second Republic of Puerto Rico was proclaimed in Jayuya, and it only came to an end when the U.S.-trained and controlled Puerto Rico National Guard dropped bombs from airplanes and killed many people.

Today, colonial officials and lackeys refer to this historical event as a small revolt by seditious nationalists, nothing more. The goal is to play down and minimize any expression of Puerto Rican nationalism and patriotism so that it can be tied to the "happy colonial" narrative peddled by the U.S. colonial regime.

What Puerto Ricans learn about Puerto Rico in school regarding history can be summed up in the following timeline:

- **Indigenous Peoples (Pre-Spanish 1493)** – emphasis on passive natives
- **The Discovery of Puerto Rico by Spain (1493-1511)** – emphasis on evil Spain
- **The Period of Spanish Colonization (1511-1898)** – emphasis on evil Spain
- **The Arrival of the Americans (1898)** – emphasis on Americans bringing democracy and civilization
- **The American Government in Puerto Rico (1898-1952)** – no mention of atrocities and repression
- **The Establishment of the Commonwealth (1952)** – an emphasis that it was democratic self-government

- **Puerto Rico: The Showcase of the Caribbean (1952-Present)** – tries to emphasize how Puerto Rico is better off than other Caribbean nations even though that is not true

In these Puerto Rican history classes, which I consider a sham and lacking in content, these historical periods are sugarcoated, and students are not taught about the colonial atrocities of the U.S. colonial regime. The colonial atrocities detailed in this book are not officially taught to Puerto Rican students, unless they are presented with this knowledge "unofficially" by family or a patriotic teacher after school.

The education system makes every effort to highlight every evil act and crime committed by the Spanish government, but regarding U.S. atrocities, massacres, and repression, nothing. The whole point is to teach children that the Americans are saviors that rescued us from our brown Hispanic Puerto Rican selves and that we should be grateful for and appreciative of their "benevolent" tutelage and colonial rule.

This colonial education is an integral part of the maintenance and fortification of the *colonial mentality* because it promotes at a young age the sense of worthlessness and being an inferior small people that need to be ruled by a foreign power. It's the same Puerto Rican sense of self-worth and narrative promoted by the early American colonial officials, many of them being white supremacists.

Many colonized Puerto Ricans have internalized this colonialist narrative so much so, that they actually *believe* they are worthless and do not deserve freedom and self-government. Many actually try to find benefits to such foreign colonial rule in order to better justify it to themselves and keep thinking, "it really isn't that bad". It's like being kept in a dungeon and beat every day, but at least the kidnapper is nice enough to bring me scraps to eat.

Sadly, even such history classes are still a threat to the colonial regime in having Puerto Ricans learn about their past. Today, the colonial education department has made Puerto Rican history an elective, not a required subject for students. Hopefully, this will be corrected soon. Due to decades of such colonial education in Puerto Rico, whole generations do not know about the Rio Piedras and Ponce massacres, the revolts against Spanish and U.S. colonial rule, the persecutions and repression against the pro-independence movement, the racist assimilation policies, imposition of English, the murders of Dr. Rhoads, and about the negative political, economic, social, and psychological impacts of colonialism. This book aims to help rectify this situation by promoting more education and discussion about these issues.

With sovereignty, Puerto Ricans would finally have an educational system that embraces and highlights Puerto Rico's great history, it's patriots, revolutionaries, and all those who fought to protect and preserve Puerto Rico's culture and language throughout the age of colonial rule.

An educational system under a sovereign Puerto Rican government will be paramount in the mission to eradicate the *colonial mentality* (a psychological disease) from future generations. Puerto Ricans need to know about their past in order to better forge a more prosperous and democratic future.

It's time to let Puerto Rico go.

SECTION 4

Invalidating the Statehooder & Colonialist Narratives

When it comes to advancing narratives, not just in Puerto Rico, but in the United States, the statehooders have an undeniable advantage in funding media campaigns and sham polls, mobilizing lobbyists, and reaching more American audiences than the pro-sovereignty movement. How has the statehood movement achieved such success in advancing their pro-statehood narrative in Puerto Rico and in the United States?

Unlike the pro-sovereignty movement, the **pro-statehood movement in Puerto Rico has *never* been persecuted nor attacked by the colonial authorities**. While there are many people who have died and suffered greatly for Puerto Rico's freedom, no one has ever been arrested, tortured, or killed by the colonial authorities for advocating statehood.

People struggle and die for freedom, yet no one would ever die for statehood. In Puerto Rico, although there are countless examples of patriots sacrificing their lives for freedom and liberty, no one is ever willing to sacrifice their lives, careers, and family for statehood. There are no martyrs or heroes in the statehood movement.

Due to advocating a belief that does not attack or threaten the premise of foreign colonial rule and being a hotbed of colonial lackeys and assimilationists, statehooders have been able to advocate their cause from the comfort of their sofas and with colonial approval. If statehooders had ever been persecuted, believe me, there would be no statehooders today.

The statehood movement is also known as one of the **most corrupt and criminal of political movements**. When statehooders (and colonialists as well) win gubernatorial elections and begin to set up their colonial cabinets and administrations, the corruption train begins. Once in power, the statehooders start to award government contracts to friends, family, and inept party loyalists. There is a *quid pro quo* as in "I give you millions of dollars in contracts or jobs to your family, and you support our electoral campaigns and lobbyists for statehood".

It is safe to say that the statehood movement has a lot of funds and access to dark money from PACs, contractors, and corrupt businesses to procure the services of various DC lobbyists to promote statehood among U.S. politicians from both parties and the American people. Along with buying lobbyist services to promote statehood, the statehooders use their millions of dollars to employ allied media companies, that in turn, subcontract to various people that provide trolls and fake social media accounts to attack opponents on social media (mainly Facebook and Twitter) and comments sections on online articles and newspapers.

The statehooders, along with ultra-right-wing foreigners from Latin America, also control radio stations, newspapers, and many other social media outlets to promote statehood and continued colonial rule. Anyone that publicly opposes statehood is verbally attacked and labeled a *communist*, *socialist*, and an *anti-American*...these are the main buzz words used in such campaigns, repeated day after day on statehooder-controlled media outlets. Many of these radio programs include only pro-statehood and pro-colonialist voices and perspectives, while totally ignoring, invisibilizing, and censuring any pro-sovereignty voices and perspectives.

One of the most prominent media voices that support statehood and attacks sovereignty is a show hosted by a life-sized puppet of an old lady (it's really a man dressed as an old lady puppet). This large puppet is used by the colonial government and pro-statehooder groups to spread rumors, tabloid gossip, attack pro-sovereignty advocates, and discredit pro-sovereignty politicians and initiatives. Yes, it's ridiculous and embarrassing, but using puppets seems to be the best way to reach the pro-statehooder political base, particularly the lunatic fringe folks. Many statehooders, as you can imagine, get a lot of their news and vitriol from this anti-freedom and sovereignty-hating puppet. Americans, are there the people you want having a say in your country's affairs and policies?

The statehooder trolls and media outlets, paid by statehooder operatives and political loyalists, employ the same script and repeat the same phrases and buzz words that attempt to influence the Puerto Rican electorate via fear, lies, and character assassinations. It would be safe to say that the statehooders, through all their dark money and corruption, have a media monopoly in Puerto Rico's communications landscape and infrastructure, which is, of course, regulated by the U.S. Federal Communications Commission (FCC).

The statehooders even use public funds to advance their pro-statehood agenda. The colonial government even created its own pro-statehood lobbying group, the *Comisión de Igualdad* (Equality Commission), to lobby for statehood (a political ideology) in Washington, DC, using millions of dollars of public funds, which is illegal, but who cares. Imagine if the Democrats created their own democrat lobbying group using federal and state funds, would the Republicans say something about that? Of course, they would, along with notifying law enforcement and media outlets about such an illegal and egregious use of public funds.

In Puerto Rico, the Feds just look the other way concerning such matters since they usually ignore statehooder illegalities (remember, statehooders and other colonialists are the "yes-men" that help administer and legitimize the colony), especially if these illegal and corrupt acts do not involve federal funds.

To support such multifaceted lobbying efforts, the pro-statehood Senate President, also called "*el tiburón*" (The Shark) in the statehooder underworld, even opened his own office in Washington, DC. Do other state legislative leaders have their own office in Washington, DC spending public funds? If that wasn't enough, the colonial government even operates the Puerto Rico Federal Affairs Administration (PRFAA) to represent Puerto Rico and advance policies that would support the government, and of course, they hire lobbyists as well. Statehooder politicians and loyalists appointed to "serve" in the U.S. very often enjoy the high life and lobster dinners on the backs of Puerto Ricans.

These pro-statehood operatives and lobbyists from Puerto Rico and the Beltway then flood the U.S. media and the offices of Democrats and Republicans with visits and briefs that are centered on the two principle statehooder narratives. Unlike the statehooder media and influence machine, pro-sovereignty groups do not have access to large sums of funds, resources, and access to lobbyists in DC.

The main goal of the statehooders is to make sure that only *their* narrative and perspective is available to American politicians, U.S. media outlets, and the American people. In Washington, DC, statehooders also attempt to place fellow statehooders in high-level federal positions. This book aims at making Americans and others aware that there is a pro-Sovereignty and pro-Democracy narrative that needs to be heard.

As mentioned before, when lobbying for statehood in Washington, DC, and speaking to American media outlets, the statehood movement's carefully selected **narrative** centers on two main appeals: The *Emotional-Military Appeal* and the *Equality/Civil Rights Appeal*. Let's learn more about them.

1. *The Emotional-Military Appeal*: "*the Puerto Ricans who have given their lives in the U.S. military in defending our freedoms*". The premise of this appeal rests on the belief that since Puerto Ricans have been drafted and served in all U.S. wars since WWI as cannon fodder and expendable lives, Puerto Ricans now have a *right* to statehood, irrespective of what Americans may think.

This appeal also uses an emotional aspect in that it tries to link the American patriotic concepts of "serving in the military" and "spilling blood for the U.S." with the concept of "statehood as a right". This appeal is usually used and works best with military service members, veterans, and some conservatives. This appeal is very disingenuous because it implies that every veteran and military servicemember supports or should support statehood, yet totally ignores any veteran or military servicemember that opposes statehood.

This appeal rests on three false premises:

Serving in the military does *not obligate* the United States (or any country) to annex a colony into their country. Annexing a colony or any territory into another country is a national-level decision, not left to the native colonials to decide. Serving in the military, whether drafted or volunteered, is a personal contract between an individual and the U.S. military.

After serving honorably in the military, you as a veteran are entitled to certain privileges and benefits, but you are not entitled to force the United States to annex Puerto Rico. If a group of one thousand Puerto Ricans sign up to serve in the French Foreign Legion, see combat and receive French citizenship after their tour is over, does that now obligate France to make Puerto Rico a French overseas *département*? Of course not.

Statehood is *not a right*; statehood (also called annexation) is a political status that is conferred by a country on a territory. The U.S. Congress is the ultimate authority regarding whether a territory is annexed into the U.S. as a state, and since 1898, they have said *nothing* about statehood for Puerto Rico. That decision does not fall on the people living in a colony. No one can obligate the United States to annex a territory. No one can obligate France to annex a territory either, and so on. In fact, the only right recognized by international law and the United Nations is a people's *right to independence*, not to annexation (statehood).

This *"right to independence"* is based on the universally accepted notion that a rational and intelligent human being naturally wants his/her country to be free, not annexed to another country. Please remember that 99.9% of humanity lives in sovereign nations, not colonies (which are illegal under international law). Statehooders are under the fantastical delusion that all sovereign countries of the world secretly wish to be annexed by the United States.

Being a military servicemember and a veteran does *not mean that one supports statehood*. Although many veterans do support statehood, there are also many Puerto Rican veterans, active military service members, and federal employees that *oppose statehood and support sovereignty*. Throughout history, there are many examples of Puerto Ricans who served in the Spanish and American military forces who also supported independence and other forms of sovereignty for Puerto Rico.

My own grandfather, Tomás Hernández, a U.S. Army and U.S. Air Force veteran who was drafted and served in WWII and Vietnam, also advocated for Puerto Rico's independence. There are many Puerto Rican veterans like him, as he once stated to me, but they have to keep a low profile. According to my grandfather, most veterans' groups in Puerto Rico are controlled by ultra-loyalist statehooders, which shun, discriminate against, and reject any veterans who are also pro-independence advocates.

Here are a few famous and notable Puerto Ricans who served in military forces who also supported independence for Puerto Rico:

General Antonio Valero de Bernabé: Fought against the Napoleonic French forces to liberate Spain in the Peninsular War of 1808, then rebelled and fought against the Spanish Empire to liberate Mexico, Venezuela, Colombia, Peru, and other territories from Spanish rule. General Valero de Bernabé attempted to free Puerto Rico from Spain.

Pedro Albizu Campos: Served as First Lieutenant in the U.S. Army during WWI. Later became the leader of Puerto Rico's Nationalist movement and an iconic patriotic and national figure in Puerto Rican history.

José Antonio Negrón: A World War II veteran and Puerto Rican Nationalist. During the Revolution of 1950 against U.S. colonial rule, Negrón led the Nationalists against colonial troops in the mountain town of Naranjito, the last stronghold of "Free Puerto Rico".

General William Miranda Marín: Served as a Major General of the Puerto Rico National Guard. Later became the mayor of Caguas and a leading figure in the pro-sovereignty (Free Association) movement in Puerto Rico and the PPD.

2. ***The Equality/Civil Rights Appeal***: *"we Puerto Ricans are American citizens and want equal civil and political rights like all the other American citizens in the fifty states"*. The premise of this appeal rests on the belief that Puerto Ricans, as second-class U.S. citizens since 1917, are the same as U.S. citizens in the fifty states and implies that Puerto Ricans, just like African-Americans, Native Americans, and Mexican-Americans, have been discriminated

against by the U.S. government. According to statehooders, the best way to ensure that the second-class U.S. citizens of Puerto Rico enjoy the rights and benefits of first-class U.S. citizenship is to annex Puerto Rico as a state.

This equality/civil rights appeal also uses an emotional aspect in that it tries to link the concepts of "equality" and "civil rights" with the concept of "statehood as a right" in order to equate the "struggle for statehood" with the "struggle for civil rights" in the U.S.

This appeal is usually used and works best with liberals, progressives, and minority politicians and makes it hard for these groups to oppose statehood for Puerto Rico for fear of being labeled racist, anti-Hispanic or anti-Puerto Rican. Thus, you see some American politicians accepting the equality/civil rights appeal and supporting statehood in order to look like they are pro-diversity and pro-Hispanic. Statehooders will **pressure and blackmail** politicians into supporting statehood or risk being called a racist.

This book will help inform such politicians (both Democrats and Republicans) about the consequences of statehood so that these politicians may rectify their positions. This appeal, like the first one, is also very disingenuous because it implies that all Puerto Ricans, as U.S. citizens, are "yearning for equality and the same rights as their fellow citizens on the U.S. mainland." This is simply not true.

This appeal rests on three false premises:

It assumes that just because one is a *born U.S. citizen* in Puerto Rico or of Puerto Rican heritage, that you must be and want to be recognized as an American, thus ignoring over 500 years of Puerto Rican history and Puerto Rico's national identity. Puerto Ricans are U.S. citizens, not because we are *real Americans*, but because the U.S. Congress passed the Jones-Shafroth Act of 1917 and imposed U.S. citizenship on all Puerto Ricans, regardless of whether they wanted to be U.S. citizens or not. Puerto Rico's own House of Delegates rejected the imposition of U.S. citizenship, but it was still imposed.

Why should any Puerto Rican accept to have their identity determined by some old and dead white U.S. Congressmen in 1917 who needed extra bodies for the WWI war effort? Again, if China imposes Chinese citizenship on all Americans in order to make them eligible for a military draft, are Americans now *Chinese*? Of course not.

Statehooders have tried to push a narrative that frames the Puerto Rico status issue as a civil rights issue within the United States, *not* as a human rights issue where Puerto Rico, an occupied nation, would have rights under international law. Basically, they prefer that Puerto Rico be viewed as an abused family member chained up in the basement (keep it in-house) that yearns to be at the family table, not as a kidnapped victim held in bondage by another country.

Statehooders do not want the international community to become aware of and involved in the Puerto Rico status issue, yet only want American politicians and institutions to be involved since they, along with the United States, view the Puerto Rico status issue as a "domestic" problem that should only be dealt with by the United States.

When any foreign leader publicly supports Puerto Rico's right to self-determination and sovereignty, they are attacked by statehooders claiming "mind your own business", yet when an American politician publicly supports statehood in order to fish a few Latino votes, the statehooders celebrate him/her and donate to their election campaigns.

Pro-sovereignty advocates have been claiming for decades that Puerto Rico is an international issue and should be handled at the United Nations. Even the United Nations' Committee on

Decolonization supports the claim that Puerto Rico is an international issue, not a domestic one.

Of course, statehooders refuse to accept that Puerto Rico is a nation and refuse any international focus on this issue in order not to embarrass American officials. Let me explain this in a different way: If you were hiking and came upon a kidnap victim (Puerto Rico) and a kidnapper (U.S. colonial rule), would you call 911 to involve the police (the United Nations) or do nothing and walk away since the kidnapper is claiming that it is a "domestic issue"?

It assumes that the only way to put an end to U.S. government discrimination, historical abuses, and racist colonial geography-based policies of exclusion in federal funding programs, is to become a state, to merge as a sub-unit with the country you claim is discriminating and abusing you. As you can see, the statehood movement suffers from a colonial psychological combination of Battered Woman Syndrome (BWS) and the Stockholm Syndrome: where a victim becomes so defeated and passive that she believes that she is incapable of leaving her abuser, thus staying with him and defending him even after all the abuses.

These are all psychological manifestations of "learned helplessness" inherent in the *colonial mentality*, a colonial mental health condition that needs to be dealt with and eliminated if Puerto Ricans are ever to progress in the world. Sovereignty would be a big first step in the right direction in order to eliminate "learned helplessness" and the colonial mentality in Puerto Rico. With sovereignty, Puerto Rico will finally be able to rely on itself, not on the empty promises of colonial officials, to promote its interests.

The statehooders know that Puerto Rico has been abused, discriminated, and treated very badly for over a century by the United States (they mention it in all their speeches), and their solution to this problem, instead of seeking freedom from that abuse, is to *marry* him and join his family via statehood. In what world would anyone tell an abused woman that instead of escaping the abuser and starting a new life, she should marry the abuser? How many times have we seen such unhealthy situations where people stay in toxic relationships because they don't have the self-confidence to leave, fear to leave, and cannot imagine how they can ever live without that person, despite their abuses?

The statehooders see Puerto Rico as an abused and relegated girlfriend that *should* become the abused wife, since in theory, the abused wife would have access to the bank account (the U.S. Treasury) of her abusive husband (the United States). Stick by the U.S., even if it humiliates Puerto Rico every day. I have seen statehooders yell and claim "federal discrimination" by the US government, and yet they want to be part of the country that discriminates against them. I believe that such people lack self-respect and dignity as Puerto Ricans.

They want to be part of a country full of white supremacists that wish to threaten and kill Hispanics. A country full of people that constantly yell "*Speak English*" when they hear Spanish spoken in public. This does not make sense. After reading the list of atrocities and acts of repression in the previous section, why should Puerto Rico, or any Puerto Rican, keep putting up with all that abuse, humiliation, and suffering? Enough is enough.

Instead of trying to escape such colonial abuse and discrimination and start its own life in freedom with the world, the statehooders feel that Puerto Rico is worthless and inferior and can only be important if legally tied to the United States and live in its political basement. Being *just* Puerto Rican is not enough for them.

After 121 years, the United States has still not "put a ring on it" and despite statehooder attempts to pressure, cajole, and influence American politicians and the American people into a shotgun marriage with a colonized Latin American nation, the United States will never "put a ring on it".

Realizing that the United States will *never* accept Puerto Rico as a state, nor should it, it's time that Puerto Rico had some self-respect and dignity and finally began the process of transitioning to sovereignty, freedom, and democracy. Even the founder of the statehood movement, Dr. José Celso Barbosa, stated that should the United States deny Puerto Rico the possibility of statehood, Puerto Rico should seek its independence. Apparently, statehooders lack courage and blatantly ignore the very founder of their own movement.

As stated, when it comes to advancing such statehooder narratives, not just in Puerto Rico, but in the United States, the statehooders have an undeniable advantage in regards to funding media campaigns and polls, publishing mailers, mobilizing supporters and lobbyists in Puerto Rico and the United States, and reaching more American news audiences than the pro-sovereignty movement.

Now that these narratives have been dissected and explained, one can better see through all the lies and colonial politics and understand the true motivations, goals, and media strategies of the pro-statehood movement.

SECTION 5

Why Americans must Oppose Statehood & Support Sovereignty for Puerto Rico

As you have seen, there are myriad of reasons to oppose statehood and support sovereignty for Puerto Rico. This section will focus on the various reasons why Americans, both liberals and conservatives, need to oppose Puerto Rico statehood and support Puerto Rican sovereignty.

Although some reasons would impact both democrats and republicans, some reasons would have a direct impact on one political group. Puerto Rico's decolonization is a bipartisan problem with a bipartisan solution that both parties can support.

Below are various reasons why both liberals and conservatives can advance their political and economic interests and agendas by opposing statehood and supporting Puerto Rican sovereignty.

Reasons for Americans to Oppose Statehood

Why American Democrats, Liberals, and Progressives need to oppose Puerto Rico Statehood:

Annexation of an Occupied Nation: Statehood would not mean annexing an "island of U.S. citizens", as statehooders like to claim. In Puerto Rico and around the world, it would be seen as the annexation of a proud and distinct Latin American and Caribbean nation with a 500-year-old active pro-independence movement. Liberals and progressives, who abhor military occupations and colonial regimes overseas, surely do not want to fully annex a defiant Latin American country that has resisted colonial rule and assimilation into the United States. Statehood would be the culmination of colonial occupation and would be fought actively and tirelessly by Puerto Ricans.

Corrupt & Colonialist Statehooders: The pro-statehood party leadership (made up of both Democrats and Republicans) is comprised of the most anti-democratic, corrupt, colonialist, fundamentalist, clownish, and inept leaders imaginable that support statehood so that they can have direct access to federal funds and be able to influence federal laws and policies in their own selfish interest.

Foreign Policy: Regarding foreign policy, the pro-statehood party leadership is known for supporting right-wing military dictatorships and civil rights violations throughout Latin America. In fact, both the pro-statehood party and the pro-Commonwealth party have a long history of persecution and human and civil rights violations against pro-sovereignty and pro-democracy supporters and activists in Puerto Rico.

Healthcare & Women's Rights: Regarding healthcare, although most Puerto Ricans would support a universal singer-payer national healthcare system, the statehood party has various donors and corrupt relationships with many health insurance providers, thus blocking all attempts at any sensible healthcare reform in Puerto Rico.

Also, Christian fundamentalists seem to flock to the statehood party where they attempt to infringe on a women's right to choose, impose their extremist morality, discriminate against the LGBT community, and try to have a say regarding what a woman can do with her body. Amazingly, these statehooders also promote outlandish legislation and policies regarding women's rights, domestic violence, incest, and rape that make the Deep South seem liberal.

Labor: Regarding labor and socio-economic policies, the statehood party is well known for being anti-labor and has implemented various laws that strip workers of their rights and benefits.

Electoral Reform & Democracy: Regarding electoral reform, both the pro-statehood party and the pro-Commonwealth party have a record for blocking all reforms that would jeopardize their control of Puerto Rico's bipartisan colonial political system. Due to these two colonial parties, Puerto Rico's electoral law does not allow electoral alliances nor proportional representation since such alliances would give pro-sovereignty and smaller groups more power.

In 2005, the people's democratic will (83.9% in favor) regarding the implementation of a unicameral legislature was literally ignored as if it did not even happen by these supposed paladins of democracy within both parties.

The statehood party favors the electoral participation of prisoners (convicted felons, murderers, etc.), yet does not favor the electoral participation of the Puerto Rican diaspora since these stateside Puerto Ricans are beyond their control and influence (and usually turn out to be pro-sovereignty supporters).

It is common knowledge in Puerto Rico that the statehood party makes promises and arrangements with prison gangs regarding convict privileges and in return, these convicted felons vote as a block for statehood and statehooder candidates, so much so, that the "*convicted felon vote*" is pretty much guaranteed for the statehood party. Prison gang loyalty and orders even extend into the voting booths. If the prison gang leader says "vote for statehood", the prisoners in that specific gang had better vote for statehood. Welcome to democracy in the U.S. colony of Puerto Rico.

Voting Rights & Suppression: Regarding voting rights, the statehood party has a history of voter suppression, voter fraud, voter intimidation, and limiting the number of possible political parties and the number of absentee voters. Infirm and bedridden elderly and dead people amazingly turn out in droves to vote for the statehood party and their corrupt and inept politicians.

Senior citizen homes are often visited by statehooder candidates in order to instill fear into the elderly about "communist and separatist takeovers", "threats to U.S. citizenship", and have them vote for statehood.

Remember, many of these elderly people lived through the era of terror and repression against nationalism, and to this day, they still fear the possibility of being labeled a "separatist" and being persecuted and arrested; and the statehooders know this. What better way to show your loyalty to the colonial regime and our American rulers than to vote for statehood? Both the pro-statehood party and the pro-Commonwealth party have been known to undercount opposition votes, and sometimes, whole ballot boxes mysteriously end up in remote creeks, only to be discovered months after the election has already happened.

Environment: Regarding the environment, the statehood party is known for ignoring and watering down environmental laws and regulations, particularly to please foreign companies or elite political donors.

Energy Policy: Regarding energy, the statehood party, instead of harnessing the massive power of Puerto Rico's potential renewable energy sources (solar, wind, and tidal), plans to rebuild the same crumbling energy system and have the country become more dependent on liquified natural gas (LNG) in order to placate certain American politicians and energy interests. Remember, for both the pro-statehood and pro-Commonwealth parties, a self-sufficient and energy independent Puerto Rico is against their political and financial interests.

Criminal Justice: Regarding criminal justice, the statehood party is supportive of private prisons, using police officers to squash dissent and protests, making laws that would allow discrimination in the public sector, and using security forces to persecute and intimidate pro-sovereignty activists and supporters.

Education Policy: Regarding educational policy, the statehood party dismantled Puerto Rico's public-school system by closing hundreds of schools and hoping to create a new for-profit charter school system. This policy led to many educational and community problems, particularly when the American secretary of education appointed by the statehooder government was arrested by the federal government for diverting millions of dollars that were destined for Puerto Rico's children.

Why American Republicans and Conservatives need to oppose Puerto Rico Statehood:

The U.S.A. as a Multinational State: The annexation of Puerto Rico as a U.S. state would turn the United States overnight from a national state to a multinational state (one government, two nations), like the old Yugoslavia and the Soviet Union as regards political ethnic policies and problems. Let me repeat this: with a Puerto Rican state, the United States will effectively become a country made up of two distinct nations.

Puerto Ricans would not just become "Hispanic-Americans", they will remain Puerto Ricans and fight in Congress against assimilation and to have Puerto Rico's national identity and Spanish language recognized at the federal level. From the outset, the U.S. would gain a new state full of active and defiant Puerto Rican secessionists and nationalists ready to take aim at continued federal and colonial rule and all policies and notions of assimilation.

Free Enterprise: While conservatives support free-market capitalism, free enterprise, deregulation, and labor restrictions, Puerto Ricans generally support state capitalism, government intervention in the economy, public regulation, and the benefits and services of a welfare benefactor state. Even the supposed "conservative" statehooders usually support what Republicans would call "big government" since they use Puerto Rico's public agencies to hire their unqualified and inept party supporters and lackeys, not professional public servants.

As a U.S. colony, Puerto Rico is a colonial captive market and unable by federal law, to engage in the very free trade and free-market capitalism that such conservatives profess for Americans and the world.

Federal Government & State's Rights: While conservatives generally support policies that favor a smaller federal government, Puerto Ricans generally support policies that favor a larger federal government and more public agencies to work on important socio-economic issues.

As a state, Puerto Rico would favor a more powerful federal government on issues of federal funding and socio-economic initiatives, yet would also carry the *State's Rights* banner when it came to issues such as Spanish as the official state language of government and the recognition of Puerto Rican culture and history throughout the government and education. If a monolingual English-speaking American needed to interact with the state government or state courts for any reason, a translator would probably be provided.

Also, English-speaking American students would be mandated to take Spanish as a Second Language (SSL) course if they were to enter the Puerto Rican public education system. Puerto Ricans would expect nothing less, especially when monolingual Spanish-speaking Puerto Ricans must go to English as a Second Language (ESL) courses in the public schools of the fifty states.

Puerto Ricans will *not tolerate* any threats to the primacy and official position of Spanish as the principal language of instruction in public schools just because an English-speaking Johnny Johnson from Omaha moves to Puerto Rico. Little Johnny will be expected to go to special SSL courses so that he can learn Spanish and eventually mainstream into full Spanish language subject classes in Math, Sciences, and History, among other classes.

U.S. Official Language Policy: Statehood would open the Pandora's box of U.S. official language policy by having a Puerto Rico state government that would operate, in theory, entirely in Spanish. Any sort of imposed English-Only policy from the federal government will be fought and defeated in Puerto Rico (as has happened in the past).

Unlike conservatives, most Puerto Ricans would be extremely against having Spanish (and other non-English languages) not used on government language forms and the public domain. Many people joke that in Puerto Rico, English-Only laws go to die. Also, Puerto Rico would be the main force to have the federal government declare English and Spanish as the two official languages of the United States, creating a fully bilingual federal government (just like the bilingual federal government of Canada operates in English and French).

Puerto Ricans would struggle, together with other Hispanic groups, to give Spanish equal status with English at the federal level and state level of various states such as Florida, California, Texas, Arizona, New Mexico, and others. Conservative concerns that such official bilingualism would contribute to eroding the white Anglo and European-American culture and status of English as the national language of the United States would not stop Puerto Ricans at all.

If the United States annexes and brings in Puerto Rico into the union, Puerto Ricans will preserve their national culture, struggle against assimilation, and work to "Hispanicize" the United States in their own image. Believe me, as a professional diaspora Puerto Rican, those would be our goals if annexed into the United States.

American Unity: Puerto Rico statehood would also take aim on American unity by insisting that Puerto Rico maintain its own national Olympic team and international sports sovereignty (even though no other state has that right).

More Access to Federal Funds: The statehood party, as previously mentioned, aims to create a "State of Puerto Rico" that would have access to billions of more dollars of U.S. taxpayer funds (free gringo money as they say) for welfare and nutritional assistance programs. For many statehooders, the whole end goal of statehood is not to become an "American" or "join the American family", but to take more federal funds from the U.S. Treasury and pay as little taxes as possible by living under or at the poverty line. Unbeknownst to American politicians and officials, this is what statehooders *actually* tell their supporters in Puerto Rico.

American Assimilation Problems: The majority of Puerto Ricans abhor and detest any notion of assimilation into the U.S. mainstream culture. Even statehooders in Puerto Rico tell their followers that they would not need to assimilate to become a state. Why would the U.S. annex an occupied colony that has historically fought against and defeated various past assimilation policies? These past attempted assimilation policies ranged from educational, language, and cultural policies, and they were all soundly defeated by mass protests, civil disobedience, and ignoring such ridiculous colonial laws.

Remember, in Puerto Rico, the U.S. flag is routinely called "*la pecosa*" (freckles), people mock U.S. holidays, call Americans "gringos" on a regular basis, English is not used at all by the vast majority of Puerto Ricans, and although they are U.S. citizens (by a congressional decree in 1917 to conscript soldiers), the vast majority of Puerto Ricans, even after 121 years of colonial rule, continue to refer to themselves solely as Puerto Ricans (Boricuas), not Americans.

Honestly, I have never heard a Puerto Rican call themselves a "Puerto Rican-American". Americans need to fully understand that Puerto Ricans are a proud and unassimilable nation.

Immigration Policies: Regarding immigration to the United States, Puerto Ricans (although U.S. citizens) are generally sympathetic and supportive of the plight of illegal immigrants, particularly those from Latin America that cross the border in search of "a better life". Puerto Ricans are generally supportive, as is the larger Hispanic community, of sanctuary cities, and the provision of drivers' licenses to illegal immigrants.

Remember, although Puerto Ricans are U.S. citizens, they are generally viewed as foreign non-English-speaking immigrants by most other U.S. citizens, and many times discriminated against them for speaking Spanish in public and for being "Hispanic" by racists and other white supremacists in American society.

Gun Control Policy: Regarding Gun Control and the Second Amendment, Puerto Ricans are generally *not* considered "gun nuts" like many gun-totting Americans nor believe the Second Amendment to be the word of God. Puerto Ricans, in my experience, are more supportive of background and psychological checks, stricter gun control laws, and the banning of military assault rifles for personal non-police or military use.

Historically, Puerto Rico never had a "hunting culture" or "gun culture" like the one that developed in the United States. In Puerto Rico, no one "goes out hunting" with rifles or military assault weapons. Due to such lax federal gun control laws and inept federal control of Puerto Rico's maritime borders, various legal and unregistered illegal firearms now exist in Puerto Rico and are used in a large number of crimes.

All in all, Puerto Ricans are more supportive of more strict gun control legislation, ranging from more background checks to Japanese-style mandatory checks, training, government approval, and limiting the number of firearms and munitions that a citizen can legally own. As a state, Puerto Ricans would greatly affect the reach and "sacredness" of the Second Amendment, be a nightmare for the NRA and American gun rights advocates and become the tip of the spear for stricter federal gun control legislation.

The entire notion that *"guns are my birthright as an American"* has no place in Puerto Rican history nor Puerto Rican culture…it is essentially an alien concept that must be derailed.

Healthcare Policy: Regarding healthcare, most Puerto Ricans would welcome a Canadian-style universal single-payer national healthcare system in Puerto Rico, particularly after the disastrous American-modeled private insurance healthcare system currently failing Puerto Ricans with poor service, high costs, long wait times, and driving doctors and other medical professionals out of the country. In the United States, the universal healthcare system that most Puerto Ricans desire is considered "socialized" medicine by conservatives.

Fiscal & Monetary Policy: Regarding fiscal and monetary policy, both the pro-statehood and pro-Commonwealth parties, together with the federal government, have been responsible for Puerto Rico's unsustainable and unpayable colonial public debt, debt that they refuse to audit and incurred with Wall Street firms and investor groups knowing full well that Puerto Rico had no source of repayment.

The statehood party, led by various mafioso types, particularly is known for its corrupt and irresponsible fiscal policies and disasters and lack of financial transparency that aims at driving the Puerto Rican economy into the ground. Conservatives, are these the corrupt and inept Puerto Rican politicians you want having a say in the overall debt and fiscal policies of the United States?

Economic Development Policy: Regarding economic prosperity and development, the statehood party blocks all attempts at Puerto Rico developing its economy and creating wealth since, for them, Puerto Rico can *only* exist as a captive colonial market for American products. The statehooder economic plan positions Puerto Rico as a consumer, not a producer of goods and services, continually begging for more federal funds.

With a weak and dependent planned economy that rewards outsiders with tax credits and subsidies while penalizing Puerto Rican businesses with higher taxes and permits, statehooders hope to create more poverty that would drive more and more Puerto Ricans into collecting food stamps, welfare, and other federal subsidies.

Statehooder political calculations rely on more poverty creating more dependency on federal funds, thus more support for statehood since they promise voters that statehood will bring in an additional $10 billion in more federal funds for welfare and food stamps.

The statehood party's entire economic plan rests not in developing Puerto Rico's factors of production, human capital, and exportation, but in *begging for and demanding more and more federal funds* (free gringo money) from Congress. Conservatives, are these the corrupt and inept Puerto Rican politicians you want having a say in American economic prosperity and development policies?

Energy Policy: Regarding energy policy, the statehood party supports increased privatization, yet this goes at odds with what most Puerto Ricans desire, which is increased nationalization due to the inept and disastrous results of privatization, dumping of coal ash and the poisoning of communities, and the increased costs of electricity generation across Puerto Rico. When the statehooders come to power, they defund public services and make them ripe for privatization.

The majority of Puerto Ricans desire a complete reform of the energy system, the adoption of renewable energy production, and are decidedly against any form of nuclear power, "clean coal" technologies, fracking, and oil drilling off Puerto Rico's coasts.

Border Policy: Regarding border policy and drug interdiction, the U.S. federal government agencies of CBP and ICE control and oversee Puerto Rico's porous maritime borders. Once narcotraffickers achieve bringing drugs into Puerto Rico from South America via the sea and the airports (sometimes with the aid of corrupted federal agents), sending all those drugs to the U.S. is a matter of domestic postal service.

There are various narco trade networks that operate in Puerto Rico and take advantage of the U.S.-Puerto Rico colonial relationship to ship drugs into the United States. This advantage would continue if Puerto Rico were made into a state since CBP and its cadre of underpaid agents would still oversee the borders. Remember, once in Puerto Rico, such drugs and other contraband can easily be shipped and mailed to the U.S. via domestic service.

International Events: Regarding international sporting events, the statehood party constantly tells its supporters that as a state, Puerto Rico would continue to have its own national Olympic team and compete at such international sporting events as a sovereign nation. Now, are other states allowed to have Olympic teams? Of course not. The Amateur Sports Act of 1978 denies states such a right and acknowledges that all Americans in the United States are to compete internationally with Team U.S.A., not a state team.

If Puerto Ricans are forced to compete under the Team U.S.A. banner, please understand that if a Puerto Rican wins a medal, they *will* unfurl the flag of Puerto Rico, not the United States, on the podium and sing the national anthem *La Borinqueña*. Any Puerto Rican that did that would become an instant superstar and celebrated patriotic hero or heroine in Puerto Rico. Also, the statehood party tells its supporters that even as a state, Puerto Rico would still be able to compete in other international events, competitions, and forums under its own national banner.

Affirmative Action Policy: Although conservatives reject all forms of affirmative action based on race, gender, or ethnicity in education and employment, Puerto Ricans generally support, advocate, and promote such affirmative action policies since they, as part of the greater Hispanic community, benefit from it in advancing their educations and careers.

Although conservatives fear that such affirmative action policies will lead to the "cultural balkanization" of the United States, Puerto Ricans see no problem with that since such "cultural balkanization" would be regarded as "embracing cultural diversity and the advancement of minorities" and supported by the vast majority of Puerto Ricans.

If the United States makes Puerto Rico a state, the federal government would literally be embracing such "cultural balkanization" as official policy. Like most Hispanics, Puerto Ricans want to celebrate their language and culture in public and benefit from every possible opportunity to advance in society and business.

Birthright Citizenship: Although many conservatives reject the concept of "birthright citizenship" for children of illegal immigrants, Puerto Ricans generally support such policies because they believe that it helps such families, usually Hispanic, to remain in the United States and progress economically.

United Nations: Although many conservatives believe that the United States should secede from the United Nations or at least defund it due to perceived wrongs and lack of support to various American initiatives, Puerto Ricans are generally supportive of the United Nations, its policies, and programs.

American Politics: As a state, Puerto Ricans are more likely to vote for Democratic, liberal, or independent candidates, not Republican or other conservatives. In Puerto Rico, the Democratic Party is viewed as more accepting of minorities, Hispanics, and concerned about important socio-economic issues, while the Republican Party is viewed as a party of racists, white supremacists, rednecks, and uncultured people that hate Puerto Ricans.

Of course, you'll always find some Puerto Rican colonial lacky or pitiyanki that thinks he/she is an "American" and will just support the Republican Party in hopes of being selected as a token Hispanic Republican leader in Puerto Rico, but generally, most Puerto Ricans, particularly young people, would never vote Republican in any election. As a state, Puerto Rico would have two senators and six or seven democratic representatives, more than many Republican-led states who would lose congressional representation.

This one fact has been one of the major reasons why Puerto Rico statehood, even with the support of dark money, has never made it past the U.S. Senate....American congressman and others in political circles know that a Puerto Rican congressional delegation would forever shift the balance of power, to the detriment of the Republican Party, other conservatives, and other "Red" districts.

The 1989 negotiations in Congress regarding Puerto Rico's status were derailed when statehooders demanded statehood to be an option that the United States *had* to accept. The United States does *not want* statehood for Puerto Rico, yet the Congress allows this political and colonial charade to continue by not decolonizing Puerto Rico and beginning the transition to sovereignty.

Democrats should not be celebrating either, since a Puerto Rican democratic congressional delegation would usher in calls for bilingual federal Spanish-English official language policy, recognition of Puerto Rico as "a distinct nation and people" within the United States, defend a Spanish-speaking Puerto Rican state government, and be tireless promoting more autonomy or secession and independence from the very floor of Congress. To the "horror" of many Americans, these Puerto Rican congressmen and women would be giving speeches in Spanish in Congress on a regular basis.

Also, there are no rules saying that a Congressman or woman needs to be fluent in English. In other words, for both Democrats and Republicans, a Puerto Rican congressional delegation would be a headache and problem to the entire American political system.

My recommendation to Americans: cut your losses and decolonize Puerto Rico *now* by contacting their congressional representatives and urging them to begin the transition to sovereignty.

Reasons for Americans to Support Sovereignty

Why American Democrats, Liberals, and Progressives need to support Puerto Rico's Sovereignty:

Liberation of an Occupied Nation: If liberals and progressives really value freedom, democracy, and the end of humiliating colonial rule under the U.S. flag for both Americans and Puerto Ricans, then they should support a transition to Puerto Rican sovereignty. With a process of decolonization, the United States would finally be helping Puerto Rico transition from a powerless colonial territory to a new democratic and sovereign republic.

Sovereignty for Puerto Rico would be either full independence or a sovereign free association relationship with the United States, just like Palau, Micronesia, and the Marshall Islands. With free association, Puerto Rico would be sovereign, democratic, and have a treaty-based relationship with the United States as an ally and strategic partner.

If the United States really wants to promote democracy overseas, unloading and decolonizing its largest and most populous colonial territory would be a great start, particularly in the eyes of Puerto Rico and the world. A sovereign Puerto Rico would finally be able to overturn all anti-democratic colonial era laws and replace them with new national democratic laws and policies.

As a sovereign nation, Puerto Rico would finally be able to develop its economy, increase entrepreneurship and exports, interact with foreign nations and markets, better attract tourism and foreign investment, and become a member of the United Nations. A sovereign Puerto Rico would surely be a strong U.S. ally and strategic partner in Latin America. Americans, please ask yourself: is it better to have Puerto Rico as a strategic partner and ally or as a bankrupt and undemocratic colonial territory that embarrasses the United States around the world?

The End of Corrupt Statehooders: With sovereignty, Puerto Rico's political status would finally be resolved. Those statehooders who wish to live the "American Dream" as Hispanic-Americans can move to the United States and achieve their "personal" statehood...and of course, it's just a plane ride away. Those former statehooders that wish to remain in and contribute to Puerto Rico, would be welcomed.

With sovereignty, Puerto Rico would be able to implement various strict anti-corruption, political and campaign financing, government procurement, and anti-graft measures and laws that both corrupt colonial parties have never wanted to implement during colonial rule. In a sovereign Puerto Rico, partisan politics would be outlawed in public agencies, and a professional merit-based Civil Service would be established.

Foreign Policy: With a sovereign Puerto Rico, the days of the United Nations' Committee on Decolonization demanding the United States to decolonize and free Puerto Rico would be over. With sovereignty, Puerto Rico would become a United Nations member and support its global programs and initiatives regarding democracy, development, and security.

As a sovereign nation, Puerto Rico would finally be able to establish its own merit-based Diplomatic Service to serve and advance Puerto Rican national interests overseas at Puerto Rican embassies, consulates, and other diplomatic missions.

Healthcare & Women's Rights: Unhindered by American federal and retrograde policies regarding healthcare and health insurance monopolies with corrupt lobbyists, a sovereign Puerto Rico would finally be able to establish and implement its own sensible healthcare reform and the universal singer-payer national healthcare system Puerto Ricans so desperately want and need to meet the healthcare crisis currently afflicting the country.

Unrestricted by federal policies and politics regarding discrimination and women's rights, a sovereign Puerto Rico would not only adopt strict anti-discrimination measures for all societal groups and communities but would also be responsible in finally protecting a woman's right to choose what she does with her body, as supported by the majority of Puerto Ricans.

Death Penalty: Currently, as a U.S. colony or a state, federal death penalty statutes apply to Puerto Rico, even though the majority of Puerto Ricans are against the death penalty. A sovereign Puerto Rico would ensure that Puerto Rican lives would never again be threatened by such barbaric, uncivilized, and retrograde capital punishment laws.

Labor: A sovereign Puerto Rico would legally overturn all the colonial labor laws that destroyed workers' rights and benefits but would also support and promote the growth of businesses and entrepreneurship.

Electoral Reform & Democracy: As noted earlier, both the pro-statehood party and the pro-Commonwealth party have a record for blocking all reforms that would jeopardize their control of Puerto Rico's imposed bipartisan U.S.-modeled colonial political system.

A sovereign Puerto Rico could finally initiate the process of electoral and campaign finance reform that Puerto Ricans demand without being constrained by loopholes permitted in federal laws like *Citizens United* that facilitate corruption in the United States and Puerto Rico.

A sovereign Puerto Rico could finally establish a unicameral legislature, initiate constitutional reforms, a democratization of the political structures, reestablish the Puerto Rican parliament, proportional representation, run-off elections, limit the power of political parties, only allow candidates on ballots (not parties), part-time citizen legislators with no benefits, strict term limits, and other electoral and democratic reforms.

A sovereign Puerto Rico, as a true transnational nation, could even implement legislation that would strengthen economic links and allow the over six million strong Puerto Rican diaspora in the United States to participate in Puerto Rican national elections and politics with the establishment of diaspora voting districts and diaspora absentee voting, as is done in many countries that have and value their large diaspora populations. Even the United States allows and encourages overseas Americans (expats) to participate in federal and state elections.

Voting Rights & Suppression: Unlike the corrupt and anti-democratic statehooders, the democratic leaders of a sovereign Puerto Rico would finally strengthen and expand voting rights and transparency, prohibit voter suppression, facilitate absentee voting for overseas Puerto Ricans, allow same-day voter registration, mandate an Election Day holiday, fight against vote buying and electoral corruption and fraud (like having dead people vote for the statehood party), institutionalize electoral observers, and strengthen voters confidentiality and electoral security.

Also, a sovereign Puerto Rico would depoliticize the national electoral commission and create a new structure that is independent, not controlled by political parties, and administered by actual electoral professionals, not political party loyalists, as is done today under the colonial regime.

Environment: Regarding the environment, a sovereign Puerto Rico would finally strengthen and implement environmental laws and regulations, not be tied down by republican EPA regulations, establish a cadre of professional environmentalists and environmental security agents to enforce the country's environmental laws.

Energy Policy: Regarding energy, a sovereign Puerto Rico would have the power and authority to harness the massive power of Puerto Rico's potential renewable energy sources (solar, wind, and tidal), to rebuild a new electrical infrastructure, and not become dependent on liquified natural gas (LNG) and fracking companies.

With sovereignty, Puerto Rico could become self-sufficient and energy independent with other renewables such as hemp and kelp ethanol, biodiesel, and other agro-energy resources, all produced in Puerto Rico by Puerto Ricans.

Criminal Justice: Regarding criminal justice and security, a sovereign Puerto Rico would be able to finally reform the colonial criminal justice system, reform the corrections system, and reform the police and internal security agencies. Such reforms would focus on professionalization, anti-corruption measures, and the establishment of merit-based national security service and structures.

Education Policy: Regarding educational policy, a sovereign Puerto Rico would overturn the corrupt charter school and voucher system and policies, reform the private school system, reestablish and strengthen the public school system, and ratify new legislation that would strengthen the institutional autonomy and funds of the University of Puerto Rico, the same national public university that the statehooders tried to defund, privatize, and destroy.

Also, a sovereign Puerto Rico would finally be able to overturn the colonial bilingual language law, recognize Spanish as the sole official national language of the Republic, and implement a new language law that recognizes regional official languages (such as English and French) and promotes multilingualism in all Puerto Rican schools and government.

A sovereign Puerto Rico would also be able to overturn inept U.S. modeled colonial education policies (No Child Left Behind and other retrograde conservative policies) and finally implement a Puerto Rico-based national education policy and national curriculum that focuses not only on math, sciences, and technology, but also on Puerto Rican culture and identity, Puerto Rican values and civics, Puerto Rican and world history, global studies, economics, entrepreneurship, financial literacy, environmental studies, agriculture, and international affairs, among others.

Free of the U.S. modeled retrograde and corrupt colonial education system, Puerto Ricans would finally be able to establish a world class level educational system that rewards teachers, serves students, and is based and inspired on the successful educational models of Singapore, Finland, Japan, and other educationally successful countries.

Why American Republicans and Conservatives need to support Puerto Rico's Sovereignty:

The Unity of the United States: For Republicans and other conservatives, the annexation of Puerto Rico would turn the United States overnight from a national state to a multinational state (one government, two nations), thus destroying what conservatives consider to be the pillars of American culture and national unity.

Remember, Puerto Ricans are *not* Americans. Conservatives and all Americans must realize that Puerto Ricans are *not* Americans and will never assimilate into generic "Hispanic-Americans". Puerto Ricans are a proud, distinct, and unassimilable Latin American and Caribbean nation, not a mere group of ethnic minorities that speak Spanish.

During the massive protests of the Puerto Rican Summer Revolution of 2019 that ousted the corrupt pro-statehood governor from power, there were *no* USA flags in sight, only Puerto Rican flags and other nationalist and patriotic flags were used. Puerto Ricans call Puerto Rico their *país* (country) and *nación* (nation), not a *territory* as viewed by American officials.

I have never heard any Puerto Rican ever say that they "love their territory". Over 121 years of U.S. colonial rule, persecutions, arrests, murders, and colonial assimilation campaigns, were not able to destroy Puerto Rico's national identity and struggle for freedom.

With annexation, the U.S. would gain a new state full of active and defiant Puerto Rican secessionists and nationalists ready to take aim at continued federal rule, American assimilation policies, and all aspects of the conservative American agenda and the Republican platform.

If the United States wishes to destroy itself from within with ethnic strife and Québec-style politics in the U.S. Congress, then annexing Puerto Rico is the way to go. If conservatives wish to save the United States from such a fate, then please start the process of transitioning Puerto Rico to sovereignty now.

Free Enterprise: With sovereignty, Puerto Rico would finally be able to enjoy and participate in free enterprise and the free markets that conservatives always talk about. As a colony or state, Puerto Rico's businesses and entrepreneurs would be limited by overreaching byzantine federal laws and policies meant for American businesses not hampered by the Jones Act and other detrimental federal laws.

With sovereignty, Puerto Rico would be able to establish a vibrant and global business climate that embraces free markets and foreign investments yet protects and promotes Puerto Rican businesses and economic interests.

Federal Government & State's Rights: With a sovereign Puerto Rico, conservatives will not have to worry about an entire Puerto Rican democratic congressional delegation supporting policies that would increase the size and authority of the federal government. Although supportive of State's Rights regarding language and cultural issues, Puerto Rico would most likely not be in favor of the State's Rights argument used to protect the perceived constitutional rights of gun rights advocates, affirmation action policies, and other such state policies.

A Puerto Rico state government would use the State's Rights argument to establish Spanish as the language of state government and education. English would be a required class, but not the main language of instruction in Puerto Rico. Puerto Ricans would never support such an idea or policy.

U.S. Official Language Policy: With a sovereign Puerto Rico, the United States and conservative groups would not have to worry about the opening of the Pandora's box of U.S. official language policy by having a Puerto Rico state government that would operate, in theory, entirely in Spanish.

A "State of Puerto Rico" would continuously undermine English-Only policies, laws, and initiatives and advocate for official Spanish-English bilingualism at the federal level for all federal agencies and all federal documents, events, forums, and forms.

Conservative concerns that such official federal bilingualism would contribute to eroding the white Anglo and European-American culture and status of English as the national language of the United States would be realized and would not stop Puerto Ricans at all. If conservatives wish to have English remain the national language of the United States for the foreseeable future, Republicans in Congress need to begin the decolonization process and transitioning of Puerto Rico to sovereignty now.

American Unity: If conservatives want to avoid the international spectacle of having a future Puerto Rican athlete in Team U.S.A. raise the Puerto Rican flag at the Olympic medal podium and sing *La Borinqueña*, Americans need to begin the decolonization process and transitioning of Puerto Rico to sovereignty now.

End Federal Funds to Corrupt Statehooders: If conservatives want to save billions of dollars of U.S. taxpayer funds and stop funding the corrupt statehood party and its lackeys, Puerto Rican sovereignty is the way to go. For most statehooders, the whole end goal of statehood is not to become an "American" or "join the American family", but to take more federal funds from the U.S. Treasury and pay as little taxes as possible by living under or at the poverty line.

In any process to transition Puerto Rico to sovereignty, the United States must assume its responsibility as the "administrating power" and support the new Republic of Puerto Rico as an ally with financial assistance (such as block grants in a Treaty of Free Association) for a determined period of time to help build up Puerto Rico's economy after 121 years of colonial rule and wealth extraction. Acquired rights, such as social security and veterans' benefits, would continue to be sent to Puerto Ricans who contributed to those systems.

Regarding corruption, a sovereign Puerto Rico could also establish its own independent and non-partisan Singapore-modeled anti-corruption police, strengthen the powers and scope of the Office of Government Ethics, mandatory sentences for acts of corruption, and fully implement various anti-corruption laws and measures that the statehooders and colonialists have been against and preventing for years. A strong and prosperous Puerto Rican economy that can hold corrupt officials accountable for their crimes would be in a better position to attract investments and import American goods and services and is in the interests of both conservatives and liberals.

Avoid American Assimilation Problems: If conservatives want to avoid bringing in a distinct nation into the union that abhors assimilation into American society and attacks one of the very pillars of American identity, then they should support and advance Puerto Rico's sovereignty and freedom.

Remember, Puerto Ricans have historically fought against and defeated various past American assimilation policies in Puerto Rico, policies that ranged from educational, language, and cultural policies and were all defeated by mass protests and civil disobedience. Although they are U.S. citizens by a congressional decree in 1917, even after 121 years of colonial rule, continue to refer to themselves solely as *Puerto Ricans (Boricuas)*, not Americans.

In general, Puerto Ricans regard the forced assimilation policies that have been imposed on immigrants and Native Americans as disgusting and dictatorial. Americans need to fully understand that Puerto Ricans are a proud and *unassimilable* nation. Think about this: many stateside Puerto Ricans (the diaspora), although born and/or raised in the United States, despise assimilation and colonial rule, are proud of their Puerto Rican culture and identity, continue to refer to themselves as only Puerto Ricans, and are generally supportive of sovereignty for Puerto Rico, their *nation*. Yes, many first, second, and third generation Puerto Ricans born and raised in the United States continue to regard themselves as *Puerto Ricans* and call Puerto Rico their *nation*.

Immigration Policies: Regarding immigration to the United States, Puerto Ricans are U.S. citizens and therefore, cannot be deported. Even in a sovereign Puerto Rico, Puerto Ricans would have dual citizenship (American citizenship and Puerto Rican citizenship), and with a Treaty of Free Association, both peoples would be able to enjoy free transit to the other associated country.

Also, in a sovereign Puerto Rico, Puerto Ricans will have the option and freedom to renounce their U.S. citizenship if they so wanted. Just as all U.S. citizens who reside overseas, Puerto Ricans with U.S. citizenship would also be expected to pay IRS federal taxes.

Only those Puerto Ricans who renounce their U.S. citizenship would be exempt from paying U.S. federal taxes, although they would still, of course, have to pay Puerto Rican national taxes. As a sovereign country and different international jurisdiction, Puerto Rico would have its own immigration authorities that would work together with U.S. immigration authorities to stop any illegal immigration from Puerto Rico to the United States and vice versa.

Gun Control Policy: Regarding Gun Control and the Second Amendment, conservatives should support sovereignty for Puerto Rico in order to avoid pro-gun control Puerto Ricans impacting the agenda of many American gun rights advocates. Puerto Ricans, in my experience, are more supportive of background and psychological checks, stricter gun control laws, and the banning of military assault rifles for personal non-police or military use.

With sovereignty, Puerto Rico can finally establish the strict gun control laws and measures that Puerto Rico needs to clamp down on illegal weapons and the illegal arms trade in Puerto Rico. Puerto Ricans are more supportive of more strict gun control legislation, ranging from more background checks to Japanese-style mandatory checks, training, government approval, and limiting the number of firearms and munitions a citizen can legally own.

The entire notion that "*guns are my birthright as an American*" is considered foreign and dangerous to most Puerto Ricans. As conservatives, are these the pro-gun control voices you want deciding your gun control debate?

Healthcare Policy: Regarding healthcare, most Republicans and other conservatives are known as being against policies like Obamacare and other forms of so-called "socialized" medicine and support the privatization of healthcare. In Puerto Rico, most people would welcome a Canadian-style universal single-payer national healthcare system in Puerto Rico, particularly after the disastrous American-modeled private insurance healthcare system currently failing Puerto Ricans. As a sovereign country, Puerto Rico would be able to establish and promote its own universal healthcare system for Puerto Ricans without impacting the healthcare agendas and interests of Republicans and conservatives in the United States.

Fiscal & Monetary Policy: Regarding fiscal and monetary policy, a sovereign Puerto Rico would be able to establish and implement a process to restructure its financial system and properly work the myriad of issues regarding the unsustainable and unpayable colonial public debt, debt that the colonial government refuses to audit and which was incurred with Wall Street firms, corrupt bankers, and investor groups knowing full well that Puerto Rico had no source of repayment. As a colony, Puerto Rico is currently ruled by an unelected federal control board (the junta) that has gutted the Puerto Rican economy and put its future in peril.

A sovereign Puerto Rico would expel the corrupt unelected federal control board, audit the debt, arrest the corrupt bankers and other criminals that created such illegal debt, and begin the process of classifying such debt as "colonial odious debt", which under international law and American legal precedents, a sovereign Puerto Rico would *not* have to pay, thus being able to use its funds and economic resources to grow and strengthen its economy.

A sovereign Puerto Rico could finally not only establish a fiscally responsible government with short, medium, and long-range fiscal planning, but also generate more revenues through industrial development, tourism, foreign investments, education, and other national development policies and initiatives.

Economic Development Policy: Regarding economic prosperity and development, a sovereign Puerto Rico that has full control of its borders, trade, and economic variables would finally have the power to develop its own economy, create wealth, and increase exports to many international markets, particularly the United States. With a Treaty of Free Association, the United States and Puerto Rico could even establish their own free trade agreement that would promote trade in both economies.

As a colony or state, Puerto Rico would be dependent on federal funds and other federal transfers and under the nefarious and colonialist maritime Jones Act of 1920, which currently controls Puerto Rico's trade and shipping industry to the detriment of Puerto Rican consumers and the Puerto Rican economy.

As a sovereign country, Puerto Rico could finally have a strategic national economic development plan that would address all sectors of the economy, promote free trade, promote and advance entrepreneurship, foreign investment, tourism, blue economy initiatives, a shipping and maritime industry, food and energy self-sufficiency, and develop economic links with the stateside Puerto Rican diaspora, thus benefitting various state and regional economies and Puerto Rico.

Before the U.S. invasion and occupation of 1898, Puerto Rico was self-sufficient in food production and even exported products to Europe and American markets. Now, under the U.S. Flag and colonial rule, Puerto Rico can barely feed itself and is dependent on U.S. shipping companies.

This humiliating and unsustainable situation must end. The current statehooder economic plan positions Puerto Rico as a mere consumer, not a producer of goods and services, continually begging for more federal funds and at the mercy of federal laws that do not consider Puerto Rico's needs.

As conservatives, I believe you would prefer to work with entrepreneurs and investors from a sovereign Puerto Rico rather than corrupt statehooders and colonialists begging for more and more federal funds and subsidies that help keep Puerto Rico in colonial poverty.

Energy Policy: Regarding energy policy, a sovereign Puerto Rico would focus on building a new energy infrastructure that would rely upon various sources of renewable energy such as solar, wind, tidal, ethanol, biodiesel, and even geothermal.

A sovereign Puerto Rico would free itself from the "oil cartel" that currently controls Puerto Rico's energy policies and chart its own energy policy in tandem with regional and American partners, particularly American manufacturers of renewable energy equipment and infrastructures such as solar panels, solar arrays, wind turbines, and other equipment. Remember, the majority of Puerto Ricans desire a complete reform of the energy system, the adoption of renewable energy production, and are decidedly against any form of nuclear power, "clean coal" technologies, fracking, and oil drilling off Puerto Rico's coasts.

Border Policy: As an international maritime jurisdiction, Puerto Rico would establish its own border patrol and immigration agencies and formulate its own border policies. As a foreign jurisdiction, it would be more difficult for drugs and other contraband to enter the United States than if Puerto Rico were a domestic jurisdiction as a colony or a state.

Since Puerto Rico is really an archipelago of various islands, Puerto Rico would have a maritime and air border policy focused on the maritime ports of entry and the major airports. As a sovereign nation outside American jurisdiction, Puerto Rico would stop being a major narco trade and smuggling route into the United States market, thus decreasing substantially the number of illegal drugs that enter the United States.

The United States and a sovereign Puerto Rico could even establish a joint U.S.-Puerto Rico Maritime Border Task Force to coordinate drug interdiction efforts in Puerto Rico and the Caribbean region with federal agencies if needed. Although statehooders try to obtain more federal funds and political standing by selling the idea to American politicians that Puerto Rico is "America's Caribbean Border", it would be more cost-effective and politically expedient for the United States to support and assist a Puerto Rican maritime border patrol (as a partner nation) than to spend billions of dollars and federal resources (funds, agents, ships, vehicles, and planes) trying to patrol the Caribbean Sea from Washington, DC.

So even for the conservative military and law enforcement folks, Puerto Rican sovereignty is in their best political, economic, and security interests. Better to have a strong and security-oriented Puerto Rico as a major ally and strategic partner than a weak and dependent colonial Puerto Rico draining the U.S. Treasury as a major narco route into the United States.

Sovereignty would add another layer of security and border patrol jurisdiction between the U.S. and Puerto Rico regarding illegal entries of drugs. Conservatives, if you are serious about border security, you must support the transition to Puerto Rican sovereignty.

Affirmative Action Policy: Conservatives are known to reject all forms of affirmative action based on race, gender, or ethnicity in education and employment. With the annexation of Puerto Rico as a state, the United States would gain a new state where over 95% of the population, Puerto Ricans, would be considered "Hispanic" and thus minorities able to take advantage of federal and state affirmative action policies in Puerto Rico and throughout the United States.

This "State of Puerto Rico" would be a champion to protect and expand all affirmation action policies that would benefit Puerto Ricans, Hispanics, and all other minorities as classified by federal regulations. Even though Puerto Ricans would be the majority ethnic group in Puerto Rico, they would be classified as *minorities* by the federal government.

Unlike Hawai'i, where Americans and other foreign settlers moved in and made the Hawaiian people a 9% poor minority in their own country, Puerto Ricans will *not* allow their demographic decline and displacement by Americans in Puerto Rico and would respond with political and cultural resistance, as has happened in the past. Puerto Ricans are adamant that *Puerto Rico is for Puerto Ricans*, no more, no less. As beneficiaries of such affirmation action policies, Puerto Ricans would celebrate, not fear, the "cultural balkanization" feared by conservatives, particularly white Americans.

Like most Hispanics, Puerto Ricans want to celebrate and use their language and culture in public and benefit from every possible opportunity to advance professionally in society and business. Conservatives, if you do not want to speed up the "cultural balkanization" of the United States, you need to pressure your politicians and representatives in Congress to start the transition to Puerto Rican sovereignty now.

Birthright Citizenship: As mentioned before, Puerto Ricans are U.S. citizens (birthright citizens since 1917) and therefore cannot be deported. Even in a sovereign Puerto Rico, Puerto Ricans would have dual citizenship (American citizenship and Puerto Rican citizenship) and with a Treaty of Free Association, both peoples would be able to enjoy free transit to the other associated country.

During the negotiations in the transition to sovereignty, the United States may want those Puerto Ricans born after the proclamation of the Republic to not have automatic birthright U.S. citizenship. These individuals would only have Puerto Rican citizenship, yet these individuals can still obtain U.S. citizenship (via the Consular Report of Birth Abroad process) at some point since their parents would in theory still be U.S. citizens, and any child born to a U.S. citizen abroad is also considered a U.S. citizen. Dual citizenship seems to be what most Puerto Ricans will accept and be accustomed to over time.

Many Americans, particularly conservatives, may be troubled that all Puerto Ricans currently have U.S. citizenship and how this may play into the future, but let's remember: U.S. citizenship was unilaterally imposed by Congress on all Puerto Ricans in 1917, over the objections of Puerto Ricans and even Puerto Rico's House of Delegates at the time.

United Nations: As mentioned before, Puerto Ricans are generally supportive of the United Nations, its policies, and programs. Conservative foreign policy initiatives and goals involving foreign wars and occupations will not receive major support from Puerto Ricans, particularly a Puerto Rican democratic congressional delegation.

A sovereign Puerto Rico, as a U.N. member state, can be a partner of the United States in many policies and initiatives, but Puerto Ricans in Congress would severely limit and derail conservative foreign policy aspirations. With Puerto Rican sovereignty, the United States can have a partner in regional and global initiatives, but with statehood, the United States will have a *Boricua Trojan Horse* affecting U.S. foreign policy debates.

American Politics: For Republicans and other conservatives, the most important and primal reason to support Puerto Rico's transition to sovereignty regards the impact that annexation and statehood would have in Congress, the Republican Party, and the balance of power in the United States. As a state, Puerto Ricans are more likely to vote for Democratic, liberal, or independent candidates, not Republican or other conservatives.

In Puerto Rico, the Democratic Party is viewed as more accepting of minorities, Hispanics, and concerned about important socio-economic issues, while the Republican Party is viewed as a party of racists, white supremacists, rednecks, and uncultured people that hate Puerto Ricans. Although conservatives will disagree with this perception, this is how most Puerto Ricans (in Puerto Rico and the United States) view the Republican Party and other such conservative groups and organizations.

Most Puerto Ricans, particularly young people, would *never* vote Republican in any election. The very few Puerto Rican Republicans that do exist, such as the colonial Resident Commissioner Jennifer González and former colonial governor Luis Fortuño, are considered by most Puerto Ricans as sellouts, colonized individuals, not in touch with reality nor their culture, assimilationists, and opportunists who try to position themselves as the "token" Latinos or Latinas of the Republican Party. There are also a few conservative Democratic Puerto Ricans who fit this category and aim to be the "token" Latinos or Latinas of the Democratic Party, yet these token Latino politicians are not taken seriously in Puerto Rico.

As a state, Puerto Rico would have two senators and six or seven democratic representatives, more than many Republican-led states who would lose congressional representation and districts, particularly the large and least populated states of the Midwest (which so happen to be states where white Americans, conservatives and liberals, are the great majority of the population).

In essence, a majority Hispanic "State of Puerto Rico" would have a Boricua democratic congressional delegation larger than various "Red" states of the United States, thus having the power to dramatically impact the conservative agenda and advance such important Puerto Rican issues such as federal bilingual language recognition, a Spanish language state government and courts system, more federal funds for Puerto Rico and stateside Puerto Ricans, mandatory Puerto Rican culture and history courses and Spanish as a Second Language (SSL) classes for all non-Spanish-speaking American students in Puerto Rican schools, and more affirmative action protections for Puerto Ricans. In Puerto Rico, "We the People" really means *"We Puerto Ricans"*.

As a conservative, these are the principal reasons why Puerto Rico statehood, even with the support of dark money, corrupt politicians, and lobbyists, will and must never be supported by the American political establishment and the American people, particularly conservatives due to the various reasons I have laid out and explained in detail.

The United States does *not want* statehood for Puerto Rico, Puerto Ricans do *not want* statehood, and support for sovereignty has been *increasing* with every referendum. The United States needs to realize this and start decolonizing Puerto Rico and beginning the transition to sovereignty now.

My recommendation to all Americans, conservatives, and liberals:

Cut your losses and decolonize Puerto Rico *now* by beginning a transition to sovereignty. Contact your state and congressional legislators and let them know that you support Puerto Rico's transition to sovereignty and are expressly against statehood and the current corrupt colonial regime that humiliates and denigrates both the United States and Puerto Rico on the world stage.

Understand that the real benefits of Puerto Rican sovereignty (as detailed above) far outweigh the supposed benefits of statehood, particularly in regard to American political, economic, fiscal, foreign, and national unity interests.

Understand that there are many professional, capable, respected, responsible, and committed Puerto Rican stakeholders (intellectuals, academics, diplomats, security professionals, former federal officials) that can serve as interlocutors between the United States and Puerto Rico via a Joint U.S.-Puerto Rico Decolonization & Sovereignty Task Force or commission to start these negotiations today.

Understand that the Puerto Rican Summer Revolution's patriotic fervor and ousting of the corrupt pro-statehood governor on July 24th, 2019 began a peaceful national revolution and activated and inspired all sections of Puerto Rican civil society.

The massive ongoing civic rebellion and disobedience campaigns against the colonial statehooder government, the corrupt bankers and officials responsible for the colonial debt, the colonial lackeys, and the imposed unelected federal control junta is a sign that the time has finally come to decolonize Puerto Rico.

Continued colonial rule under the guise of "commonwealth" is now unsustainable. The statehood movement is *discredited,* and sovereignty, freedom, and democracy are Puerto Rico's only viable option.

Americans, please understand that it's time to let Puerto Rico go.

SECTION 6

Developing a PREXIT Strategy & Why National Sovereignty is the Only Viable Option for Puerto Rico

With the advent of the Puerto Rican Summer Revolution of 2019, Puerto Ricans are finally uniting and rising up via patriotic and creative protests and various ongoing civic disobedience campaigns against not just corrupt politicians, but against the corrupt pro-statehooder administration, the unelected federal control board (the junta), and U.S. colonial rule. Puerto Ricans have had enough of corrupt and undemocratic colonial governments and politicians and want a change *now*.

If we learned anything from the Puerto Rican Summer Revolution, it is that successful protests and non-violent civic campaigns are led, not by political party leaders, but by the people themselves who quit fear, realized their own power in numbers (*somos más y no temenos miedo*)[65], and then harnessed the raw power of their own collective indignation, anger, creativity, love, and coordinated rage against powerful corrupt officials, colonial rule, and those who sought to control and humiliate the Puerto Rican people.

To the detriment of the colonial government, Puerto Ricans have realized that *anger defeats fear and unleashes a civic power strong enough to bring down corrupt leaders and governments.* To harness the anger is to harness the power. No amount of beatings, tear gas, propaganda, and rubber bullets can stand up to nor stop that kind of beautiful and civic power, particularly when the future of the Puerto Rican Nation is at stake.

After centuries of despotic and corrupt colonial rule, we saw the benevolent lamb of Puerto Rico realize its own power and rise up as a giant flaming and raging *Pitirre* to oust not just its corrupt colonial governor and his statehooder lackeys in twelve days, but threaten the legitimacy and authority of the U.S. colonial regime itself on the world stage[66].

Photos by Edil Sepúlveda (Summer Revolution 2019, San Juan)

After being discredited on the world stage by international media, the statehooders tried to counterattack the Summer Revolution's massive protests with a "massive" protest of their own. On September 1, 2019, the statehooders, led by a small fringe group, called for a "massive" pro-statehood protest march through the streets of San Juan's financial district which ultimately drew only a few hundred diehard old statehooders carrying U.S. flags, a far cry from the massive Summer Revolution protests that drew over a million people carrying Puerto Rican flags in San Juan and thousands more throughout Puerto Rico and the diaspora.

For the statehooders, the massive protest marches of the Summer Revolution were a direct threat to the notion that Puerto Ricans are loyal to U.S. colonial rule…and they were right; it was a direct threat. While the statehooders tried to demonstrate a show of force, the rest of Puerto Rico and the world just laughed and ignored them. Without fear and violence, the statehooders are finding it very difficult to draw large crowds and supporters.

As a colony under U.S. rule, the buck ultimately stops with the United States regarding Puerto Rico's decolonization. Understanding this situation, Puerto Ricans and American officials need to develop and implement what I like to call a **PREXIT Strategy**, the actual plan that initiates the decolonization and transition process from a colonial territory to a sovereign Republic of Puerto Rico as an independent country or a country in sovereign free association with the United States.

As we have seen and noted, Puerto Rico needs to rapidly *exit* the American colonial basement, and PREXIT will achieve this. We cannot allow the horrors of colonialism change who we are as the Puerto Rican nation and thus embrace sovereignty and democracy as birthrights denied to us, but no more. We do not beg for freedom; we take it.

There is currently a bill in the U.S. House of Representatives, H.R. 900, that would authorize a referendum in Puerto Rico and would provide Puerto Ricans only with the sovereign political status options of **Independence** or **Free Association**, status options that are non-colonial and favorable to both American and Puerto Rican decolonization interests. Keep in mind that the current territorial Commonwealth is a colonial non-sovereign regime, and statehood is not in the interests of both the United States and Puerto Rico, as meticulously explained in this book.

Congressional ratification of H.R. 900 would be the most unequivocal sign and statement from the U.S. government that it was finally ready to start Puerto Rico's decolonization process and transition to sovereignty. Although they believe they can, Puerto Rican statehooders cannot *force* and unilaterally *impose* statehood on the United States. They fail to understand that the United States is a sovereign nation, and only the U.S. Congress, not its colonial subjects, can decide if it wants to annex Puerto Rico. Slaves cannot force their masters to adopt them into their family.

After 121 years of never bringing up the issue of statehood, we can most assuredly state that the United States does not wish nor approve of statehood for Puerto Rico. It never has and it never will. Americans are smarter than what the statehooders give them credit for.

With the advent of sovereignty, the diehard statehooders and colonial loyalists can always move to and reside in any one of the fifty states where they can finally be part of the American society, they so desperately want to be a part of. With the arrival of a sovereign Puerto Rico, many thousands of overjoyed stateside Puerto Ricans would return to Puerto Rico to support the establishment of the new democratic government, organize the pillars of the new Puerto Rican economy, and strengthen family, cultural, entrepreneurial, and economic links between Puerto Rico and the United States. I would be one of them.

With the political and economic collapse of the colonial commonwealth government and the death of the statehood movement due to decreasing public support, resurgent patriotic millennials leading the civic revolution, and various federal corruption investigations and arrests of many pro-statehood leaders and contractors, **sovereignty** is now Puerto Rico's only viable option to resolve the status issue and propel Puerto Rico forward into the global economy as a free, democratic, and sovereign nation.

PREXIT STRATEGIES:

Roadmaps and Proposals for Decolonization & Sovereignty

PREXIT Strategy #1: MAP's Decolonization Roadmap

A very viable *PREXIT Strategy* and roadmap regarding Puerto Rico's decolonization and transition to sovereignty has been proposed by the Puerto Rican Action Movement (*MAP-Movimiento Acción Puertorriqueña*), a non-partisan pro-sovereignty organization made up of respected and committed intellectuals, academics, diplomats, former federal officials, and other Puerto Ricans dedicated to decolonization.

MAP's **12-Point Roadmap to decolonization and sovereignty** is viable, has been researched, and is divided into the following succeeding steps:

1. The U.S. President, as the executive power of the United States, would order the U.S. Department of State to start the negotiations for the decolonization and sovereignty of Puerto Rico.

2. The U.S. Secretary of State would then order the Office of the Assistant Legal Advisor for Treaty Affairs to commence such negotiations with the Puerto Ricans. The U.S.

Senate's Committee on Foreign Affairs would be included in this process.

3. A delegation from Puerto Rico would be invited by the U.S. Secretary of State to join such negotiations. This delegation would serve as an interlocutor and would be made up of respected and committed intellectuals, academics, diplomats, constitutionalists, legislators, and other individuals, not colonial administration officials tied to the corrupt colonial parties. This delegation could use MAP's working document (*Puerto Rican Regeneration*), another working document (such as *Propuesta de Convergencia: El país que queremos*, by Diálogo Soberanista), or a combination of working documents as agreed upon by delegation members.

4. Negotiations between the U.S. Department of State and the Puerto Rican Decolonization Delegation regarding the future U.S.-Puerto Rico relationship would begin and could last anywhere from six months to one year. During these very important negotiations, issues such as citizenship, social security, and veterans' benefits, federal block grant assistance, maritime jurisdictions, security and defense, free transit, the establishment of U.S.-Puerto Rico diplomatic relations, among other issues would be worked out.

5. A treaty or compact agreement signed by both parties, the United States and Puerto Rico, will establish a new relationship between the United States and Puerto Rico based on the sovereignties of both nations.

6. The U.S. Senate then ratifies this agreement, which then turns this treaty or agreement into U.S. law.

7. The treaty or agreement is then ratified by the people of Puerto Rico via a referendum.

8. A special general election would be held to elect the members that will form the Constitutional Assembly, which would then draft Puerto Rico's new constitution. To elect the members of the Constitutional Assembly, electors would vote for individuals, not political parties. Those elected to form the Constitutional Assembly cannot occupy any electoral position at the time they are elected. The time to draft and negotiate a new constitution would take from six months to one year.

9. After the new Puerto Rican constitution is drafted, outlining civil rights and the administrative structures and powers of the government of the Republic of Puerto Rico, a special general election would take place to approve the new constitution of the Republic of Puerto Rico.

10. After the new constitution is democratically approved by the people of Puerto Rico, a date would be selected for the ceremony that would officially declare a sovereign Republic of Puerto Rico. At this ceremony, United States sovereignty and colonial rule over Puerto Rico would officially end, and Puerto Rico's sovereignty would be declared, established, and recognized by the United States. At this moment, the U.S.-Puerto Rico relationship would shift from being colonial to one where both sovereign countries would be allies and strategic partners. That will be a glorious day.

The President of the Constitutional Assembly would provisionally become the Interim-President of the Republic of Puerto Rico and would be excluded from running for the Constitutional Presidency during the first democratic elections under the new national constitution of Puerto Rico. At this point, the new Republic of Puerto Rico would be able to join the United Nations as a full voting member state and begin the process of establishing Puerto Rican diplomatic missions in the United States and around the world.

11. The Constitutional Assembly would become the provisional legislative body of the new Republic of Puerto Rico. The provisional government will have the objective of drafting and ratifying fundamental laws and organizing the first constitutional general elections. This provisional government should have a duration of no more than one calendar year.
12. The provisional government of the Republic of Puerto Rico would hold the first general election of the constitutional government of a sovereign and democratic Republic of Puerto Rico.

PREXIT Strategy #2: The Puerto Rican Constituent Assembly as a tool for Decolonization

After the Puerto Rican Summer Revolution of 2019, as stated before, Puerto Ricans are finally uniting and rising up via protests and ongoing civic disobedience campaigns against not just corrupt politicians, but against the corrupt pro-statehooder administration, the unelected federal control board (the junta), and U.S. colonial rule. Yet, if the U.S. government does nothing to start the decolonization process or drags its feet, what can Puerto Ricans do?

Taking a page from history, Puerto Ricans can do what American patriots did in the 1770s and establish a constituent assembly (*Asamblea Constituyente*) by the people where Puerto Ricans decide, by themselves, to unilaterally begin the process of decolonization. Other pro-sovereignty advocates support a Constitutional Assembly on Status (*Asamblea Constitucional de Estatus*) regarding decolonization. This constituent assembly can be established by the current colonial government or by the people of Puerto Rico, without government approval. If selected by Puerto Ricans, the Constituent Assembly would be a powerful tool for Decolonization.

Option A

With a colonial government led by the corrupt statehood party, a constituent assembly has virtually zero chance of being established. Sadly, the statehooders are intellectually, politically, and logistically incapable of organizing any sort of independent democratic entity to resolve Puerto Rico's status problem, especially not a Constituent Assembly.

If the colonial government, led by a coalition of pro-sovereignty groups and a pro-Free Association Partido Popular Democrático, did establish a constituent assembly, it would have to determine who would be its members and what powers it would have when negotiating the decolonization process with the United States.

A Partido Popular Democrático, still led by colonialist *autonomistas* committed to the colonial Commonwealth model would be discarded as a viable partner and considered, like the statehooders, irrelevant in the future Puerto Rico. Such a government-sanctioned and funded Constituent Assembly would then negotiate directly with the United States concerning what the U.S. government is willing to consider regarding the decolonization of Puerto Rico.

With the death and discreditation of statehood and the political and economic unsustainability of the colonial Commonwealth regime, this Constituent Assembly would then begin the negotiations and process to transition Puerto Rico into a sovereign nation. This, in my opinion, would be the best option, but we should always have a contingency plan.

Option B

In the absence of a constituent assembly established by the colonial Commonwealth government, the people of Puerto Rico *can* establish their own constituent assembly, a new civic political body that would be founded by the sovereign and democratic will of the Puerto Rican people, similar to the Continental Congress founded by American patriots.

The American patriots did *not* ask Great Britain for permission to establish the Continental Congress, the patriots just recognized their own sovereignty and did it. Puerto Ricans can do it too. With option B, Puerto Ricans would literally be implementing their own unilateral decolonization.

At some point during this process, the political and international crisis and optics this plan would create would pressure and force the United States to finally pay attention to and deal with Puerto Rico's demands for decolonization and sovereignty. After 121 years of American indifference and colonial rule, the time has come for Puerto Rico to stop asking for permission.

With the establishment of a peoples-led constituent assembly, an alternate political structure and institution would be formed in Puerto Rico that would challenge the authority and legitimacy of the colonial Commonwealth government. Although the colonial Commonwealth government would seek to delegitimize and stop the Puerto Rican Constituent Assembly from existing and exercising power and authority in Puerto Rico, probably using state violence, the Puerto Rican people have already shown the world that "People Power" (*poder del pueblo*) can overcome and defeat "colonial power" when the people are united and determined to end colonial rule and forge a better future for all Puerto Ricans.

The Puerto Rican Constituent Assembly would be made up of elected citizens and community leaders that would represent not only all of Puerto Rico's 78 municipalities, but also civil society, political, cultural, socio-economic, urban, rural, and educational sectors of the country. Special community-led and participatory democratic elections in various municipalities and communities would be held to elect those community leaders that would ultimately be accountable to their local communities.

All members elected to serve on the Puerto Rican Constituent Assembly would pledge allegiance to the Puerto Rican flag and take an oath to serve solely the Puerto Rican Nation.

Even today, after the Puerto Rican Summer Revolution, various Peoples' Assembles (*Asambleas del Pueblo*) are being convened throughout Puerto Rico and the diaspora by regular citizens to discuss such political and economic issues and attempt to forge unity and possible solutions to such problems. These *Asambleas del Pueblo* are showing people that they can take the initiative to assemble themselves in a democratic entity, without colonial government approval, to tackle such problems that the colonial government seems unable and unwilling to solve.

Once the members of the Constituent Assembly are elected by the people, various community, municipal, regional, and national level structures and committees would be organized in order to facilitate coordination, logistics, and communications between all members, supporters, and citizen leadership structures across Puerto Rico and the diaspora via social media and other alternative communications and organization networks.

If every one of Puerto Rico's 901 barrios had a representative, a committee, and the presence of the Puerto Rican Constituent Assembly, it would have more reach and coordination in Puerto Rico than the current colonial government.

How would such a Puerto Rican Constituent Assembly be funded? Surely, without funds from the United States or the colonial Commonwealth government, our efforts would fail, unless committed and resourceful Puerto Ricans came together to fund it themselves.

In order to avoid politicization, internal ego conflicts, and disunity, I would propose that known political party leaders not make up the leadership of the Constituent Assembly, yet they should be available as advisors. Leadership positions in all organizations, committees, and structures should only be available to respected and accountable community and recognized non-partisan national leaders, not old political caudillos and party hacks.

Once the Constituent Assembly is organized and in operation, a parallel provisional Puerto Rican government would be established with: an executive branch (*Consejo Nacional*) with various parallel institutions, a legislative branch (*Asamblea Nacional*), and a judicial branch comprised of a Peoples' Court (*Tribunal del Pueblo*) where corrupt and criminal officials that escaped justice would be tried by a peoples' jury until a proper justice and judicial system could be established.

The Constituent Assembly, with the support of Puerto Rican constitutionalists and community activists, would also begin the process of drafting a new national Puerto Rican constitution.

The main goals of the **Puerto Rican Constituent Assembly** would be:

- Decolonization and the establishment of a sovereign Puerto Rican nation-state.
- The drafting and adoption of a new national constitution designed by Puerto Ricans and for the Puerto Rican people.
- The establishment of a new system of government and administration based on republican, parliamentary, and democratic principles.
- The coordination of special elections, throughout Puerto Rico, to elect new legislators to Puerto Rico's new citizen legislature (National Assembly or Parliament).

- The launching of peaceful civic actions and civil resistance campaigns to end the colonial regime and pressure the United States to finally sit down at the negotiating table with the Puerto Rican Constituent Assembly in order to work out a proper timeline and transition process from colonial rule to sovereignty.

Governmental and Economic Proposals for a Sovereign and Democratic Puerto Rico

Despite the lack of vision and proposals for a future sovereign and democratic Puerto Rico from the two traditional colonialist political parties whose only idea of economic development involves begging Congress for federal funds and consolidating dependence on the United States, other more responsible, visionary, and pragmatic political and non-partisan civil society organizations have developed such national proposals.

Such proposals, such as the Puerto Rican Independence Party's platform on decolonization and national development, the National Hostosian Independence Movement's proposal *"Otro Puerto Rico es Possible"*, and the Sovereigntist Union Movement's platform and proposal *"Plan de Construcción Nacional"*, are required reading for those working these issues and have all contributed to the discussion regarding the administrative organization and policies of a sovereign and democratic Puerto Rico.

All these historic proposals have greatly influenced the most recent comprehensive proposals for a sovereign and democratic Puerto Rico, particularly the below detailed proposals of the Puerto Rican Action Movement and Diálogo Soberanista.

In this section, I will also detail and summarize another new and comprehensive proposal, *"El Plan Nacional Estratégico para un Puerto Rico Soberano"* (The National Strategic Plan for a Sovereign

Puerto Rico), that I developed after years of research and work on this issue.

The Puerto Rican Action Movement's Proposal for Puerto Rican Regeneration

The Puerto Rican Action Movement (*MAP-Movimiento Acción Puertorriqueña*), is a non-partisan pro-sovereignty organization and think tank made up of respected and committed intellectuals, academics, diplomats, and other Puerto Ricans dedicated to decolonization.

The MAP has elaborated and published a highly regarded proposal for a sovereign and democratic Puerto Rico titled "**Puerto Rican Regeneration**" (*Regeneración Puertorriqueña*).

This proposal details how a sovereign Puerto Rico would successfully tackle issues of decolonization, social justice, healthcare reform, education reform, the strengthening of the University of Puerto Rico, economic growth and development, electoral reform, legislative reform, judicial reform, international relations and diplomacy, public service reform, socio-economic reform, regionalization, environmental reform, cultural development, citizenship policy, immigration policy, maritime border policy, and security and defense reform and development, among other issues.

To review and consider the MAP's proposals, please access the following link: https://www.elmappr.com/la-regeneracion

Diálogo Soberanista's Proposal of Convergence

(*Propuesta de Convergencia: El país que queremos*)

Diálogo Soberanista is a non-partisan pro-sovereignty coalition made up of various pro-sovereignty and patriotic organizations and supporters throughout Puerto Rico. Similar to the MAP, Diálogo Soberanista is made up of respected and committed intellectuals, academics, lawyers, teachers, prominent activists, workers, entrepreneurs, and other Puerto Ricans dedicated to decolonization and Puerto Rican sovereignty.

Diálogo Soberanista's proposal, "*Propuesta de Convergencia: El país que queremos*", is excellent and very comprehensive regarding various aspects of a future sovereign and democratic Puerto Rico. Among other initiatives and policies, Diálogo Soberanista's wide-ranging proposals include:

- A proposal for a democratic, inclusive, and participatory government of Puerto Rico.
- A proposal for a Constituent Assembly.
- A proposal for a new Puerto Rican constitution.
- A proposal for a unicameral legislature.
- A proposal of an executive branch made up of a Presidency, ministries, and secretariats.
- A proposal for an independent judiciary.
- Various proposals regarding government transparency and responsibility.
- Various proposals regarding public agencies, the annual national budget, and public debt.
- Various proposals for proper and democratic electoral reform.
- A proposal regarding the territorial subdivision structures of municipalities and regions.

- A proposal and various ideas for a sustainable economic development plan.
- Various proposals regarding economic strategies to fully develop and advance the Puerto Rican economy and the creation of jobs across all sectors.
- Various proposals to develop and promote community self-sufficiency, cooperatives, businesses, and entrepreneurs in Puerto Rico.
- Various proposals for public service reform and socio-economic reform.
- Various proposals for agricultural and environmental reform.
- Various proposals regarding Puerto Rican cultural development.
- Various proposals regarding citizenship and immigration policy.
- Various proposals regarding veterans, public security, and defense reform.

El triunfo del pitirre: de dictadura colonial a soberanía democrática

(*Triumph of the Pitirre: From Colonial Dictatorship to Democratic Sovereignty*)

The upcoming book "*El triunfo del pitirre: de dictadura colonial a soberanía democrática*", by Javier A. Hernández, details a comprehensive national strategic plan for Puerto Rico in regards not only to decolonization, but involving various proposals for government structures and administration, democratization, revenue generation, economic growth and development, fiscal reforms, and diplomatic relations.

Along with presenting "*El Plan Nacional Estratégico para un Puerto Rico Soberano*", the book also strives to explain the Puerto Rico status problem through historical, political, economic, and personal lenses and attempts to answer the many questions and concerns Puerto Ricans and others have regarding sovereignty, colonial rule, the colonial mentality, the struggle against assimilation, political culture, the process of decolonization, and how Puerto Rico would use its sovereignty to become a successful and prosperous nation.

Among other initiatives and policies outlined and explained in the book, *El triunfo del pitirre* recommends various across-the-board and detailed proposals for a sovereign, democratic, stable, progressive, and economically prosperous Puerto Rico. *El triunfo del pitirre*, along with answering the most frequent questions and addressing the most important issues regarding a future sovereign Puerto Rico, lays out the plans and proposals that will allow readers to envision how stable, democratic, and prosperous Puerto Rico can become if it were a sovereign nation.

Below is a brief yet detailed summary of some of these comprehensive proposals, initiatives, and policies that *El triunfo del pitirre* addresses and clarifies for a sovereign, democratic, and better Puerto Rico:

1. Government Structures of the Republic

A proposal for a democratic, federalist, parliamentary, and participatory **government structures and institutions** for the Republic of Puerto Rico which take into account the finest models of democratic governance, public and fiscal administration, and best practices from various successful nations ranging from Singapore, Switzerland, South Korea, Taiwan, and Ireland to Israel, the Nordic countries, Costa Rica, Uruguay, Panamá, and the United States, among other countries.

2. A Viable National Reconstruction Plan

A proposal for a **National Reconstruction Plan**, based on the experiences and best practices of various nations, particularly post-WWII Germany, Japan, South Korea, and Singapore.

After WWII, these nations were decimated political and economic backwaters, yet today they are recognized as economic powerhouses. Decolonization and sovereignty would allow Puerto Rico to start over and implement a comprehensive National Reconstruction Plan that's focused solely on:

- infrastructure development,
- political internationalization,
- global trade and exports,
- security alliances,
- industry and economic development,
- education,
- multilingualism,
- workforce development,
- transportation,
- maritime development,
- and an effective and stable democratic and legal system.

Systems would have to be implemented to promote a strong, democratic, visionary, and responsible Puerto Rican leadership. Such a National Reconstruction Plan would assure the Puerto Rican people that the new Republic of Puerto Rico would become a successful country with a growing economy.

3. The Treaty of Free Association between Puerto Rico & the United States

A proposal for **U.S.-Puerto Rico relations** and policies under a *Treaty of Free Association* between two sovereign nations. Under this proposal, the Republic of Puerto Rico would be in "free association" with the United States as an important ally and strategic economic partner in Latin America and the Caribbean.

Even if Puerto Rico were to become an independent republic without free association, pro-independence organizations have stated that they would be committed to a *Treaty of Friendship and Cooperation* with the United States.

4. A New Puerto Rican National Constitution

A proposal for a **new Puerto Rican constitution** and other organic foundational laws regarding democracy, national government powers and authority, the parliamentary model of government, the powers and responsibilities of regional governments, human rights, and the political and civil rights of all Puerto Ricans.

This new Puerto Rican constitution would be the supreme law of the nation and be based on the popular sovereignty of the Puerto Rican people. A draft national constitution for Puerto Rico, redacted by me, is available for review at: www.PrexitBook.com.

5. The National Decolonization Plan

A comprehensive and multifaceted proposal regarding the **decolonization** process and policies aimed at strengthening Puerto

Rican national identity and ridding Puerto Rico of the symbols and humiliating legacies of colonial rule such as, but not limited to:

- the **officialization of Spanish** as the sole National Language of Puerto Rico, although I do propose and detail legislation for the officialization of important "*regional languages*" such as English, French, and other languages for use in bilingual government documents and signage, to advance mandatory foreign language education at all levels, to promote foreign business investments, and the development of a multilingual Puerto Rican workforce;

- the **officialization of national, regional, and municipal flags**, coat-of-arms, anthems, emblems, and other important symbols;

- the **purging and removal of statues** and street names of foreign presidents, colonizers, tyrants, white supremacist governors, murderers, and colonial lackeys and replaced with the names of Puerto Rican patriots, revolutionaries, abolitionists, indigenous Taino chieftains (caciques), cultural icons, and other heroes and heroines in Puerto Rican history;

- the "*puertoricanization*" of geographical and urban place names and signage. I would propose the removal of the colonialist-inspired *Paseo de los Presidentes* and replaced with the patriotic *Paseo de los Próceres y Patriotas Puertorriqueños*;

- the establishment of a **National Pantheon of the Republic** and various other monuments dedicated to Puerto Rican patriots and the long struggle against Spanish and U.S. colonial rule;

- the **official recognition of the modern Taino language** (*Tainonaíki*) and Taino indigenous organizations and institutions;

- more autonomy and funding for the **Institute of Puerto Rican Culture** and various other cultural agencies and organizations;
- the founding of a **National Museum of Puerto Rican History & Culture** (*Museo Nacional de Historia y Cultura Puertorriqueña*);
- and the establishment of a **patriotic and non-colonial curriculum** and educational system based on Puerto Rican values and international standards;
- the founding of a **National Museum of Indigenous Peoples of Borikén** (*Museo Nacional de Pueblos Indígenas de Borikén*);
- the establishment of a **Truth & Reconciliation Commission** (TRC) that would further investigate colonial crimes and human rights abuses during colonial rule, yet would also offer certain individuals the opportunity to apologize for any colonial crimes or treasonous activities they committed and seek reconciliation with their friends, family, and society.

  The TRC would also collect testimonies from perpetrators and victims, initiate a disappeared persons initiative, initiate a photographic and collective memory project, and focus on political assassinations, extrajudicial killings, tortures, disappearances, persecutions, use of police dossiers (*carpetas*), displacements, use of terrorist methods and tactics, and other human rights violations executed by the colonial government, right-wing paramilitary groups, foreign state agencies, foreign terrorist groups, and any national resistance organizations.
- the establishment of a new **National Coat-of-Arms** for the Republic of Puerto Rico. The current and historical Puerto Rico Coat-of-Arms would be maintained but used as the symbol and Coat-of-Arms of the San Juan National District.

I propose the following Coat-of-Arms for the Republic of Puerto Rico, designed by me in 2013, which incorporates many national symbols such as the Pitirre, flags of Puerto Rican history, the Taino Sun symbol (Yukiyú), the Taino language, and other important aspects and symbols. This proposal is currently used by many pro-sovereignty advocates.

For those that wish to download and use the image of the proposed National Coat-of-Arms for the Republic of Puerto Rico (public domain) for personal, political, or commercial purposes, please go to the following website:

http://www.EscudoPitirre.com

6. The Puerto Rican Parliament

A proposal for a **unicameral Puerto Rican Parliament** made up of three representational counsels where elected parliamentary delegates would represent the national districts, regional governments, and civil society, yet would vote on all legislation simultaneously. These councils within the unicameral Parliament would be the National Council, the Regional Council, and the Civil Society Council.

The Puerto Rican Parliamentary system that I propose would be based on proportional representation and allow electoral alliances and voting blocs between parties and civic organizations.

The Three Representational Councils of the Unicameral Puerto Rican Parliament

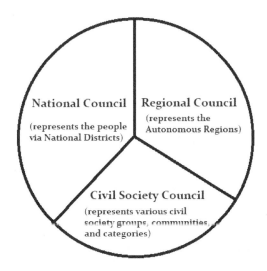

Puerto Rican regional governments would also utilize the parliamentary model of government. Other major reforms would be legislative term limits, run-off elections, citizen-legislators, the requirement of a majority, not plurality of the vote, and citizen initiatives and referendums, among others.

7. The Puerto Rican Presidential Council

A proposal for an executive branch made up of a multi-member **Presidential Council** or **Constitutional Presidency**, and various ministries and secretariats. Under the parliamentary system that I propose, the members of the Presidential Council would be elected members of parliament who would also be selected to head the executive ministries via a meritocratic selection process.

A Constitutional Presidency model would be made up of a ceremonial President as Head of State and a Prime Minister (the leader of the largest voting bloc and elected by the Parliament who would be the Head of Government) and various government ministers.

8. The Puerto Rican Judiciary System

A proposal for an **independent and non-partisan three-tiered judicial system**, the election of judges, and judicial term limits, among other issues of judicial reform. The highest court in Puerto Rico for civil, criminal, and constitutional matters would be the Supreme Court of the Republic. Other special tribunals would be established, as needed.

9. The Puerto Rico Postal Service

A proposal for the establishment of a **Puerto Rico Postal Service (PRPS)**, a national postal system for courier service, parcels and cargo, and the utilization of a new letter/number-based postal code system specific to an address' region, municipality, and local community.

The PRPS that I propose would be an independent government corporation in a public-private partnership or joint agreement with either the United States Postal Service or any one of the major international parcel delivery service companies such as FedEx, UPS, DHL, among others. The public-private partnership or joint agreement would involve the logistics and delivery of parcels and cargo outside of Puerto Rico.

With such an agreement, the PRPS, headquartered in San Juan, would focus on intra-archipelago courier and mail service within Puerto Rico, while the PRPS partner would be responsible for international postal, express, and shipping services. In time and with experience, the PRPS would establish its own Puerto Rican logistics and supply chain management company specializing in international courier, parcel, express, and sea and air mail in the Latin American and Caribbean region.

10. Government Transparency & Anti-Corruption Plan

Various proposals regarding **government transparency**, corruption, ethics, professional responsibility, and the establishment of a merit-based Civil Service and Diplomatic Service.

Regarding corruption, I propose and detail the enactment of various anti-corruption laws, the strengthening of an independent and non-partisan Office of Government Ethics, and the establishment of an independent and Singapore-modeled anti-corruption police that would only answer to the Presidential Council (or Constitutional Presidency) and have the power and authority to investigate any government agencies, transactions, government contractors, and public officials throughout the Puerto Rican government without fear of partisan and criminal influences.

11. Puerto Rico's Colonial Debt

Various proposals regarding public agencies, the annual national budget, and public debt. I propose that a sovereign Puerto Rico, using principles of international and United States law, declare all colonial debts of the previous Commonwealth regime as **"illegal and odious debt"** since *non-sovereign colonial regimes do not have the sovereign nor legal authority to take on debt in their own name.*

This very basic legal precedent and principle is lost upon and ignored by the federally imposed, unelected, corrupt, and conflict of interest-ridden Fiscal Control Board (la junta) that is hellbent on having Puerto Ricans pay for an illegal colonial debt. Puerto Rico would work with creditors and other banking institutions to resolve these important colonial debt issues.

12. Puerto Rico's Electoral System

Various proposals for proper democratic **electoral reform**, a new Electoral Code, and the establishment of an independent and non-partisan National Electoral Commission administered by actual electoral professionals.

13. Establishment of the Puerto Rican Scouts

A proposal to establish the **Puerto Rican Scouts** (*Scouts de Puerto Rico*) throughout Puerto Rico for male and female Boricua youth. These Puerto Rican Scout troops would learn skills and develop the scouting spirit and Puerto Rican pride, identity, and civics among Puerto Rican scouts and promote experiences and programs between other scout troops in order to develop solidarity, relationships, and lasting friendships.

The Puerto Rican Scouts would be part of the international scouting movement. With the Puerto Rican Scouts, male and female Puerto Rican youths interested in scouting would not have to join the foreign Boy Scouts and Girl Scouts of America in order to enjoy the scouting experience.

14. Decentralization of the National Government

A proposal to decentralize Puerto Rico's national government via "**administrative democratic decentralization**" by declaring San Juan as the *Administrative Capital* with all the executive ministries; Ponce as the *Legislative Capital* and seat of the Puerto Rican

Parliament; and Mayagüez as the *Judicial Capital* and seat of the Supreme Court of the Republic.

Each of these cities would be a "constitutional capital" of Puerto Rico. With this decentralization, all national power, politics, and economic resources are not centered in San Juan, thus involving other regions in the democratic administration of the national government and its economic development policies and programs.

15. The Establishment of Autonomous Regions

A proposal regarding the **regional territorial subdivision** of Puerto Rico into eight Autonomous Regions[67] (*Regiones Autónomas*) in Puerto Rico, one San Juan National District (*Distrito Nacional*), and an Autonomous Region for the diaspora, among other forms of territorial administration.

These proposed Autonomous Regions would have constitutionally delegated regional sovereignty, a regional government, a regional parliament, and be made up of various municipalities. In homage to our native Taino ancestors, I propose that the Autonomous Regions be named after the 15th century Taino regions (*yukayekes*) they would geographically cover and administer.

Two to four bordering municipalities would also constitute multi-jurisdictional Provincial Districts (*Provincias*) within each Autonomous Region, which would serve as electoral and judicial districts and function as inter-municipal councils and shared services commissions.

Like U.S. states and Spanish autonomous communities, the Autonomous Regions would have exclusive and shared authorities with Puerto Rico's federalist national government as outlined in the constitution.

These Autonomous Regions would be the following:

Map detailing the proposed Autonomous Regions, the San Juan National District, and the three constitutional capitals of the Republic of Puerto Rico. A larger map will be available in the Addendum and on www.PrexitBook.com.

Autonomous Region	Capital
Distrito Nacional de San Juan Bautista	San Juan
Región Autónoma de Aymánio-Mabó	Río Piedras
Región Autónoma de Majágua-Aramaná	Bayamón
Región Autónoma de Abacóa-Cibúco	Arecibo
Región Autónoma de Yagüécax-Aymáca	Mayagüez
Región Autónoma de Guaynía-Otoáo	Ponce
Región Autónoma de Jatiboníku-Guamaní	Aibonito
Región Autónoma del Turábo-Macáo	Caguas
Región Autónoma de Daguáo-Insulares	Río Grande
Región Autónoma de la Diáspora Puertorriqueña	New York & Orlando

16. The Autonomous Region of the Puerto Rican Diaspora

A proposal for the establishment of an **Autonomous Region of the Puerto Rican Diaspora** (PRD) with transnational political structures, community structures, cultural and educational institutions, budgets, resources, and voting districts so as to better integrate the vast overseas Puerto Rican communities, organizations, and businesses into the national political and economic framework of the new Puerto Rican government. The PRD's administrative capital will be New York City, NY, and its legislative capital will be Orlando, FL.

Although its affiliated Puerto Rican citizens[68] would reside overseas, particularly in the United States, the *Autonomous Region of the Puerto Rican Diaspora* would have elected parliamentary delegates serving in Puerto Rico's Parliament representing the over six million Puerto Ricans of New York, New Jersey, Connecticut, Massachusetts, Florida, Texas, Virginia, Hawai'i, and various other states.

Large and organized Puerto Rican communities in the Dominican Republic, the U.S. Virgin Islands, Canada, Spain, and other countries and territories would also be represented within the structures of the PRD.

The *Autonomous Region of the Puerto Rican Diaspora* would administer and be made up of the following institutions and entities:

- the **PRD Executive Council** (*Consejo Ejecutivo*) headquartered in New York City, NY. Although the PRD leadership will be elected by the vast diaspora electorate, all PRD departments and services will be staffed and administered by qualified Puerto Rican professionals hired by the PRD within the framework of the Puerto Rico Civil Service. New York City-based Executive Council regional government departments would include:

1. Administration
2. Revenue & Economic Development
3. Health & Social Services
4. Arts & Cultural Affairs
5. International Relations
6. Tourism
7. Education
8. Language Affairs
9. Communications
10. Security
11. Youth Affairs
12. Political Affairs
13. Workforce Development
14. Business Affairs
15. Historical Patrimony
16. Taino Affairs
17. Diaspora Affairs

- the **PRD Regional Parliament** (*Parlamento Regional*) headquartered in Orlando, FL will only convene once a quarter and on any additional special sessions;
- an executive government office in San Juan, PUR to represent PRD interests and initiatives in Puerto Rico;
- a parliamentary delegation office in Ponce, PUR to coordinate national legislative policies and represent diaspora interests;
- four diaspora regional government offices in New York, Philadelphia, Orlando, and Chicago to serve the large Puerto Rican communities of those regions;

- a network of PRD-affiliated Puerto Rican cultural centers in the top 25 communities in the United States with large Puerto Rican populations, along with centers in St. Croix and Hawai'i. These cultural centers would be staffed, have resource libraries, media/computer centers, performance areas, and classrooms;
- a network of Spanish-English Dual Language Puerto Rican K-12 charter schools (*Escuelas Hostosianas*) in Puerto Rican communities and administered by a Puerto Rican educational non-profit organization;
- a PRD-sponsored diaspora branch of the Puerto Rican Scouts (*Scouts de Puerto Rico*) throughout all the Puerto Rican diaspora communities for male and female Boricua youth. The various well-funded diaspora Puerto Rican Scout troops would learn skills and develop the scouting spirit and Puerto Rican pride, identity, and civics among Puerto Rican scouts and promote experiences and programs between diaspora scout troops and Puerto Rico-based scout troops in order to develop Puerto Rican solidarity, relationships, and lasting friendships;
- a PRD University Scholarship Fund;
- a PRD Business Directory (online and PDF);
- a PRD Government Procurement Registry, where both the PRD and Puerto Rican national governments would be able to contact, hire services, and establish G2B contracts with diaspora businesses, professionals, and service providers via transparent procurement platforms;
- a network of Puerto Rican import and export enterprises and platforms to facilitate trade and business between Puerto Rico and the various Puerto Rican diaspora communities;

- a *PRD Entrepreneurship Program* that would facilitate courses and seminars regarding the establishment of small businesses in the various Puerto Rican communities;
- a PRD Chamber of Commerce;
- a biweekly bilingual newsletter to all affiliated citizens, nationals, and supporters announcing events, policies, programs, news, and contacts;
- a network of **regional operational districts** that will organize and coordinate the political and administrative structures of the PRD. The seven regional districts of the PRD, which also function as regional electoral districts, will coordinate with all the state-level organizations (*state congresses / congresos estatales*)[69] within their jurisdiction. These state congresses would organize, coordinate, and be made up of all the various affiliated Puerto Rican political, community, educational, cultural, social, and business organizations within that state.
- a PRD flag and symbols;

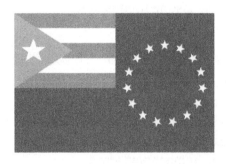

Flag of the Autonomous Region of the Puerto Rican Diaspora

Like the other regions of Puerto Rico, the Autonomous Region of the Puerto Rican Diaspora will have an official flag, emblem, buildings, and properties.

The Autonomous Region of the Puerto Rican Diaspora will adopt a bilingual Spanish-English language policy in its administration, services, and educational institutions.

Larger Puerto Rican communities would organize themselves as "*comunidades autónomas*"[70] and establish direct links with their state congress and their regional district. Regarding parliamentary representation at the PRD Regional Parliament, each state congress will elect one delegate; each regional district will elect two delegates, and each *comunidad autónoma* will elect one delegate. Regarding parliamentary representation at the Puerto Rico Parliament, each regional district will elect two delegates (for a total of fourteen diaspora delegates).

Any organized *comunidad autónoma* outside of the United States (such as the Puerto Rican community in the U.S. Virgin Islands and others) will elect one delegate to the PRD Regional Parliament. Puerto Rican political parties and voting blocs would also operate within the political structures of the PRD.

Regarding funding, the PRD would rely not just on funds from the Puerto Rican government, but its own internally-generated funds as well, such as special annual diaspora taxes that would be paid by affiliated Puerto Rican citizens and nationals in the United States and around the world.

The annual diaspora tax payment would go to a PRD General Fund and be used to pay for all the PRD's services and programs throughout all the regional districts. Such Puerto Rican diaspora economic development would also ripple and generate economic growth in the states as well, creating "buy-in" from state authorities.

With such funding, the PRD could establish its own **universal diaspora family health insurance plan** for Puerto Rican citizens and nationals (affiliated to Puerto Rico's universal healthcare system); develop a **PRD Business Development Fund** to support new

Boricua entrepreneurs; develop a **PRD Cultural Arts Development Fund** to support new Boricua artists, artisans, and cultural organizations; and establish its own **political action committee (PAC)** to promote Puerto Rico & Puerto Rican diaspora political and economic interests in the U.S. Congress and various state capitals.

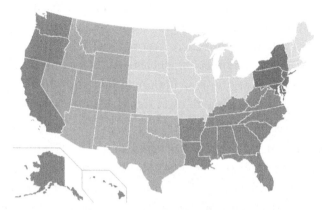

Districts of the Autonomous Region of the Puerto Rican Diaspora (PRD)

- Northeast District
- Mid-Atlantic District
- Southern District
- Midwest District
- Southwest District
- Mountain District
- Pacific District

Under this unique, inclusive, and progressive diaspora policy, Puerto Rico would be the first country in the world to not just extend voting rights and legislative representation to its overseas citizens, but also establish a non-territorial first-level regional administrative entity for its diaspora with full parliamentary representation on par with other Puerto Rican regional governments.

As a transnational and diasporic nation, Puerto Rico exists wherever Puerto Ricans are around the world. Every Puerto Rican, culturally and spiritually, embodies a piece of Puerto Rico. With such a diaspora policy and diaspora diplomacy initiatives, Puerto Rico's democracy and vibrant globalized economy would include, advance, and benefit *all* Puerto Ricans.

17. Law to Promote the Return of Puerto Ricans

A proposal for legislation (*Ley del Regreso Borincano*) that would promote the **return of professional stateside diaspora** Puerto Ricans to reside and work in Puerto Rico via limited subsidies and tax incentives and credits for any new businesses (particularly service and export-oriented) they establish in Puerto Rico. Such legislation would help reverse Puerto Rican demographic decline related to the political and economic failures of colonial rule.

Professional stateside Puerto Ricans would also benefit from this policy if they are certified to work as teachers, doctors, nurses, police/security, farmers, engineers, scientists, professors, and other very important professions needed in Puerto Rico.

18. Development Plan for Vieques, Culebra & Mona

A comprehensive proposal regarding the demarcation, economic development, and security of **Vieques, Culebra, Mona**, and various other Puerto Rican islands via the following policies:

- improving the **road, port, and sanitation infrastructures** in Isabel Segunda (Vieques), Esperanza (Vieques), and San Idelfonso (Culebra);
- the modernization and **expansion of the main ports** of Vieques and Culebra;
- the official recognition of **Puerto de la Libertad David Sanes Rodríguez**, on Vieques' northwest coast;

- the establishment of a community and municipal-owned **Vieques & Culebra Maritime Transport Cooperative** that would provide ferry and maritime transport services between Vieques, Culebra, Ceiba, and Fajardo;
- the establishment of a **Vieques & Culebra Community Development Fund**;
- the establishment of a **hospital and trauma center** in Vieques and Culebra;
- the establishment of various **conservation areas** such as Monte Pirata Natural Conservation Area, the Vieques Natural Conservation Area, the Bahia Ferro Natural Conservation Area, the Punta Este Conservation Zone, the Esperanza Nature Reserve, Monte David Nature Reserve, the Cacimar Nature Reserve, and the Culebra Natural Conservation Area;
- the establishment of the **Manatee Sanctuary Maritime Reserve** on the northwestern coast of Vieques;
- the establishment of various **Nature Restoration Zones** for highly contaminated areas resulting from U.S. Navy bombardments and environmental violations;
- the modernization and **expansion of the regional Vieques and Culebra airports**;
- the conversion of the derelict former U.S. Navy Camp Garcia facilities and airport area into the **Puerto Rico Spaceport** (*Puerto Espacial de Puerto Rico*), under the authority of the Office of Spaceport Administration;
- the establishment of the **University of Puerto Rico-Vieques campus**, a school of maritime sciences, and an oceanographic center;
- the establishment of a **Monument to the Vieques Struggle**;

- the establishment of the joint-municipal **Vieques & Culebra Electric Energy Cooperative (VCEEC)** that would administer the Vieques Solar Farm, Culebra Solar Farm, and the Vieques Wave Energy Park;
- the establishment of a **network of community gardens**, parks, and forests in Vieques and Culebra;
- the establishment of **hiking and biking trails** in Vieques and Culebra;
- the establishment of a **Vieques & Culebra Community Land Trust** that would oversee, preserve, and manage various municipal and community-owned residential, agricultural, and forest properties;
- the reorganization of the Caja de Muertos Natural Reserve into the **Abeyaney[71] Natural & Maritime Reserve**. Caja de Muertos would be officially renamed Abeyaney;
- the establishment and organization of the **Territory of Aymoná** (Territorio de Aymoná) made up of the islands on Mona, Monito, and Desecheo. The Territory of Aymoná[72] would be under the direct authority of the Republic of Puerto Rico and administered by the Aymoná Territorial Commission[73], based in Mayagüez and Puerto Stahl[74].

An appointed Administrator would be in charge of territorial administration, logistics, services, and community affairs. The Administrator would be appointed to a four-year term and would reside in Puerto Stahl with his/her family.

The two incorporated settlements on Mona would be **Puerto Stahl** (Playa Pájaros) and **Poblado Aymoná** (Playa Sardinera). The Territory of Aymoná would encompass the Mona & Monito Natural Reserve, the Desecheo Natural Reserve, the marine reserves around these islands, the Tourmaline Reef Marine Reserve, and the three Marine Protection Areas of Bajo de Sico, Tourmaline, and Abrir la Sierra.

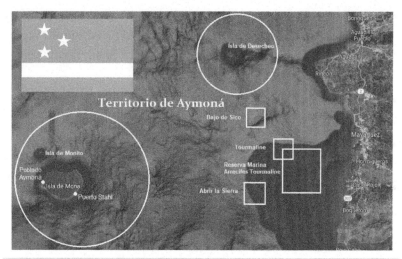

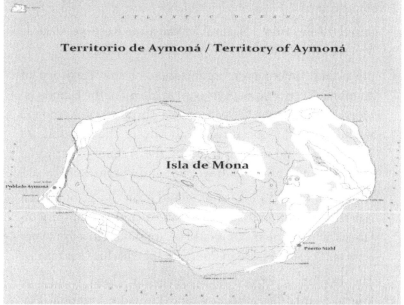

As the administrative center of the Territory of Aymoná, **Puerto Stahl**, on the eastern coast of Mona, would have a modern pier, residential quarters, administrative buildings, a town square, communications, a medical clinic, a mechanics station, a café and small grocery store, a renovated lighthouse, a weather station, off-grid water/energy generation facilities, a diversified agroecological farm and tropical fruit orchard, a Puerto Rico Maritime Security Service (MSS) security post, and an emergency rescue squad.

Poblado Aymoná, on the western coast of Mona, would house other residential quarters and scientific research facilities, a small pier for research vessels, a small airfield and helipad, off-grid water/energy generation facilities, a community center, a library, and an office center.

Staffed and managed by a small and dedicated cadre of government employees and contractors on renewable one-year tours, the Territory of Aymoná would host and support Puerto Rican and foreign scientists and researchers working on projects related to environmental sciences, conservation, botany, tropical zoology, oceanography, marine biology, and other life, botanical, and maritime sciences.

Along with providing security to the two settlements, the MSS security outpost in Puerto Stahl would provide security services and enforce maritime and fishery regulations in the waters of the Territory of Aymoná and the Mona Passage. A passenger ferry service between Mayagüez and Puerto Stahl would transport visitors and supplies 1-2 times a week.

19. Puerto Rico's Maritime Economic Development Plan

A proposal regarding the use, demarcation, economic development, and security of Puerto Rico's immense maritime **Exclusive Economic Zone (EEZ)**, various Fishery Protection Zones, Maritime Nature Reserves, Marine Reserves, Mangrove Conservation Areas, Critical Habitat Reserves, Coastal Nature Reserves, Coastal Erosion Protection Zones, Marine Sanctuaries, Whale Sanctuaries and Breeding Areas, Sea Turtle Nesting Zones, and Maritime Conservation Zones and areas to protect Puerto Rico's marine life, reefs, and maritime resources.

Currently, as a U.S. colony, Puerto Rico's EEZ is under the colonial, and economically stagnant dominion of the United States called the "U.S. Caribbean Region".

Under the jurisdiction of the Republic of Puerto Rico and a Puerto Rican leadership focused on real economic development, the EEZ would be generating billions of dollars for Puerto Rico's economy via various maritime "blue economy" initiatives.

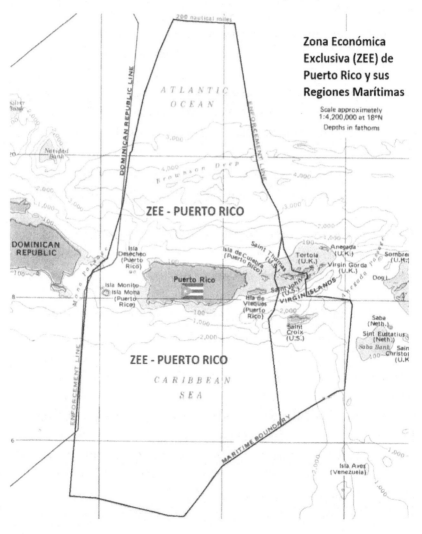

Under colonial rule, Puerto Ricans have been taught to view themselves as small and insignificant, a minority group of small people on a small island. To the joy of our colonial overloads, this perspective helps to consolidate and fortify their rule and the colonial mentality of Puerto Ricans since small people usually have small aspirations.

Puerto Ricans need to understand that Puerto Rico is actually bigger than they thought it was. We have to do away with the 100x35 mentality and begin to view and internalize the above map of Puerto Rico as one which encompasses both *insular* Puerto Rico and *maritime* Puerto Rico.

This map of Puerto Rico needs to be in every classroom so that young Puerto Ricans can see how large Puerto Rico actual is and can begin to break down the colonial mentality and internalized "smallness". The geographic area of insular Puerto Rico (including all of our smaller islands) is 9,104 km2 (3,515 sq mi). The area of maritime Puerto Rico occupies Puerto Rico's territorial sea, the maritime contiguous zone, and our huge Exclusive Economic Zone (EEZ), which encompasses 177,685 km2 (68,605 sq mi).

Combining these areas, one can see that Puerto Rico's total insular and maritime area encompasses **186,789 km2 (72,120 sq mi)**. Even beyond insular and maritime Puerto Rico, we Puerto Ricans also have the large, growing, and vibrant 5,588,664 strong Puerto Rican diaspora[75] or *"Overseas Puerto Rico"* established mainly in the United States. Most countries do not have such a large overseas diaspora community, particularly a patriotic diaspora community very strongly committed and involved in the affairs of the home country, which for us is Puerto Rico.

This total insular and maritime area 186,789 km2 of Puerto Rico is larger than the land areas of Singapore, Belgium, the Netherlands, the United Arab Emirates, Portugal, and England, among other countries. Within the areas of insular and maritime Puerto Rico, the government of the Republic of Puerto Rico would have sovereign control over resources and activities and could establish hundreds of economic development and energy generation projects that would also create thousands of professional jobs and generate large revenues for the government (some of which are discussed below).

Statehooders and colonialists will undoubtedly question and ridicule such aspirations and will continue to promote the retrograde idea that a small country, like Puerto Rico, cannot economically survive or progress in the world economy, yet all evidence points to the fact that many of today's richest and successful countries are in fact small countries.

Remember, most pro-statehood leaders are inept and small-minded, and people with small minds and no vision have small aspirations. While statehooders and colonialists aspire only to receive more federal funds and food stamps from the United States and American taxpayers, pro-sovereignty advocates aspire to make Puerto Rico into a prosperous and regional economic powerhouse.

We cannot allow the small-minded corrupt statehooders and colonialists to limit Puerto Rico's aspirations and economic potential. Of the top twenty richest and most successful countries in the world, twelve of them are actually small countries[76].

Singapore, which is roughly the size of the San Juan metropolitan area, is a very successful modern country and major economy of Southeast Asia

Comparison between Puerto Rico and the San Juan Metropolitan Area with Singapore

	Puerto Rico	Singapore
Area (km2)	9,104 km2	725.1 km2
GDP (2018)	$101.131 billion	$372.807 billion (2019)
GDP per capita	$31,603	$65,627
Population (2018)	3,195,153	5,638,700
Political Status	U.S. Colony (called Commonwealth)	Sovereign Republic

	San Juan Metropolitan Area	Singapore
Area (km2)	722.67 km2	725.1 km2

For this calculation, the San Juan Metropolitan Area is composed of the municipalities of San Juan, Bayamón, Guaynabo, Cataño, Carolina, Trujillo Alto, and Toa Baja.

Thus, one can see that Singapore, although having the same area (km2) as seven (7) Puerto Rican municipalities, is still able to establish itself not only as a stable, successful, and democratic country but as an economic power in Southeast Asia and on the world stage. Despite its small land area and greater population, Singapore has approximately 3.6 times the total GDP of Puerto Rico, and its GDP per capita is more than double the Puerto Rican GDP per capita.

According to the statehooders and the colonialists, the success of Singapore defies logic and is not supposed to happen because Singapore is small. Singapore used to be a poor mafia-controlled corrupt and colonial outpost (just like Puerto Rico), but with sovereignty, a strong visionary and patriotic leadership, a meritocratic civil service, and a viable and diversified economic development plan, Singapore became the great success it is today.

The *"we are too small to be free"* argument falls flat when presented with facts and reality. Statehooders and colonialists fail to realize that **Puerto Rico's greatness and potential is not measured in the size of its territory, but in the greatness, dignity, and power of the Puerto Rican nation. Puerto Rico's greatest asset is its people**.

In fact, in today's world, being a small insular nation like Puerto Rico at the crossroads of major international shipping lanes and at the center of four giant continental markets is an amazing asset and blessing that Puerto Ricans need to take advantage of, yet we can only do that with sovereignty.

With sovereignty, Puerto Rico could become the *"Singapore of the Atlantic"*, but under incompetent statehooder and colonialist administrations of the U.S. colonial regime, Puerto Rico has become a corrupt, colonial, and bankrupt embarrassment due to the utter failure of U.S. colonial policies and the massive corruption scandals and schemes of the local colonial lackeys, the very colonial lackeys that wave American flags with one hand, while stealing funds from Puerto Ricans with the other. Puerto Ricans, we need to end this pathetic colonial situation if we are to forge the country and economy that we deserve.

Regarding maritime economic development, I propose the development of sustainable ocean farming within Puerto Rico's EEZ and demonstrate how this would support national food sovereignty and exportation goals.

I detail how a network of various oceanic farms covering 10,000 maritime acres would generate 250,000 tons of kelp/seaweed (for energy and export) and 2.5 billion units of seafood (shrimps, shellfish, oysters) for Puerto Rico's national and export markets.

I also propose the following policies to ensure Puerto Rico's maritime environmental and economic development efforts:

- the establishment of a **Puerto Rico Fisheries & Aquaculture Administration** that would be responsible for private and commercial fishing regulations, fishing and aquaculture policy enforcement, state-owned oceanic farms, domestic fishing fleets and licensing, and the conservation and sustainable utilization of the fishery and marine resources of Puerto Rico's EEZ and territorial waters;

- the establishment of the **Puerto Rico Office of Maritime Transport Logistics**, associated with an Institute of Maritime Transport (IMT) where professional maritime transport technicians would earn specialized degrees and certifications in shipping, the maritime industry, maritime laws and protocols, and transport logistics, administration, and geography;

- the establishment of a state-owned international shipping corporation, **Navieras Trans Oceánicas de Puerto Rico (TransOcPR)**, that would become the principal cargo shipping company (among many others) exporting Puerto Rican goods to various foreign markets;

- with the **modernization and expansion of the ports of San Juan, Ponce, Mayagüez, and Ceiba,** Puerto Rico could become a major international transshipment hub in the Atlantic Ocean between Europe and the Panama Canal, particularly when two major international shipping lanes (the Mona Passage and the Anegada Passage) pass right through Puerto Rico's EEZ.

- the establishment of an **offshore transshipment hub** that would expand port capabilities and increase the amount of cargo tonnage Puerto Rico would redirect to their final destinations around the world;

- the establishment of the **Puerto Rico Maritime Security Service (MSS)** that would provide physical and transport security in Puerto Rico's EEZ to protect major international shipping lanes, fishing vessels, and provide search and rescue support;

- the establishment of various **Maritime Security Zones (MSZ)** on the borders of Puerto Rico's EEZ to support international drug interdiction and maritime security efforts;

- the establishment of a **Joint U.S.-PR Search and Rescue Region (SRR)** comprising the Puerto Rican EEZ and the U.S. Virgin Islands EEZ that would be supported by the MSS and the U.S. Coast Guard;

- the proper demarcation of **Puerto Rico's EEZ maritime boundaries** with the Dominican Republic, Venezuela, the U.S. Virgin Islands, and the British Virgin Islands via bilateral agreements and treaties;

- the proper oceanographic, geologic, and **topographic mapping** of Puerto Rico's EEZ and seafloor, particularly the Puerto Rico Trench, the Mona Canyon, the Mona Seamount, the Muertos Trough, the Virgin Islands Basin, and the vast Caribbean Basin regions;
- the establishment of **Special Protection Areas (SPA)** and **Maritime Research Areas (MRA)** within Puerto Rico's territorial waters and EEZ to protect marine wildlife communities and support maritime scientific research;
- seek to extend Puerto Rico's sovereign rights over natural resources of the seabed via U.N. recognition of an **Extended Continental Shelf** zone up to 350nm on the northern section of the EEZ;
- the establishment of various **new submarine energy cables** to support Puerto Rican energy exports to various energy markets;
- the demarcation of various **offshore leased oceanic blocks** for fishery, energy, and other commercial activities. Energy blocks would host offshore wind farms and energy platforms. Licensees would pay Puerto Rico billions of dollars to operate in these areas;
- the establishment of an **EEZ Joint Development Zone** between Puerto Rico and the Dominican Republic;
- the establishment of a **Pollution Prevention Zone (PPZ)** over international waters north of Puerto Rico. In the PPZ, Puerto Rico would have no sovereign rights over the water or seabed resources but would assert rights and responsibilities related to pollution, floating plastics, and ocean clean-up activities in the North Atlantic;
- the establishment of a **Caribbean Sea Conservation Area (CSCA)** between Puerto Rico and various other Caribbean nations and territories;

- regarding the Sargasso Sea, Puerto Rico would become a member of the **Sargasso Sea Commission (SSC)**, offer the SSC headquarters facilities in San Juan and an oceanic research station platform within Puerto Rico's EEZ, and together with Bermuda and the SSC, establish and oversee a Sargasso Sea Conservation Area (SSCA);
- along with the various planned Maritime Conservation Zones to protect current reefs and marine ecosystems, Puerto Rico would establish various **artificial reef projects** throughout Puerto Rico's territorial waters to create new marine ecosystems and increase diverse marine life in the Caribbean.
- the establishment of a **maritime alliance** between Puerto Rico and Panama via the founding of a joint state-owned maritime assets and services corporation, various joint maritime investments, and the formation of various joint shipping and maritime transport networks, ports, and transshipment hubs;
- the establishment of the **School of Maritime Transport Studies** (*Escuela de Estudios de Transportación Marítima*) at the University of Puerto Rico's Río Piedras campus.

20. Puerto Rico's Energy Independence & Development

A proposal to make Puerto Rico **energy independent** via the generation and utilization of diversified renewable power sources such as solar, wind, marine (tidal, wave, thermal exchange, and currents), geothermal, biodiesel, and ethanol (which would be produced in Puerto Rico through the industrial hemp and kelp marine farming industries).

For example, among many proposals, I detail how 60 100 MW onshore and offshore ocean thermal exchange conversion (OTEC) maritime energy plants would generate 6,000 MW of installed generation capacity, enough to replace all fossil fuel dependence and usher in Puerto Rico's energy independence, without even considering the MW contributions of other renewable energy sources such as a national and regional network of renewable energy (solar and wind) microgrids and various joint projects with major companies[77].

I also propose the following initiatives:

- the establishment of a **Puerto Rico National Energy Development Strategy**;
- the establishment of independent and regional and municipal government **renewable energy generation assets and networks** that would sell their energy to Puerto Rico under various power purchase agreements;
- the establishment of a state-owned energy company that would own and develop various Puerto Rico and international **energy generation, transmission, distribution, and investment assets**, energy equipment, and research projects;
- the establishment of a new and stronger **Puerto Rico Energy Commission** to regulate the energy sector and support the transformation towards modernization and renewable energy;
- a comprehensive **energy security initiative** that would protect electrical stations and plants from criminal and atmospheric events;
- a **subterranean transmission and distribution cable network** to reduce vulnerabilities from rains, storms, and hurricanes, particularly when one realizes that more than 90% of Puerto Rico's current transmission and distribution system is above ground and exposed to such threats that could lead to blackouts during emergencies[78];

- the **halting of irresponsible privatization** of the energy industry and establishing various community and cooperative energy agreements and networks to promote local ownership and development of local energy assets;
- the **institutional autonomy and depoliticization** of the Puerto Rican Energy Authority;
- national legislation by Puerto Rico to consolidate and support the transformation, modernization, diversification, and **sustainability of Puerto Rico's electrical grid**, distribution system, and overall energy sector;
- the establishment of a **Puerto Rican Marine Energy Center** tasked with researching and exploring marine energy technologies.

I also detail how Puerto Rico can develop a **tidal energy project** similar to Scotland's MeyGen Tidal Energy Project that will have an installed capacity of 398 MW by 2020[79]. Since Puerto Rico has various tidal zones throughout its national coastal territory, just 5 of such tidal energy projects would increase Puerto Rico's installed energy capacity by 1,990 MW.

Puerto Rico could also partner with Irish company Ocean Energy (OE) for the establishment of a network of various wave energy buoys[80] (with a potential energy output of 500 MW) within Puerto Rico's territorial waters and vast EEZ.

With 12 of these 500 MW OE buoys, Puerto Rico could generate 6,000 MW of installed generation capacity, enough to meet its electrical energy needs. With 24 of these 500 MW OE buoys, Puerto Rico could meet its energy needs and export another 6,000 MW of electrical energy to various Caribbean nations, South America, and even to the African energy market via undersea transmission cables to West Africa, particularly Senegal, Mauretania, and other countries[81]. Another potential market for surplus Puerto Rican energy could be Spain and the European Union, whose current cost of electricity is very expensive.

Regarding solar energy, I propose the **establishment of various small solar farms**, solar microgrids, regional solar parks, solar panels on all government buildings, solar tax credits, a state-owned solar energy corporation, solar power installation certification, progressive solar net metering policy, a solar energy research center, and 3 large solar energy farms with a capacity for 530 MW on 14 sq. km. each, generating a total capacity of 1,590 MW.

Regarding geothermal energy, I propose the establishment of the **Puerto Rico Geothermal Energy Complex (PRGEC)** that would be modeled on other successful geothermal projects, particularly from Indonesia, the Philippines, Iceland, Mexico, and the United States. The PRGEC that I detail would be similar to Mexico's Cerro Prieto Geothermal Power Station, which has an installed capacity of 720 MW. With three such geothermal projects, Puerto Rico would be able to generate 2,160 MW in additional energy capacity for the national grid, energy reserves, or export.

Regarding **ethanol production**, I detail how Puerto Rico could dedicate 10 million maritime acres (via undersea grid vertical columns) within its EEZ to produce sugar kelp and produce over 20 billion gallons of ethanol (which would generate annual revenues of $2.4 billion). Such ethanol could be converted into biodiesel for Puerto Rico's national transportation and fuel market or exported around the world to major continental markets such as North America and Europe. With such massive ethanol production via ocean farming in our EEZ, Puerto Rico would become the largest producer of ethanol in the world, surpassing both the United States and Brazil.

21. The Technological & Scientific Development Plan

Various comprehensive proposals regarding **technological and scientific development**, exploration, education, and innovation via the following policies and initiatives:

- the establishment of the **Puerto Rico Institutes of Science**;

- the establishment of the **Puerto Rico Scientific Innovation Fund** and the **Puerto Rico Advisory Council for Scientific Development**;
- the establishment of a **Scientist & Researcher Visa** in order to attract such important individuals from around the world to work and reside in Puerto Rico;
- the establishment of the **Puerto Rican Botanical Institute** and the National Botanical Gardens;
- the establishment of the **Puerto Rican Institute of Geology**, which would carry out a comprehensive and full-scale study of Puerto Rico's geologic profile and resources;
- the establishment of the **Puerto Rican Institute of Tropical Medicine**;
- the establishment of the **Office of Oceanographic & Atmospheric Affairs**;
- the establishment of the **Puerto Rico Scientific Development Fund**;
- the establishment of the **Scientist Protection Program**, where controversial and/or threatened scientists and researchers would be allowed into Puerto Rico, given new identities, and allowed to work on their leading-edge research and innovations in peace and security, particularly those involving renewable energies, among others;
- the establishment of the **Puerto Rico Office for Maritime Exploration**;
- the establishment of the **Office for Technological Innovations**;
- the establishment of the **Office of Agricultural Sciences**;
- the establishment of the **Office of Renewable Energy Innovations**;

- the establishment of the **Office of Intellectual Property Development**;
- the establishment of the **Office of Robotics & Drone Development**;
- the establishment of the **Office of Medical Development & Innovations**;
- the establishment of the **Puerto Rican Institute of Applied Linguistics**;
- the establishment of the **Office of Polar Affairs**, which would establish and operate the Puerto Rico Antarctic Base (jointly administered by the UPR and the Puerto Rican Antarctic Institute) that would support polar and climate-related scientific research and polar renewable energy initiatives, particularly wind energy platforms that would harness the immense energy of Antarctica's katabatic winds that can reach hurricane speeds of 300 km/h (190 mph) near coastal valleys.

  The Office of Polar Affairs would also establish and promote Puerto Rican shipping and trade networks and economic development projects in Greenland, Svalbard, and other Arctic regions;
- the establishment of the **Puerto Rico National Laboratories**;

22. The Aeronautical & Space Development Plan

Various comprehensive proposals regarding **aeronautical and space development**, exploration, education, and innovation via the following policies and initiatives:

- the establishment of the **Puerto Rican Institute of Astronomy**;
- the establishment of the **Puerto Rican Space Development Council**;

- the establishment of the **Arecibo Radio Telescope Authority** and research center;
- the establishment of a **School of Aeronautics & Space Sciences** (*Colegio de Aeronáutica y Ciencias Espaciales*) at the UPR-Mayagüez campus. This school would encompass the departments of Astronomy, Aerospace Engineering, Astrophysics, Astrobiology, Planetology, Physical Cosmology, Exogeology, Space Medicine, Orbital Mechanics, Space Industry & Resources, Space Technology, Astrorobotics, Space Transport Systems, and Space Logistics and Exploration;
- the establishment of the **Puerto Rico Aeronautics & Space Administration** (*Administración Aeronáutica y Espacial Puertorriqueña* - AAEP) as the independent government agency of the Republic of Puerto Rico responsible for the civilian space program, space exploration, spaceports, aeronautics, commercial space activities, and aerospace research and applications.

In the field of space research and administration, Puerto Rico's main assets are its highly skilled engineers and human capital, its infrastructure network, and its geographic location in the Caribbean.

AAEP's Office of Spaceport Administration would manage Puerto Rico's various onshore and offshore spaceports. The AAEP would be based at the Puerto Rico Space Center. The AAEP would aim to accomplish satellite launch capabilities from Puerto Rico spaceports;

- the **Puerto Rico Space Center Complex** (*Centro Espacial de Puerto Rico*), along with hosting the AAEP headquarters, would have a PRSC Visitors Complex, a Spacecraft Landing Facility, a Space Training Center, a Spacecraft Assembly Facility, a Space Technology Development Facility, an

Aeronautical & Space Exploration Museum, and the Caribbean Spaceport Complex with various launch pads and landing zones.

- the AAEP would be organized into directorates, offices, and research centers across Puerto Rico, employing thousands of professional Puerto Rican engineers, scientists, information technology specialists, and many other specialties;
- the AAEP would be led and staffed by Puerto Rican aerospace administrators, engineers, and scientists, many of whom have worked with and led various NASA projects;
- the ratification of a **bilateral agreement of cooperation**, collaboration, and mutual support between NASA and AAEP in regards to space development, research, training, mission and project support, and launch support, among others. In line with the treaty of free association between Puerto Rico and the United States, Puerto Rico would seek to become a strategic partner of the U.S. in regards to space development, research, and exploration goals;
- the establishment of an **International Space Command Center (ISCC)** where the AAEP, NASA, the European Space Agency, and other prominent national space agencies can come together to coordinate and work multinational space missions, launches, programs, and initiatives, such as the International Space Station (ISS) or future lunar orbital expeditions.

The ISCC, led by a multinational council made up of space agency representatives, would have facilities, an airfield, a port, and various spaceports to launch such multinational space missions. Puerto Rico would cede a small territory to the ISCC as an international entity.

- the AAEP will also establish several **state-owned space transportation companies**, partner with private space companies, and investment interests in various other spacecraft and equipment manufacturing and transportation companies.

The AAEP would establish bilateral agreements and joint ventures with various commercial space companies. The AAEP would also promote and support Puerto Rican aerospace companies in Puerto Rico and the diaspora, particularly in the aerospace-linked states of Florida and Texas.

The government of the Republic of Puerto Rico could even implement various special tax credits and fiscal benefits to commercial space companies that establish subsidiaries, branches, and projects in Puerto Rico.

23. Special Economic Zones & Industrial Development

A comprehensive proposal regarding the establishment of various **Special Economic Zones**, **Free Trade Ports**, and **Special Industrial Hubs** (bilateral and multilateral) to attract more foreign direct investment, generate employment, increase government tax revenues, and increase exportations from Puerto Rico's major urban trade and industrial centers.

I would propose a comprehensive investment incentive program for such SEZ and industrial hubs that would include some of the following incentives:

Incentives	Special Economic Zones (SEZ)
Corporate Income Tax	Exemption for the first five years. 50% income tax reduction in the next five-year period. At the 10-year mark, the company would receive a 6%-8% tax rate for 10 years.

Incentives	Special Economic Zones (SEZ)
Customs Duty	Exemptions on materials and equipment used during the construction period. Exemption on imported raw materials, machinery, equipment, and other specific goods for the first 5 years of commercial operation.
Land Lease	Investors can lease land for 50 years (30 years with two extensions of 10 years each).
Property Tax	Exemption for the first three years.
Tax Credits & Subsidies	Various tax credits and subsidies would be available depending on location, industry, business sector, and other factors.

This proposal also includes a detailed plan to position and ensure that Puerto Rico, via the development and expansion of the ports of San Juan, Ponce, Mayagüez, and Ceiba, becomes a major international maritime trading, export, and transshipment hub in the North Atlantic region between the major continental markets of North America, Latin America, Europe, and Africa.

24. The National Economic Development Plan

A proposal and various ideas for a sustainable long term and multi-sectorial **National Economic Development Plan** via *Operación El Nuevo Amanecer* (Operation New Dawn), based on *state capitalist* and *free market principles* and the five pillars of production, consumption, entrepreneurship, internationalization, and commerce, where Puerto Rico would not just establish and promote Puerto Rico-based businesses and industrial sectors, but would also generate billions of dollars in tax revenues for government administration, services, and the implementation of various bilateral and multilateral economic development projects.

A restructured, non-partisan, professional, multilingual, and autonomous Government Development Bank of Puerto Rico, among other agencies, will be essential in the implementation of these national and international economic development and foreign direct investment proposals and policies.

25. National Fiscal Policies & Economic Strategies

Various proposals regarding **fiscal policies** and **economic strategies** to fully develop and advance the Puerto Rican economy, increase Puerto Rico's Gross Domestic Product (GDP), and the creation of jobs across all sectors. Detailed proposals include tourism development, industrial development, infrastructure development (roads, metro rail in the San Juan metropolitan region, and a national highspeed rail system), government corporation development, municipal corporations, public-private partnership reform, taxation reform, and maritime "blue" economy initiatives and development.

Other initiatives could be the establishment of the agro-energy industry, vertical farming and urban agricultural development, a national shipping industry and maritime trade development, an agricultural revolution for our food sovereignty goals and consolidation of our coffee, cacao, medicinal cannabis, and industrial hemp industries, pharmaceuticals, technological innovation, and aerospace industries, among many other policies.

Puerto Rican economists, particularly those that support sovereignty, need to stop just analyzing Puerto Rico's limited colonial economy and also start creating economic proposals and policies that a sovereign and democratic Puerto Rico could actually implement to succeed.

This book aims at guiding these economists in the right direction. Many economists just focus on the minutia of the colonial economic debacle under U.S. rule without even considering or thinking outside the box regarding Puerto Rico's great potential as a regional economic powerhouse. Sadly, many of these economists, infected with the colonial mentality, do not have the mental aptitude nor vision to even begin this process; thus, it is the duty of those economists and researchers with actual vision to do this very important work.

In order to increase Puerto Rico's **Gross Domestic Product (GDP)**, I propose a balanced fiscal policy and progressive economic development policy that:

- increases government spending (to lower unemployment and encourage investments);
- increases national and regional tax revenues;
- increases revenues from government corporations and income (profits, interest, and dividends) from public-owned foreign assets;
- promotes and funds human capital development programs;
- promotes technological innovation initiatives, incentives, and imports;
- promotes the strengthening and expansion of Puerto Rican small businesses;
- establishes a Puerto Rican pharmaceutical industry centered on the production and exportation of generic pharmaceuticals and innovations;
- increases the labor force;
- promotes the establishment of research and development centers;

- promotes international trade via the establishment of Special Economic Zones, exportation platforms, free trade agreements, international corporations, maritime initiatives, and joint ventures;
- establishes a national recycling industry and other processing industries that would reduce waste and create revenues for Puerto Rican companies and local governments;
- expands and diversifies Puerto Rico's tourism industry;
- establishes the necessary renewable energy generation systems in order to export surplus electricity to other energy markets, particularly the Caribbean and Latin America;
- promotes national and retirement savings accounts;
- establishes a tax credit and incentive system to attract foreign investments;
- establishes an alternative national community currency – the *Puerto Rican Peso* (backed by U.S. dollar reserves and agricultural commodities and administered by a non-profit cooperative network)[82] to support, strengthen, and engage regional and local economies;
- promotes competitive interest rates to increase investments and consumption from businesses and consumers;
- promotes literacy and multilingualism; and improves the overall quality of education in Puerto Rico.

26. Puerto Rico's National Taxation System

A proposal to reform Puerto Rico's **taxation system** towards a progressive state capitalist model that would include, but not limited to:
- zero income taxes for the majority of Puerto Ricans (to facilitate savings and consumption),
- no retail sales and use (IVU) tax,

- low to modest corporate taxes for domestic Puerto Rican companies and joint ventures,
- fair corporate taxes for foreign corporations operating in Puerto Rico,
- corporate tax allowances and exemptions,
- a progressive and pro-business foreign corporate tax and tax credits system,
- low capital gains tax,
- excise taxes,
- national payroll taxes,
- low per capita taxes,
- national port tariffs,
- a progressive and innovative offshore financial center policy,
- various tax credits and incentives for individuals and corporations,
- a national dividend (*bono nacional*) for all Puerto Rican citizen taxpayers from any excess post-investment profits from government-owned national and international business and investment interests,
- tax incentives to encourage the use of credit unions and renewable energy,
- and the just taxation of large multinational retail corporations and conglomerates, among other initiatives.

For example, in 2018, these large multinational corporations made $44.5 billion in profits, yet only paid $1.7 million in corporate taxes - an unjust, ridiculous, and unsustainable 0.04% tax rate[83]. With a 10% corporate tax rate (low compared to various other international jurisdictions[84]) for such multinational firms, a sovereign Puerto Rico would have generated approximately $4.44 billion in corporate tax revenues (practically 48.8% of the $9 billion budget of the colonial Commonwealth).

If a sovereign Puerto Rico instituted a 17% corporate tax rate for such multinational firms, like Singapore (a very successful pro-business and state capitalist economy), Puerto Rico would have generated approximately **$7.5 billion in corporate tax revenues** (practically 83.3% of the $9 billion budget of the colonial Commonwealth).

If a 10% corporate tax rate were applied to U.S. corporations in Puerto Rico that repatriated $334 billion from 2008 to 2017[85], a sovereign Puerto Rico would have generated approximately $33.4 billion in corporate tax revenues in this nine-year period (averaging $3.7 billion/year). For certain multinational companies, particularly those established in Puerto Rico prior to sovereignty, the Puerto Rican national government could even negotiate special G2B agreements and fiscal arrangements that would benefit both partners. All this is possible with sovereignty. With statehood or the colonial Commonwealth, this is not possible.

The recent federal decree from Washington, DC opposing and striking down the **4% tax on foreign corporations** in Puerto Rico (which currently generates about 20% of the Commonwealth's revenues) is going to further destroy Puerto Rico's fragile colonial and dependent economy. The federal government is literally taking away 20% of Puerto Rico's revenues without even offering a replacement revenue source (since colonial Puerto Rico cannot create its own revenue sources like a sovereign country could).

These inept federal officials and American spokespersons who fancy themselves the supposed "paladins of financial responsibility" have the audacity to lecture Puerto Rico about fiscal solvency, especially when the U.S. national debt is in the trillions of dollars. They destroy, limit, and choke Puerto Rico's economy, then blame Puerto Ricans for the sad state of the Puerto Rican economy (Yes, the very Puerto Ricans who are powerless to develop the economy due to the very colonial rule imposed by Washington, DC).

With sovereignty, Puerto Rico would have the power to tax such foreign corporations and generate billions in revenues without having to ask the U.S. government permission nor acquiesce to such ridiculous colonial demands and policies. This decree can be said to be the final death blow of the United States towards Puerto Rico's colonial economy. This abusive federal treatment of the "colony" makes one wonder if there's any interest in maintaining any relationship at all.

What the U.S. colonial regime giveth, the U.S. colonial regime taketh, without even considering Puerto Rico's interests and needs. This colonial racket and economic circus have been going on since 1898 when the United States invaded and forcibly occupied Puerto Rico preaching "freedom" yet only handing out poverty and colonial humiliation day after day. Puerto Rico, if it's to survive and progress as a viable country, **needs sovereignty now**.

Reduced government revenues from personal income taxes would be offset and increased with various alternative government revenue streams such as corporate taxes, general tariffs and customs fees, tourism taxes, airport fees, visa fees, profits from industrial and agricultural government enterprises, license and permit fees, and entrance/exit fees, among other initiatives (revenue sources a colonial Puerto Rico cannot implement). Also, I propose that, unlike U.S. citizens, Puerto Rican citizens who reach a certain high personal income tax rate would only be taxed on Puerto Rico-based income, not global income.

As mentioned, I propose a progressive and innovative offshore financial center policy that would attract overseas businesses and financial resources to Puerto Rico (bringing in assets to flow and grow in the Puerto Rican economy). This offshore financial center policy would be imbodied by the establishment of the **Hato Rey Financial District (HRFD)**. The HRFD would occupy a section of the Hato Rey-Río Piedras area and would constitute its own autonomous fiscal and tax territory and offshore financial center outside of the Puerto Rican tax system.

The HRFD would be administered by a Multinational Governing Board, a Secretariat, and have its own Charter of Autonomy for internal self-governance. In essence, the HRFD would be an autonomous financial microstate or *"fiscal Vatican"* with its own "international status" and jurisdiction within the borders of Río Piedras in association with the Republic of Puerto Rico. The HRFD would attract assets, funds, and investments from corporations, insurance companies, investors, banks, and millionaires from all over the world, and of course, they would utilize the professional services of various specialized Puerto Rican business and financial support companies to help manage, secure, grow, and transfer such funds.

The HRFD Secretariat would be made up of professional Puerto Rican and foreign administrators, employees, and contractors in order to carry out the HRFD's governance functions of internal administration, human capital resources, security, logistics, procurement, energy, water/sanitation, information technology, communications, external relations, business and commerce, community affairs, institution-building, investments, translation & interpreter corps, and resource allocation, among others.

As an autonomous microstate recognized and associated with the Republic of Puerto Rico, the HRFD would have its own flag and official emblem. As it aims at becoming a premier global financial hub, the HRFD would have a multilingual language policy.

The HRFD and Puerto Rico would establish bilateral agreements and a shared services commission that would provide essential services to the HRFD. The HRFD would house banks, legal offices, corporate subsidiary offices, commodities brokers, currency exchange dealers, and investment firms with the aim of becoming a major international financial hub and business center.

The HRFD, as an international entity, will be able to engage in international relations and own properties, businesses, holding companies, hotels, banks, trusts, industrial development projects, digital realty, debt services, and other business and financial instruments.

Corporations and foreign citizens with accounts within the HRFD would benefit from: no capital gains tax, no sales tax, no gift tax, no profit tax, no inheritance tax, and no corporate tax. HRFD revenues would be obtained directly from annual license and service fees for offshore companies incorporated in the jurisdiction of the HRFD. Business service transactions would still be subject to limited business transaction fees. Companies incorporated in the HRFD as "International Business Corporations" (IBC), "Private Investment Corporations" (PIC), and "Global LLCs" (GLLC) would be exempt from certain fees.

The HRFD Global Stock Exchange (HRFDX) would also be established in the HRFD and would be affiliated with the Puerto Rico Stock Exchange (PRSX). The Republic of Puerto Rico would benefit greatly from the economic flow of business and commercial transactions between the HRFD and Puerto Rico. The HRFD would provide financial privacy and security to firms and individuals with accounts.

The HRFD would be located within the larger **Río Piedras Business District (RPBD)**, which would also house banks, businesses, legal offices, corporate offices, and investment firms, but within the Puerto Rican fiscal and tax system. The RPBD would be divided into corporate office zones, commercial zones, residential zones, parks and green zones, river and environmental zones, government zones, and historical zones.

The RPBD, as an independent government agency, would be administered by a joint committee made up of representatives from the Municipio Autónomo de Río Piedras, the Región Autónoma de Aymánio-Mabó, residential communities, business groups, local civil society groups, and one representative appointed by the national government. The HRFD and the RPBD would also establish service and resource sharing agreements related to energy, police, fire service, emergency management, and medical. Both the HRFD and the RPBD would have dedicated maritime port terminals in the Bay of San Juan and a joint airport terminal that would handle joint import-export and business interests.

27. The University & Educational Development Plan

Various proposals regarding **university educational development** via educational internationalization, strengthening the institutional autonomy and expansion of the University of Puerto Rico (UPR) System, establishing the UPR as a major academic and economic motor and hub throughout Puerto Rico, the establishment of specialized universities (medical sciences, technology, and agricultural), and the establishment of university consortiums and UPR-affiliated foreign and multilingual campuses in Puerto Rico.

Other initiatives are UPR campuses and research centers in Puerto Rican communities in the United States, the establishment of a network of UPR-affiliated cooperative enterprises, the establishment of various study abroad programs to attract diaspora Puerto Rican, Americans, and international students to pursue short and long-term university studies in Puerto Rico, among other initiatives.

Along with the UPR System, I also propose the establishment of industrial and agricultural vocational schools and institutes in all of Puerto Rico's regions via the establishment of a UPR-affiliated *Hostosian National University System* throughout Puerto Rico made up of smaller and more specialized technical schools and campuses.

28. The National Revenue Plan

A detailed and comprehensive proposal on how Puerto Rico, finally free of colonial rule and having full sovereign control of its economic variables of production, its borders, tourism and visa policy, trade and shipping policy, and establishing its own customs authority, would be able to **generate enough revenue** and wealth to not only fund most of the government's annual national budget and economic development initiatives, but also become independent of federal funds from the United States.

For example, among other revenue sources, I detail how a 10.5% General Tariff on all 2016 imports (which were $43.3 billion), could generate approximately $4.4 billion for Puerto Rico's Treasury.

Most importantly, I detail and explain how a sovereign Puerto Rico customs authority (*Aduanas de Puerto Rico*), by only instituting a 10.5% General Tariff, a 3.25% General Port Tariff, and various other revenues from visa and entry/exit fees, would generate annual revenues of **$7.6 billion** (which amounts to 84.4% of the current $9 billion budget of the colonial Commonwealth).

Also, that's approximately $2.8 billion more than what the U.S. federal government sends to Puerto Rico in "federal funds".

To the joy of Democrats and Republicans, the U.S. would then be free to use such federal assistance funds to support the economic development of poor urban and rural areas of the United States, not promote dependence in colonial territories.

Yes, with sovereignty, a robust Puerto Rican customs authority can potentially generate 84.4% of the government's operating budget, without even factoring in other national revenue sources. If Puerto Rico combines the $7.6 billion from tariff/fees revenue with the $7.5 billion from a 17% corporate tax on large multinational corporations, Puerto Rico would generate **$15.1 billion in national revenue**.

With sovereignty, comes the end of colonial dependency on federal funds and the potential of actual economic development and national wealth that Puerto Ricans deserve. As a colony or a state, this $15 billion revenue would not even be part of Puerto Rico's economy.

29. Community Self-Sufficiency & Development

Various proposals to develop and promote **community self-sufficiency**, local community barrio councils, community cooperatives, businesses, and entrepreneurs in Puerto Rico via training, courses, internships, small business micro-loans, and investment funding for start-up capital.

I propose the establishment of barrio councils (*Consejos Comunitarios de Barrio*) in all of Puerto Rico's 901 rural and urban barrios. These barrio councils would be the foundation of direct and participatory democracy and community governance, involving barrio residents in local decisions and projects related to community life and socioeconomic development.

30. Business & Economic Initiatives

I also propose various **business and economic initiatives** that would facilitate and support small businesses, support e-Business services, support e-Residency services, support the establishment of location independent businesses and families, support the diplomatic service industry, support the creation of Puerto Rican multi-industrial export-oriented conglomerates, and support the Puerto Rican business community overseas via Puerto Rican Overseas Chambers of Commerce and various Economic Development Offices attached to Puerto Rican diplomatic missions, among other initiatives.

31. National Public Service & Socio-economic Reforms

Various proposals for **public national service and socio-economic reform** via the establishment of a National Service Corps (NSC), various community land and housing trusts throughout the country, and the establishment a **National Social Insurance System** (NSIS) that would not only provide social security and pension benefits to all Puerto Rican citizens, but also pay for universal education, universal healthcare, maternity and paternity leave, and a special supplemental solidarity pension for the elderly.

I would also propose a national network of public Pre-K schools to replace the federally sponsored Head Start program. This National Social Insurance System would be administered by an independent government corporation and funded by national and payroll taxes.

The **National Service Corps** (NSC) system that I propose would be a compulsory public service for all male and female Puerto Rican citizen youths. Deferments, accommodations, and exemptions would be available on a case-by-case basis. The law would require all post-high school youth (or post-undergrad youth) to enroll in the NSC for a period of two years after choosing which service branch they want to join.

Managed by the National Service Administration, the NSC *"aims to form and develop young Puerto Rican citizens committed to their country, their family, and their community and with the necessary skills and knowledge to contribute to a better Puerto Rico and the world"*.

After six months at an NSC Academy (for orientation; basic training; various civic, academic, language, and technical courses; experiential trips and activities; and team service projects), young Puerto Rican citizens, as NSC cadets, would earn a monthly stipend and work experience at one of the NSC service branches via a two-year tour of national service:

NSC-Agricultural Service

NSC-Environmental Service

NSC-Police Service

NSC-Civil Defense Service

NSC-Community Service

NSC-National Defense Service

At the conclusion of their national service obligations, young Puerto Rican citizens would be part of the NSC-Reserve, earn valuable pre/post-university work experience, learn skills and civic-work responsibility, create lasting friendships and professional contacts, develop a sense of unity and solidarity with other youths, be eligible for special NSC study abroad scholarships, preferential selection if they want to develop a career at their service branch, and a special NSC tax credit, among other benefits.

32. The National Insurance Initiative

A proposal for Puerto Rico to establish its own government-affiliated **national insurance cooperative** that would make personal and business liability, agricultural, workers' liability, life insurance, auto insurance, and home insurance available and more affordable and accessible to Puerto Rican citizens.

33. Puerto Rican Healthcare Reform

Various proposals regarding **healthcare reform** that will improve and expand Puerto Rico's healthcare infrastructure, a universal single-payer healthcare system, expand medical tourism, the reconstruction of Puerto Rico's medical sector, and various initiatives to attract doctors, nurses, surgeons, specialists, and other medical professionals to Puerto Rico. Predatory and corrupt private health insurance companies would be expelled from Puerto Rico.

Legitimate private health insurance companies with good customer service records would be allowed to operate in Puerto Rico, but only as supplemental health insurance providers and as a regulated industry.

To reduce the power and influence of such private healthcare insurance companies in the supplemental healthcare insurance sector, I propose that the government establish its own *national healthcare insurance cooperative*. All Puerto Rican citizens, whether in Puerto Rico or overseas, would have access to Puerto Rico's universal single-payer healthcare system.

34. Puerto Rican Agricultural Development

Various proposals for **agricultural development**, approval of a comprehensive National Agricultural Plan, the establishment of a government agency to oversee acres of public lands that can be used for agricultural purposes, the establishment of public-private joint agricultural corporations and community agricultural cooperatives, agroecological incentives and policies, and environmental development and protection reforms. Agricultural development goals would be:

- Consolidating and strengthening the national agricultural market.
- Supporting small farmers and agricultural enterprises with subsidies and credits.
- Establishing a National Food Sovereignty Plan.
- Accessing agricultural export markets in North America, Latin America, and Europe.
- Establishing various agricultural development communities and zones throughout Puerto Rican municipalities and regions.
- Establishing various agricultural joint ventures and agricultural reserves.

For example, I propose and detail the establishment of a public-agricultural cacao joint venture with over 34,000 acres that would generate annual revenues over $585 million and an industrial hemp government agricultural corporation with over 158,000 acres (divided into 5,000 small farms of 31 acres each) that would generate huge annual revenues over **$2.5 billion**.

The Puerto Rican Independence Party has already developed a viable proposal where the government would allocate 800,000 acres of land for agricultural production initiatives and programs.

I also detail how Puerto Rico, with one government agricultural corporation or cooperative with 90,000 acres dedicated to industrial hemp (2,000 farms of 45 acres each), would generate annual revenues over **$1.44 billion**, which are more than enough funds to replace all federal assistance and food stamp funds sent by Congress every year.

Yes, with one 90,000-acre industrial hemp operation (for processing and exports), Puerto Rico would literally not need such federal funds since it would be able to generate enough profits and revenues to pay for such services and resources itself.

35. Protection of Puerto Rico's National Patrimony

Various proposals regarding the **protection of Puerto Rican patrimony**, historical sites, monuments, and the development of community education and cultural arts via the establishment of municipal and regional library systems, the development of Puerto Rico's General Archives (*Archivos Generales*), the development of a National Library (*Biblioteca Nacional*) and a national library system, a national museum network, and the protection of various indigenous and historically significant areas.

Under sovereignty, all federal parks and U.S. National Park Service assets and facilities, such as El Morro, San Cristobal, and El Yunque, would be transferred over to Puerto Rico for Puerto Ricans to manage, preserve, and develop.

36. Puerto Rican & United States Citizenships

Various proposals and policies regarding **Puerto Rican citizenship**, dual citizenship, Puerto Rican nationals, passports, and immigration and naturalization policy for those that wish to immigrate to Puerto Rico and acquire Puerto Rican citizenship.

Regarding the acquisition and maintenance of U.S. citizenship in a sovereign Puerto Rico[86], I present various proposals (based on

current U.S. policies) that may be considered in any sovereignty negotiations with the United States:
- All Puerto Ricans born in Puerto Rico would be considered automatic Puerto Rican citizens by the government of the new Republic of Puerto Rico. All Puerto Rican citizens would be entitled to the new Republic of Puerto Rico birth certificates, identity documents, and Puerto Rican passports and afforded the service and protections of Puerto Rican diplomatic missions around the world.
- All Puerto Ricans born in the diaspora that have at least one Puerto Rican parent or grandparent, would be considered Puerto Rican citizens by the government of the new Republic of Puerto Rico if they voluntarily apply for it and go through an expedited diaspora citizenship process. Diaspora Puerto Ricans born in the United States would also have the option of obtaining the status of Puerto Rican national[87], but not citizenship.
- The Republic of Puerto Rico would officially recognize the principle of dual and multiple citizenship as an important aspect of global mobility and internationalization. Along with U.S. citizenship, the Republic of Puerto Rico would recognize that many other Puerto Ricans also have Spanish and European Union citizenship, among others.
- The U.S. and Puerto Rico would establish a protocol within the Treaty of Free Association that would formalize, not just the free transit of U.S. and Puerto Rican citizens between both nations, but also a reciprocal consular support policy[88].
- The U.S. government would allow Puerto Ricans born prior to sovereignty to maintain their U.S. citizenship and expect them to pay federal taxes on their global income (expat taxes) and would be considered U.S. citizens residing

overseas. Puerto Rican U.S. citizens who refuse to pay federal taxes would be investigated and/or audited by the IRS office in Puerto Rico. Remember, it was the U.S. itself that imposed U.S. citizenship on all Puerto Ricans in 1917 without the consent of Puerto Rico.

- Just like U.S. citizens that reside in other countries, any U.S. citizen residing in Puerto Rico would be able to vote in federal U.S. elections via absentee voting *only* if they have residency in a state and/or via their parent's last state of residence address[89].

For example, if a U.S. citizen is eligible to vote in Florida or New Jersey, he/she can also vote absentee as a U.S. citizen residing overseas in Puerto Rico or France. Under current U.S. policy, a Puerto Rico-born U.S. citizen with no eligibility to vote in any state will encounter issues and problems when trying to vote in federal elections since voting is tied to the state of residency or last state of residency.

Such a Puerto Rico-born U.S. citizen can legally acquire the right to vote absentee by first establishing residency in any of the fifty states, then moving back to Puerto Rico where said individual will technically be considered an expat U.S. citizen residing overseas. As such, he/she will be able to take advantage of the Federal Voter Assistance Program (FVAP) and procure all the absentee voting forms necessary to vote in federal elections.

Such expat U.S. citizens would be able to vote for President and other federal and state representatives of the state where they reside. If this expat U.S. citizen in Puerto Rico also has Puerto Rican citizenship (as a dual citizen), he/she would also be able to participate in Puerto Rico elections if desired. This expat U.S. citizen would also be responsible for any federal and state income taxes[90].

- Puerto Ricans born after the declaration of sovereignty would only have Puerto Rican citizenship at birth, regardless of whether one or both parents are U.S. citizens. U.S. citizenship would only be acquired by Puerto Ricans born in Puerto Rico if their U.S. citizen parents go through the **consular report birth abroad process**. Regarding employment with the Puerto Rican government's Civil Service and Diplomatic Service, only Puerto Rican citizenship would be considered a requirement.

- Foreigners born in Puerto Rico after sovereignty is declared would only be Puerto Rican citizens at birth, not U.S. citizens.

- Such federal tax-paying Puerto Rican U.S. citizens who reside in Puerto Rico would be able to transfer their U.S. citizenship to their Puerto Rico born children by registering their birth at the U.S. Embassy in San Juan via a *Consular Report of Birth Abroad* (FS-240) form[91], just like any child born to a U.S. citizen overseas.

- Puerto Rican dual citizens (with both U.S. and Puerto Rican citizenship) would be responsible for paying both federal/state and Puerto Rican income and other taxes.

- Puerto Ricans would also have the option to renounce their U.S. citizenship at any time, thus becoming only Puerto Rican citizens. As Puerto Rican citizens, these individuals would only pay Puerto Rico taxes, not federal or state taxes, since a Puerto Rican citizen would no longer be a person taxable by the United States. Whether or not a Puerto Rican decides to maintain their U.S. citizenship or renounce it is, I believe, a personal decision with many family, personal, work, and professional considerations to take into account.

To **renounce their U.S. citizenship in a sovereign Republic of Puerto Rico**, Puerto Ricans would have to go through a simple 5-Step Renunciation Process[92]:

1. For a Puerto Rican to renounce his/her U.S. passport, he/she will need to already have a Puerto Rican passport, and he/she will be required to bring this with them to their renunciation appointment.

2. He/she would prepare the DS-4079 and other renunciation forms, which are all available online[93].

3. He/she would call and set up the Renunciation Appointment at the closest U.S. embassy or consulate. In Puerto Rico, it would be the U.S. Embassy in San Juan.

4. When he/she attends the Renunciation Appointment at the U.S. Embassy in San Juan, he/she will need to take both their U.S. and Puerto Rican passports, their birth certificate, and any other requested form. At the end of the Renunciation Appointment, he/she will be provided with a DS-4083 form called the Certificate of Loss of Nationality (CLN). The CLN will need to be approved by the U.S. State Department, and this can take several months. The CLN will be their evidence of the date he/she formally signed the renunciation form.

5. The final step in the renunciation process is filing their last U.S. tax return for the year they renounced. Once their CLN is approved by the U.S. State Department and he/she has filed their last U.S. tax return, he/she would finally only be a Puerto Rican citizen with a Puerto Rican passport and would never again have to file a U.S. tax return, pay federal and state income or payroll taxes, be subject to a military draft or Selective Service obligations, or vote in any federal and state elections.

37. Puerto Rican Veterans, Security & National Defense

Various proposals regarding **veterans, public security, and defense reform** which would include:

- a restructuring of the **Puerto Rico Police**,
- the establishment of a modern and well-funded **National Police Academy**,

- regional police forces,
- **emergency management** and services reform,
- the establishment of a **National Security Service** (for national felony and state offenses and liaisons with U.S. federal security agencies),
- a **Naval Defense Corps** and **Maritime Security Service** (to protect Puerto Rico's coasts, EEZ, and maritime interests),
- a professional **National Defense Forces** (to protect Puerto Rico's national sovereignty, territorial integrity, advance Puerto Rican interests, and support national and regional emergencies),
- bilateral U.S.-PR training facilities, among other security agencies and policies.

I would also propose the establishment of a **Puerto Rico Security Council**, made up of representatives of all the Puerto Rican security, military, emergency services, and intelligence units that would advise the Presidential Council on all security matters regarding Puerto Rico, the Caribbean, and its allies.

All these security and defense agencies would be under the authority of the Ministry of Justice, Security & National Defense. All colonial Puerto Rico National Guard assets, properties, and responsibilities, before being dissolved, will be transferred to the NDF.

The **Puerto Rico National Defense Forces (NDF,** *Fuerzas de Defensa Nacional Puertorriqueña*) that I propose would be a professional and dedicated military force made up of ground forces, air force, naval forces, and other specialized units. The issue of Puerto Rico establishing its own armed forces is very controversial, particularly among pro-sovereignty organizations and advocates.

Some pro-sovereignty advocates prefer that Puerto Rico establish its own armed forces, while other pro-sovereignty advocates support the demilitarization of Puerto Rico, meaning that Puerto

Rico would have no armed forces and in case of invasion or war, would have to rely on another country (or regional alliance) to come to our aid.

My personal opinion on this matter is that Puerto Rico *should* establish and maintain its own armed forces to defend Puerto Rico's sovereignty, territorial integrity, and national interests. If Puerto Rico were ever attacked and invaded, are we to depend on foreign countries to come rescue us when these same countries did nothing when Puerto Rico was occupied and administered by a colonial regime? No, of course not. No country will come to our aid.

Only Puerto Ricans care about Puerto Rico and Puerto Ricans should have the capabilities and resources to defend Puerto Rico and ensure our freedom, sovereignty, and democracy. Once free, we need to ensure that we never become a colony again of *any* country. Puerto Rico *needs* its own armed forces to protect Puerto Rico from foreign threats, terrorism, ensure our democratic system, and provide support and emergency response efforts on Puerto Rican territory.

Below is a preliminary proposed organizational structure for the NDF (the Puerto Rican Armed Forces), inspired by the organizational structures and models of small, yet robust military and security forces of countries like Israel, Singapore, Taiwan, and other nations:

- **NDF-National Militia**: land-based militia corps organized in regional commands, infantry corps, brigades, international peacekeeping forces, emergency management groups, and engineering corps. Diaspora Puerto Ricans will also be able to volunteer to serve in the NDF via the Diaspora Program.
- **NDF-Maritime Force**: sea-based Naval Defense Corps, Maritime Security Service, maritime medical groups, Maritime Operations Group, and maritime service battalions.

- **NDF-Aeronautics Force**: made up of the Puerto Rico Air Force, NDF Drone Brigade, NDF Helicopter Squadrons, and the Aeronautics Operations Group to defend Puerto Rico's air space and aerospace interests.
- **NDF-Gendarmerie**: border and port security force, protection of government and NDF facilities, and a division that handles internal affairs and NDF investigations.
- **NDF-Strategic Operations Corps**: an elite unit of Puerto Rican militia and special operations experts.
- **NDF-Foreign Brigade:** an auxiliary service branch primarily made up of volunteer foreigners (mainly Spanish-speaking Latin Americans, Hispanic-Americans, and Equatoguineans) who contract and enlist to serve in the NDF as professional militia for a period of six years to augment the National Militia in domestic and overseas missions.

  At the conclusion of their service with an honorable discharge, the foreigner with civil residency will be rewarded with Puerto Rican citizenship, the right to reside/work/vote in Puerto Rico with his/her family, and a service benefits package. Other qualified and talented foreigners would be considered as well.
- **NDF-Peacekeeping Brigade:** an auxiliary service branch of the National Militia made up of professional militia personnel trained to support UN Peacekeeping missions overseas.
- **NDF-Counterterrorism Group:** would plan and conduct all antiterrorist and counterterrorist operations, WMD operations, perform hostage rescues, special reconnaissance, and direct-action operations.
- **NDF-Expeditionary Force:** the only NDF unit authorized to operate in overseas military missions in defense of Puerto Rican sovereignty, territorial integrity, and Puerto Rican

national interests and in support of allied and United Nations forces to defend democracy, world peace, and security.

- **NDF-Joint Strategic Operations Command:** the NDF component command that plans and conducts joint special operation exercises and training, ensures communications compatibility across all joint forces, and oversees all special missions in Puerto Rico and overseas. The NDF-JSOC would have operational relationships with other Puerto Rico and foreign security forces and special units.
- **NDF Reserves:** a reserve division made up of NDF veterans and citizen volunteers.
- **NDF-General Staff:** the supreme administrative command of the NDF and composed of the following directorates:
  - **Operations Directorate:** responsible for operations planning and strategy, coordination with other security forces, drafting recommendations for the government, and NDF security issues.
  - **Planning Directorate:** responsible for military organization, infrastructure, and strategic and tactical planning.
  - **Intelligence Directorate:** an independent service responsible for military intelligence activities and threats to national security, led by the Defense Intelligence Unit.
  - **Personnel Directorate:** responsible for the coordination of all human resources, placements, employment issues, and NDF service conditions. The Education Corps is tasked with the academic and military education of militia soldiers and commanders and the development of national values and morale among the troops of the NDF via courses, cultural activities, and experiential learning trips.

- o **Information Technology Directorate:** responsible for NDF information and communications systems, cybersecurity threats, cyber defense projects, and encryption technologies.
- o **Technological & Logistics Directorate:** responsible for NDF logistics regarding administration, resources, medical/healthcare services and facilities, emergency resources and reserves, transport and shipping logistics, construction of facilities, physical security, and fuel and maintenance of NDF vehicles.
- o **Tribunals Directorate:** responsible for the NDF Military Tribunal and the lower military district courts.
- o **Academy & Training Directorate:** responsible for all NDF military training academies, officer schools, facilities, programs, and professional development centers, particularly the NDF Language Institute and the NDF Institute of Strategic Studies. The NDF's premier military training institute would be the Gen. Antonio Valero de Bernabé Military Academy.
- o **Security Industry Directorate:** responsible for the coordination of various Puerto Rican security and defense technology companies and various joint projects with foreign security companies. This directorate would be composed of a Puerto Rico Security & Defense Industry Council and Research & Development Units.

The Puerto Rico National Defense Force (NDF) would be led by a Secretary of Defense & National Security, a Joint Chief of Staff, and the Minister of Justice, Security & National Defense. Under the doctrine of "*Total Defense*", the NDF will only defend Puerto Rico's sovereignty and territorial integrity, support emergency situations, and participate in international peacekeeping missions.

If Puerto Rico's national security and existence is ever threatened by an external nation or entity, Puerto Rico may declare war if approved by the Puerto Rican Parliament. The NDF will be designed to be a major employer and integral economic motor of Puerto Rico, helping to stimulate the national economy and regional economies.

Organizationally, each Autonomous Region of the Republic would also constitute an NDF Regional Command with its own National Militia Infantry Brigade and Armored Brigade. A Maritime Regional Command, based in San Juan, would be established over the entirety of Puerto Rico's EEZ. As constitutional capitals and major urban areas, the cities of San Juan/Río Piedras, Ponce, and Mayagüez would also have their own dedicated Artillery Brigades, Engineering Corps, and Medical Corps.

The NDF should be a small, yet professional and properly trained military force that is centered on the quality of its soldiers, not their quantity. The NDF would be made up of professional career officers and soldiers, National Service NDF cadets, and various Foreign Brigade enlistees. The NDF would also be able to call upon the NDF Reserves and various other volunteer and security units. All Puerto Rican citizens should take courses and training regarding the strategies and tactics of civil resistance in case they are ever called upon to defend Puerto Rico or its democratic government.

I believe that the NDF should cooperate and take advantage of overseas training and security cooperation opportunities, yet I must be adamant that such training and cooperation cannot occur with organizations with a long and horrid human rights record, such as the infamous former School of the Americas, now called the Western Hemisphere Institute for Security Cooperation (WHINSEC), and others. The NDF, if it is to be a professional and credible organization, must not ever associate itself with organizations, training centers, and institutes known for promoting anti-democratic coups and human rights violations in foreign nations.

Regarding community-security engagement, Puerto Rico can establish *Citizen-Public Security Commissions* in all municipalities to encourage security and community collaboration, communication, and planning. Puerto Rico's National Defense Force can also help establish a *Caribbean Maritime Security Task Force* made up of various Puerto Rican maritime units, the U.S. Coast Guard, and maritime security units of allied nations in order to promote stability and regional security for the entire Caribbean basin.

Regarding Puerto Rican U.S. veterans, Puerto Rico would establish a **National Veterans Community Housing Trust** to eliminate homelessness among former U.S. military members by making them co-homeowners of actual residential units; legislate a special veterans tax credit; establish a **Puerto Rico-Veterans Affairs Commission (PRVAC)** where all issues regarding veterans services and benefits in Puerto Rico are discussed and managed; establish dedicated regional veterans hospitals and clinics; and establish the channels for any Puerto Rican U.S. veteran (from any military service branch) to be able to advise and provide professional counsel, based on their valuable experiences, regarding the establishment and structures of Puerto Rico's proposed National Defense Force.

I would also establish a **National Monument to Puerto Rican Veterans** that would honor *all* Puerto Rican veterans that served in the Spanish Imperial Forces, the U.S. Armed Forces, various Latin American armed forces, the Puerto Rican armed forces, and any other armed forces where Puerto Ricans served. Another initiative I would support would be to allow deported U.S. veterans from Latin American nations to seek asylum and immigrate to Puerto Rico.

39. Puerto Rico & Taino Community Relations

I propose that the government of the Republic of Puerto Rico finally **recognize the existence of indigenous Taino communities** in Puerto Rico; recognize the Taino language as the "indigenous language of Borikén"; integrate "Taino & Indigenous Studies" into the Puerto Rican national curriculum; establish and recognize indigenous sovereignty within the Constitution of Puerto Rico; and commit resources to the preservation, progress, support, and organization of indigenous administrations in recognized territories within Puerto Rico.

Puerto Rico would also establish and promote relations, projects, and initiatives between Puerto Rico's Taino communities and other indigenous Caribbean peoples such as the Garifuna, the Guajiro-Wayuu, Kalinago, and various other peoples.

Once established, these indigenous community administrations would have a constitutional relationship and formal association with the Republic of Puerto Rico.

40. The Establishment of a new National Calendar

With the advent of sovereignty and freedom, Puerto Rico will need a new *decolonized* **calendar of public holidays** that finally celebrates Puerto Rico, its people, and its history, not the history and important dates of the colonial regime. Since the establishment of the U.S. colonial regime in 1900, Puerto Ricans have been forced to celebrate and observe the foreign holidays of the United States, even when these do not coincide with nor reflect Puerto Rican history or values.

Particularly infuriating and awkward was having to observe and "celebrate" the 4th of July in Puerto Rico, a holiday meant to celebrate the independence and freedom of the United States, yet for decades, those that advocated Puerto Rican independence and freedom in Puerto Rico would be arrested and persecuted by this very colonial regime. For example, U.S. President's Day and Thanksgiving or *Zangüívin*, have no bearing on Puerto Rican history at all and would be replaced.

All holidays in Puerto Rico would be either public holidays (where most banks and government agencies are closed) or observed holidays (where government agencies are open). For a few observed holidays (*in italics*), I would support a partial closure where schools and select government agencies would operate until noon.

Below is a proposed national calendar of 15 public (in red bold) and 19 observed holidays and commemorations for the Republic of Puerto Rico that I believe most Puerto Ricans would be content with:

January 1st	New Year's Day	Año Nuevo
January 6th	Three Kings Day	Día de los Tres Reyes Magos
January 8th	Birthday of Eugenio María de Hostos	Conmemoración del Natalicio de Eugenio María de Hostos
January 24th	Birthday of Arturo Alfonso Schomburg & Day of Afro-Boricua Heritage	Conmemoración del Natalicio de Arturo Alfonso Schomburg y Día de la Herencia Afro-Boricua
February 14th	Valentine's Day	Día de San Valentín
February 17th	Birthdays of Blanca Canales & Julia de Burgos Remembrance of María de las Mercedes Barbudo	Conmemoración de los Natalicios de Blanca Canales y Julia de Burgos Recordación a María de las Mercedes Barbudo
March 21st	*Remembrance of the Ponce Massacre of 1937*	*Recordación de la Masacre de Ponce de 1937*

March 22ⁿᵈ	Emancipation Day	Día de la Abolición de la Esclavitud
March 24ᵗʰ	Commemoration of the Yauco Revolt of 1897	Conmemoración de la Intentona de Yauco de 1897
April 14ᵗʰ	*Birthday of Antonio Paoli & Day of Puerto Rican Music*	*Conmemoración del Natalicio de Antonio Paoli y Día de la Música Puertorriqueña*
April 15ᵗʰ	Birthday of José de Diego	Conmemoración del Natalicio de José de Diego
April 19ᵗʰ	Good Friday	Viernes Santo
April 21ˢᵗ	Easter Sunday	Domingo de la Resurrección
May 12ᵗʰ	Mother's Day	Día de las Madres
May 27ᵗʰ	Memorial & Veterans Day	Día de los Veteranos y la Recordación de los Muertos en Guerras
June 18ᵗʰ	Father's Day	Día de los Padres
July 15ᵗʰ	Birthday of Luis Muñoz Rivera	Conmemoración del Natalicio de Luis Muñoz Rivera
July 24ᵗʰ	*Birthday of Abelardo Díaz Alfaro & Day of Puerto Rican Literature*	*Conmemoración del Natalicio de Abelardo Díaz Alfaro y Día de la Literatura Puertorriqueña*
July 25ᵗʰ	Day of the Martyrs for Puerto Rican Freedom	Día los los Mártires por la Libertad de Puerto Rico

July 27th	Day of Marcos Xiorros & the Afro-Boricua Resistance	Día de Marcos Xiorro y la Resistencia Afro-Boricua
August 5th	Commemoration of the Battle of Arecibo of 1702	Conmemoración de la Batalla de Arecibo de 1702
September 2nd	Labor Day	Día de los Trabajadores
September 12th	*Birthday of Pedro Albizu Campos*	*Conmemoración del Natalicio de Pedro Albizu Campos*
September 14th	Birthday of Lola Rodríguez de Tió	Conmemoración del Natalicio de Lola Rodríguez de Tió
September 23rd	Commemoration of the Grito de Lares	Conmemoración del Grito de Lares
October 14th	Taino Heritage & Indigenous Peoples' Day	Día de la Herencia Taina y de los Pueblos Indígenas
October 24th	Remembrance of the Rio Piedras Massacre of 1935	Recordación de la Masacre de Río Piedras de 1935
October 28th	Birthday of Luisa Capetillo & Day of Women's Rights & Emancipation	Conmemoración del Natalicio de Luisa Capetillo y Día de los Derechos y la Emancipación de la Mujer
October 30th	Commemoration of the Grito de Jayuya & the Puerto Rican Revolution of 1950	Conmemoración del Grito de Jayuya y la Revolución Puertorriqueña del 1950
October 31st	Halloween	Día de Brujas

November 19th	Day of Puerto Rican Culture & National Identity	Día de la Puertorriqueñidad
November 25th	The International Day to End Violence Against Women	Día Internacional de la Eliminación de la Violencia contra las Mujeres
November 28th	Day of the Puerto Rican Family (fourth Thursday in November)	Día de la Familia Puertorriqueña
December 24th	Christmas Eve	Noche Buena
December 25th	Christmas Day	Navidad
December 31st	New Year's Eve	Fin de Año

Of course, the eventual date of Puerto Rico's Declaration of Sovereignty and the Founding of the third Republic of Puerto Rico would be an official national public holiday.

41. Puerto Rican Educational Reform

Various **educational reform** proposals, particularly the establishment of a national curriculum based on Puerto Rican values and the highest international standards, the transition from a test-based education model to a project-based education model, the modernization of public school buildings, special education reform, a mandatory financial literacy, economics, and entrepreneurial curriculum across various grade levels, a mandatory Puerto Rican civics, history and global studies curriculum across various grade levels, the recognition of homeschools and cooperative schools, the proper funding of all schools and teachers' salaries.

Puerto Rico would ensure the implementation of a **Multilingual Education Language Policy** that would promote language learning for all students and require that all students be fluent in Spanish (our national language) and proficient in two other foreign languages (English, French, Portuguese, German, Mandarin Chinese, Japanese, etc.) of their choosing in order to graduate high school.

This multilingual language policy, which I call the *Política Lingüística para un Puerto Rico Global*, would be inspired and pedagogically modeled after the European Union's multilingual education language policy. Such a multilingual Puerto Rican workforce will be an important pillar of Puerto Rico's world class human capital resources and its global commercial initiatives and projects.

42. Puerto Rican Diplomacy & Foreign Policy

Various proposals regarding **Puerto Rican foreign policy**, the establishment of the Ministry of Foreign Affairs and International Cooperation, the establishment and training of a professional and multilingual Diplomatic Service, the establishment of a Diplomatic Academy, the establishment of embassies and other diplomatic missions, and recommendations of other possible alliances, cooperation and trade agreements, reciprocal agreements, free transit and visa waiver agreements, international tax treaties, extradition agreements, regional arrest warrant treaties, international conventions, and memberships in regional and international organizations such as:

- the **United Nations (UN)** and **UNESCO**
- the **Caribbean Community (CARICOM)**
- the **Community of Latin American & Caribbean States (CELAC)**
- the **Association of Caribbean States (ACS)**
- the **Organization of Eastern Caribbean States**
- the **Organization of Ibero-American States**

Along with Puerto Rico's important strategic ally relationship with the United States via a Treaty of Free Association, I propose the establishment of a bilateral inter-governmental organization between Puerto Rico and Spain, a **Spanish-Puerto Rican Commonwealth** (*Mancomunidad Española-Puertorriqueña*) that would promote the economic, cultural, historical, educational, regional, and business interests of both nations.

With such a Spanish-Puerto Rican Commonwealth, Puerto Rico would provide Spain a gateway to U.S. and Latin American markets, while Spain would provide Puerto Rico a gateway to the markets of Spain and the European Union. Such a Spanish-Puerto Rican Commonwealth would be able to promote and facilitate the free transit of students, tourists, and businessmen and women between Puerto Rico and Spain.

A sovereign Puerto Rico would finally be able to assume leadership positions and responsibilities in regional Latin American and Caribbean political and economic organizations. Puerto Rico can also work to host various regional and international summits, conferences, and events, becoming a major political, diplomatic, and economic hub in the Caribbean region.

Another bilateral inter-governmental organization that I propose to be established is the **Antillean Confederation** (*Confederación Antillana*) between Puerto Rico and the Dominican Republic. Similar to the Spanish-Puerto Rican Commonwealth, the Antillean

Confederation would promote the economic, cultural, historical, educational, regional security, and business interests and initiatives of both Puerto Rico and the Dominican Republic.

The Antillean Confederation was first contemplated in the 1800s and supported by great historic statesmen and patriots such as Ramon E. Betances, José Martí, Eugenio M. De Hostos, Gregorio Luperón, and José De Diego and included Cuba, the Dominican Republic, and Puerto Rico.

The modern version that I propose would initially unite only Puerto Rico and the Dominican Republic, with the eventual incorporation of Cuba due to economic integration concerns. The Antillean Confederation would have observer status at the United Nations and develop strong political and economic relations with CARICOM and the CELAC.

I propose that the Secretariat of the Antillean Confederation be based in the city of Santo Domingo with other important institutions and agencies based in Havana and San Juan. Every year, the Antillean Confederation would hold a Regional Summit where various heads of government and select ministries would meet to discuss regional affairs.

Regarding membership in other regional organizations, I must caution a future Republic of Puerto Rico in regards to joining the **Organization of American States (OAS)**. As evidenced by its historical record and recent actions regarding the massive civic protests in Chile and Ecuador and the 2019 military coup d'état in Bolivia, the OAS is no longer a relevant nor trusted regional inter-governmental organization. Its support of right-wing dictatorships and military juntas throughout Latin America and its decades of silence in regards to Puerto Rico's decolonization and sovereignty totally discredits it from being an impartial broker and promoter of peace and security in the region.

How can anyone take the OAS seriously when they publicly state that "the social and political crisis in Bolivia is not a coup, but rather simply soldiers and police taking power by force.[94]" That's like saying that a slave is not actually a slave, but rather a human owned by another human that is forced to work for free, cannot leave the property without permission and does not have authority over his or her own body, yet utilizing the ridiculous logic of the OAS, that's not a slave.

The OAS states that it stands for democracy, yet it never mentioned nor acknowledged the crass lack of democracy in the U.S. colony of Puerto Rico right on its doorstep.

All the colonial persecutions – No OAS.
All the tortures of sovereignty supporters – No OAS.
All the killings of sovereignty supporters – No OAS.
The denial of self-determination – No OAS.
The denial of a decolonization process – No OAS.
The fact that Puerto Rico was invaded and is currently occupied by an OAS member state – No OAS.

If Cuba, Venezuela, or Bolivia had a colony in Latin America, do you think the OAS would stay silent? Of course not. In all of its existence, the OAS has never once held hearings nor passed a resolution regarding the U.S. colonial regime in Puerto Rico, the persecutions of independence advocates, the colonial tortures, the political prisoners, and lack of democracy in Puerto Rico. I understand one does not want to annoy and anger your largest donor.

Currently, the OAS budget is approximately $85 million, with the United States contributing about $50 million or 58.2% of the OAS budget. With so much United States influence over the OAS agenda and its policies, the OAS is considered by many in the region as an appendage of the U.S. Department of State. It seems that a country that donates $40million - $50 million to the OAS budget will never be scrutinized, even if it maintains colonies in Latin America.

Is the OAS agenda and institutions for sale? If Puerto Rico were to contribute $60 million to the OAS, would Puerto Rico then be able to control the OAS the agenda, actions, and policies of the OAS? As a sovereign nation in free association with the United States, Puerto Rico will not need OAS structures and institutions in communicating directly with the United States government.

Today, with the end of the Cold War, the OAS has tried to reshape its image and mission into one of democratization and election monitoring, although in my opinion, the Carter Center has a better track record of observing electoral processes than the entire OAS.

My recommendation for a future Republic of Puerto Rico in regards to joining the Organization of American States (OAS) is to either not join it or join, but only as a Permanent Observer, a position that could be easily staffed from the Embassy of Puerto Rico in Washington, DC. Anything of relevance that is discussed at the OAS is also discussed at the United Nations.

Another option could be to join the OAS, but with the express intent of reforming it into an actual impartial and democratic inter-governmental organization that is trusted and would actually promote democracy, transparency, cultural and language rights, rule of law initiatives, environmental protection, regional emergency preparedness initiatives, regional security, and economic development in the region.

To accomplish this, Puerto Rico and a few other Latin American nations could contribute 75%-80% of the OAS budget and advocate for the OAS to transfer its headquarters to a Latin American capital, maybe Mexico City, Panama, or even San Juan. If this reform is not possible, then the route of non-voting Permanent Observer should be selected.

Puerto Rico should focus its diplomatic efforts with the United Nations (UN), the Caribbean Community (CARICOM), and the Community of Latin American and Caribbean States (CELAC), among the other mentioned regional organizations. Within CARICOM and the CELAC, Puerto Rico has an opportunity to contribute greatly to such regional organizations, particularly in regards to economic development initiatives, democratization, trade policies, regional security, health policies, and environmental and cultural policies.

I recommend that Puerto Rico establish diplomatic relationships with all the countries and territories of the world, particularly in Latin America and the Caribbean, irrespective of whether the government is right-wing or left-wing in order for Puerto Rico to maintain its credibility and promote and establish commercial and economic development projects, companies, and multilateral economic initiatives.

If a specific government, either right-wing or left-wing, operates beyond what Puerto Ricans consider to be the norm of a proper democratic government or violations of human rights, Puerto Rico will have the ability to manage such diplomatic relationships and establish channels of communications, if needed.

Such international memberships and diplomatic relations would help advance Puerto Rican political and economic interests in Latin America, the Caribbean region, and around the world. To further such interests, I propose that Puerto Rico establish diplomatic missions in every Latin American and Caribbean nation and territory, in major world economic capitals and hubs (such as New York City, Brussels, and Tokyo), and promote shared and regional diplomatic missions with allies in other parts of the world, if possible.

Along with establishing **embassies** in large economic hubs and various countries, Puerto Rico should also establish **consulates** in other large cities; various **Economic Development & Cultural Affairs Offices**; **Tourism Offices** in Madrid, Paris, Berlin, Rome, Tokyo, Tel-Aviv, and the Nordic countries; and **Diplomatic Presence Posts (DPP)** in other cities and regions of the world.

Such DPPs would be under the authority of the nearest Puerto Rican diplomatic mission, staffed by one or two diplomatic service officers, and not be able to issue visas. Along with other diplomatic missions, such DPPs would help promote business contacts, inform Puerto Rico of political and economic opportunities, establish communications between Puerto Rico and local communities, and support trade and economic development projects with various other regions of Africa, Latin America, Eurasia, Oceania, and North America.

As stated before, Puerto Rico's diplomatic relations with the United States would be outlined and detailed in the Treaty of Free Association between the two nations. As allies and strategic partners, the United States would establish an embassy in San Juan, while Puerto Rico would establish an embassy in Washington, DC.

Outside of Latin America, Puerto Rico should also establish close relationships with Canada, Singapore, Japan, South Korea, the European Union, the African Union, and various other countries, territories, international organizations, and regional inter-governmental organizations in order to promote joint economic development initiatives, trade agreements, and other Puerto Rican interests.

Under the parliamentary federalist government that I propose for the Republic of Puerto Rico, the Autonomous Regional governments of Puerto Rico would also be able to establish their own para-diplomacy and international relations initiatives and projects in the areas of education, tourism, business, and economic development, with the final approval and support of Puerto Rico's Ministry of Foreign Affairs & International Cooperation.

CONCLUSION

The main goals of this book are for the reader to realize the colossal mistake it would be for the United States to annex Puerto Rico as a U.S. state and to consider and accept that sovereignty is the only viable option, not only to decolonize Puerto Rico, but to promote U.S. and Puerto Rican political and economic interests that would result from decolonization.

This book not only outlined and detailed various PREXIT strategies and sovereignty proposals, but also presented a vision and viable plans to forge and support Puerto Rico's path to sovereignty as a free, democratic, and economically prosperous Republic of Puerto Rico as an ally and strategic partner of the United States. As you must have seen, a world of economic opportunities awaits a sovereign Puerto Rico.

With sovereignty, Puerto Rico would finally have the power and authority to transition from a corrupt and bankrupt colonial territory ruled by foreign politicians and colonial lackeys to a democratic nation with a globalized economy ruled by Puerto Ricans that actually serves Puerto Ricans, Puerto Rican businesses, and Puerto Rican interests. With sovereignty, Puerto Rico would finally be free to forge its own destiny and become a force for freedom, democracy, and decolonization in the world.

Puerto Ricans need to believe in themselves and in their own strength and capacities as a people to build and create the country that we need not only to survive, but to progress through history.

Americans and Puerto Ricans need to contemplate and anticipate the negative political, economic, and cultural dire consequences of statehood, not just for Puerto Rico, but for the United States. Annexing Puerto Rico (an occupied Latin American and Caribbean nation) into the United States would be a colossal mistake that would forever negatively impact American politics, economics, and society.

The majority of Puerto Ricans would consider statehood the culmination of colonialism and would actively struggle and fight against it. Imposing statehood on Puerto Rico would be tantamount to imposing British rule on Ireland and French rule on Algeria. Statehood is bad for Puerto Rico and bad for the United States as well. It's just not a good idea for either party.

The recent major civic protests of the Puerto Rican Summer Revolution of 2019 led to the resignation of the corrupt pro-statehood governor and the subsequent political debacle of the corrupt pro-statehood colonial government. In both Puerto Rico and the United States, the statehood movement has been discredited, disgraced, and has utterly failed as a viable option for Puerto Rico.

Sadly, the U.S. government and its politicians currently lack the courage to confront the statehooders and tell them that statehood will never happen. Even when the statehooders try to manipulate and steal elections and plebiscites through voter fraud and fear campaigns, they still fail, and everyone knows it.

In Puerto Rico, statehood is a dying ideology and political platform pretty much supported only by the colonized and scared old guard, the lunatic fringe, convicts, deceased voters, corrupt politicians, colonial lackeys (*lacayos*), uneducated party loyalists (*batatas*), violent pro-colonial political thugs (*turbas*), business opportunists trying to score contracts with corrupt politicians, assimilationists who hate their own Puerto Rican culture, political opportunists looking for federal handouts and photo ops, and colonialist veterans who think they are still fighting the Cold War.

With nursing homes and geriatric care centers in Puerto Rico considered the last solid bastion of the diehard statehood movement, one can see why the statehood party dedicates resources and time in organizing this fearful, colonized, and non-mobile electorate. Using fear, jingles, threats, fallacies, and Cold War narratives, many elderly Puerto Ricans vote for the statehood party, even against their own interests as the statehood party takes aim at reducing pensions and degrading healthcare. Today, this is literally the largest "base" of the statehood party in Puerto Rico.

Americans and a growing number of Puerto Ricans, particularly the younger and professional generations, do not support statehood and are finally beginning to consider sovereignty as the best viable option for Puerto Rico and their families. No amount of statehooder and colonialist terror, fear, and ineptitude could have stopped the inevitable rise of sovereignty and patriotism among the Puerto Rican people in Puerto Rico and the diaspora.

Sovereignty will usher in the cultural, political, and economic rebirth of Puerto Rico, offering us the opportunity to forge and build the nation that we need, the nation that we deserve. Just as the Puerto Rican people united and rose up against the corruption and ineptitude of the statehooder colonial government, Puerto Ricans need sovereignty and freedom in order for us to finally have the tools to build the great country Puerto Rico was always meant to be. Colonialism will be our past, while freedom and democracy will be our future - a future where Puerto Rico rules itself in harmony with all the other nations of the world, without being ruled by any.

With sovereignty, Puerto Ricans would be able to aspire and work towards greatness, freedom, and the pursuit of happiness for all Puerto Ricans. Once sovereign and free, no country wishes to return to the humiliation of foreign colonial rule. Yes, we'll have problems like any country does, but they'll be *our* problems to deal with and find solutions for. Puerto Rican problems need Puerto

Rican solutions, and we can only accomplish that with the powers of sovereignty.

Remember, no Johnny Johnson from the United States really gives a damn about Puerto Rico as the past 121 years of colonial rule have demonstrated. Puerto Ricans, we need to look out for ourselves because no one else will do it for us. Lost at sea in the proverbial colonial storm, we must reach the safety and security of the port of sovereignty in order to save our families and our great Puerto Rican nation.

Throughout this book, I demonstrate how U.S. colonial rule in Puerto Rico has been a blatant political, economic, and cultural failure. Only sovereignty, freedom, and democracy can help Puerto Rico, to not only protect its national culture, identity, and Spanish language, but also support its economic development in the world economy. I believe, like many, that some form of Puerto Rican sovereignty is inevitable and needed to finally move Puerto Rico forward in the 21st century.

We cannot expect to progress in the world while still being in colonial chains that hold us back. The naysayers and those that profit from Puerto Rico's colonial servitude must be sidelined and ignored into their own irrelevancy.

Statehooders and colonialists have had their chance to lead Puerto Rico for decades, and they have all utterly failed, leading Puerto Rico into bankruptcy, poverty, and colonial humiliation. With the statehooders and colonialists, we've reached the bottom of the legendary colonial barrel, and now there's simply nowhere else to go but up and out of the colonial debacle that holds us down as a people and begin to reach for our own freedom and future.

Under the great and generous "tutelage" of U.S. colonial rule led by the fanatical loyalists of the statehood and commonwealth parties, Puerto Rico's poverty rate is estimated to be an astonishing and deplorable 52.3%[95]. Over a century of U.S. colonial rule and this is all they have accomplished.

As an ignored colonial scab of the world's largest economy, Puerto Rico is wasting away in squalor and unable to free and develop itself due to colonial rule. In the absence of ideas and a national vision, these retrograde and useless statehooder and colonialist politicians only promote fear, persecution, mediocrity, and the begging of federal funds as their only idea of economic policy.

This ridiculousness needs to end, and we can end it. It's time for them to move aside and let patriotic and truly committed Puerto Ricans with solutions to lead the country towards its freedom and economic prosperity. If the statehooders and colonialists dream of taking more and more federal funds and food stamps on the backs of Americans, let them do it in one of the fifty states.

Puerto Rico needs committed patriots, productive workers, and visionaries, not colonial leaches and lackeys.

When statehooders and colonialists attempt to sway you to support "statehood" or continued U.S. colonial rule and tutelage, please remember the following facts and events:

- the thousands of murdered and tortured Puerto Ricans who were victims of the policies and excesses of the U.S. colonial regime;
- the thousands of Puerto Ricans jailed over the decades for owning a Puerto Rican flag;
- the hundreds of forced female sterilizations to reduce the Puerto Rican population;
- the banning of our flag, our national anthem, and national symbols;
- the Río Piedras and Ponce massacres of 1935 and 1937;
- the attempts to destroy Puerto Rican culture via assimilation policies;

- the decades of inept and humiliating colonial rule by foreign American white supremacists who were appointed "governor";
- the use of El Morro and its sacred historical grounds as a military golfing and swimming pool area for American service members and their families;
- the radiation torture and burning of Dr. Pedro Albizu Campos by U.S. colonial authorities;
- the physical and psychological tortures inflicted on pro-independence supporters, particularly those being locked up in a small cell full of millions of bedbugs that would cover and overwhelm the human body and bite the victim until they mentally and physically gave up;
- the thousands of Puerto Ricans held in concentration camps during anti-colonial revolts;
- the father who was forced to eat his own murdered son by American soldiers at the "Academy of Truth" in 1950;
- the other tortures at the "Academy of Truth" particularly the electrocutions and being forced to scream "Long Live the United States" while being beaten by American soldiers;
- the deaths and damage caused by the violent pro-statehood *turba* mobs to terrorize Puerto Ricans;
- the bombing and burning of homes and businesses of pro-independence leaders and supporters;
- the criminalization of "independence" and the illegal police dossiers (*carpetas*) used to persecute and intimidate pro-independence supporters and their families;
- federal government programs, such as COINTELPRO, used to infiltrate and weaken pro-independence and pro-sovereignty organizations in Puerto Rico;

- the colonial police executions of pro-independence supporters and activists (such as the Cerro Maravilla assassinations);
- the hundreds of kidnapped and missing Puerto Ricans because they supported independence, democracy, and human rights;
- the destruction of our economy and democratic institutions;
- the abolition of our peso currency in order to plunge more Puerto Ricans into poverty;
- the attacks on our Spanish language and the imposition of the English language;
- the infection of hundreds of Puerto Ricans with diseases by U.S. doctors for medical experiments;
- the drafting of thousands of Puerto Ricans to fight in foreign wars as colonial troops;
- the Puerto Ricans who were murdered by Dr. Cornelius Rhoads via cancer injections;
- the imposition of the colonial mentality and a colonial educational system;
- the forced usage of expensive U.S. shipping companies via the Jones Act that takes $1.5 billion out of the Puerto Rican economy every year to subsidize American shipping companies;
- the decades of U.S. Navy abuse, violence, and environmental disasters in Vieques and Culebra; and many other atrocities.

After considering this brief list of atrocities committed against the Puerto Rican people by the U.S. colonial regime over the decades, **who in their right mind would support statehood or continued colonial Commonwealth**? I have seen and heard statehooders and colonialists from both colonial parties mock and joke about how pro-independence supporters are not in the majority, yet they never want anyone to bring up or mention the previous list of atrocities.

Please remember, the statehooders and colonialists have power and influence in local Puerto Rican politics, not because of their ideas or policies, but because they are merchants of fear, purveyors of ineptitude, and ultimately standing on top of a mountain of murdered Puerto Rican patriots and martyrs that suffered prison and tortures in trying to defend the Puerto Rican nation and Puerto Rico's right to sovereignty and independence.

All the blood, murder, and grief suffered by Puerto Ricans and the statehooders are only concerned with access to additional food stamps and other federal monies. If China had committed these acts against the United States, would you expect Americans to want annexation to China as fifty new Chinese overseas provinces, or would Americans struggle for their freedom? Yes, Americans would struggle for their freedom while Puerto Rican statehooders would welcome such Chinese rule, because, as we've seen in the past, these statehooders are loyal, not to the Puerto Rican nation, but only to whoever has power.

Statehooders and colonialists claim that Puerto Rico could not survive without federal funds, yet this book proves otherwise and outlines various revenue sources and policies that would generate billions of dollars and thousands of jobs in a sovereign Republic of Puerto Rico, thus totally destroying the colonial narrative that *"a poor Puerto Rico needs the United States to survive"*. This narrative is simply not true, and Puerto Ricans need to know and realize this.

While statehooders and colonialists are consumed by fear, mediocrity, and insignificance, patriotic pro-sovereignty Puerto Ricans are consumed by love of their country, fearlessness, patriotism, national self-awareness, and a determination to make Puerto

Rico a free, democratic, and great nation in the world for the benefit of all Puerto Ricans.

Despite the terrors, fears, murders, humiliations, and submission of colonial rule, Puerto Ricans will eventually come together and forge our own great Republic that will unite us with the world and build the maritime, industrial, and economic powerhouse we aspire to become. We can do this; we just have to believe we can and actually work to make it happen.

Puerto Ricans cannot hope to reform and resuscitate a failed, indifferent, decrepit, bloodstained, and despised colonial model that has never worked for Puerto Rico's interests, particularly with the same corrupt and inept colonialist leadership that brought so much shame, suffering, and disaster to Puerto Rico. As I mentioned before, freedom and democracy are always good, and it's about time Puerto Rico finally experienced and embraced them. With your support, you too, can help eradicate colonialism and help Puerto Rico forge its path to sovereignty and freedom. We must work to overturn the colonial order and finally embrace Puerto Rican national emancipation.

As readers, thank you for your time and understanding. There are literally millions of dollars being spent by the statehooders and colonialists so that you do not hear this message of Puerto Rican freedom and democracy.

As supporters of Puerto Rico, I thank you for your support and ask you to share this book and tell more people about the struggle for Puerto Rico's sovereignty.

AFTERWARD

An Exhortation to Liberate Puerto Rico from the Barbarians

This part of the book is an open letter to the Puerto Rican people and was inspired by the last chapter of Niccolo Machiavelli's *The Prince* titled "An Exhortation to Liberate Italy from the Barbarians". Similar to Machiavelli and other Italians of his time, we as Puerto Ricans today have to struggle against the same plague that infected his beloved Italy, the plague of *colonialism* and *foreign occupation*.

As Italy was occupied by the Spanish, the Swiss, the Germans, and others, the Italian people sought ways to resist such humiliation, yet they were divided by small fiefdoms, kingdoms, and princely states that were more concerned with power and riches than the survival of the Italian nation as a whole.

In modern Puerto Rico, we Puerto Ricans are divided by political parties, colonial politics, ruled by foreigners and their local colonial lackeys, and told to put up with such humiliation because we are supposedly an inferior and powerless people that need to be ruled by the supposedly superior Americans. Who are these foreign and local barbarians that rule us through fear, violence, and terror?

For me, all those who benefit from our colonial servitude are barbarians. All those who rejoice in our humiliation and colonial enslavement are barbarians. All those who administer and enrich themselves off the colonial regime are barbarians. All those who steal money, resources, and assets from Puerto Rico are barbarians. All those who deny us freedom and democracy so that we may live in the filth of colonialism and poverty are barbarians.

All those colonialist Puerto Ricans and traitors who deny, attack, and aim to destroy the Puerto Rican nation and our national identity are barbarians. All those corrupt politicians and officials that deny qualified young Puerto Ricans work opportunities, prompting many to leave Puerto Rico, are barbarians. Puerto Ricans, if we are to survive and live in freedom, we must expel these malicious colonial barbarians from our nation.

In this last chapter of *The Prince*, Machiavelli states that "*it was necessary that the people of Israel should be captive so as to make manifest the ability of Moses; that the Persians should be oppressed by the Medes so as to discover the greatness of the soul of Cyrus; and that the Athenians should be dispersed to illustrate the capabilities of Theseus*[96]."

In order to discover the greatness of the Puerto Rican nation, it was necessary for Puerto Rico to be reduced to such horrendous colonial rule as to manifest the genius of Betances and Ruíz Belvis; that such colonial isolation, indifference, and barbarism would lead to the greatness and courage of De Hostos and De Diego; and that such colonial repression, fear, depravity, and terror would illustrate and call forth the abilities, patriotism, leadership, and bravery of Albizu Campos, Lolita Lebrón, and Blanca Canales.

Today, Puerto Rican youth in Puerto Rico and the diaspora recite quotes from Albizu Campos, have Albizu Campos posters, listen to his speeches on YouTube, and even wear Albizu Campos T-shirts. While Muñoz Marín was the voice of colonial subservience, Albizu Campos was the voice of a nation and represented the aspirations of freedom, democracy, and national salvation. Albizu

Campos allowed us to see ourselves as great, strong, brave, and deserving of freedom. In the 1990s, as a teenage Puerto Rican in Teaneck, New Jersey, I was inspired by Albizu Campos and other patriots to become the best, educated, and cosmopolitan Puerto Rican that I can be and committed myself to help free my country from colonial rule. I have never seen any Puerto Rican youth wear a T-shirt showing pride in Muñoz Marín or Barceló *El Caballo*.

Muñoz Marín may have jailed, abused, and ridiculed Albizu Campos for years while he suffered unthinkable indignities and horrors in various colonial dungeons, but in the end, it is Albizu Campos who is remembered and celebrated by the Puerto Rican youth of the 21st century, not Muñoz Marín. Muñoz Marín may have enjoyed power, wines, women, drugs, and luxury in La Fortaleza, while Albizu Campos languished in filth, disease, radiation burns, abuse, and tortures in La Princesa Prison in Old San Juan, but it is Albizu Campos who will enjoy the immortality and honor of being the Father of the Modern Puerto Rican Nation.

Muñoz Marín and the colonial regime joyfully crushed him into the ground, not realizing that Albizu Campos was not just a man, but an idea, the idea of *freedom*, and ideas are bulletproof and indestructible. They succeeded in killing Albizu Campos, but today, the colonial Commonwealth that he denounced in the 1950s is in political and economic ruins; the Partido Popular Democrático that imprisoned him is collapsing under the weight of its own colonial inconsistencies and directionless leadership; the statehooders that hated him are discredited, morally bankrupt, and most of its leadership is in federal prison for corruption; yet the idea and aspiration of *freedom* is growing in Puerto Rico and the diaspora.

Some have never forgotten Albizu Campos, while some are rediscovering him now, reading his speeches and writings, and listening to his 1950s speeches on YouTube and podcasts that still resonate today regarding Puerto Rico's colonial dilemma. As foretold by Albizu Campos himself, such colonialist politicians and lackeys are to be forgotten in time and become mere footnotes in Puerto Rican history (*pépanos en la historia puertorriqueña*), nothing more. I look forward to the day I will fly to San Juan and arrive at the Dr. Pedro Albizu Campos International Airport.

Puerto Ricans, it's time for this colonial madness to end. We must be the ones that finally put an end to this humiliating immorality called colonialism, *the slavery among nations*, if we are to be a free nation with our own sovereign, democratic, and prosperous Republic. It will not be perfect, but it'll be ours. In all the countries of the world, we are *guests*, but in Puerto Rico, we are *home*.

When Puerto Ricans unite and realize that anger overcomes fear, we can become so powerful as to oust a corrupt governor from power and expel the powerful U.S. Navy from Vieques. When the Puerto Rican nation decides to stand up and *take* its freedom and destiny into its own hands, the colonialists and lackeys will have to kneel to the power of the Republic because they will have no other choice.

These corrupt, shameless, and inept colonial lackeys rule over us year after year because Puerto Ricans, through fear, ignorance, and apathy, allow this to happen. So many Puerto Ricans electing pathetic, colonialist, and corrupt felons and gangsters into office and naïvely expecting them to govern like committed and patriotic public servants. These corrupt statehooders and colonialists are experts at peddling fear and they work and seek to make Puerto Ricans fear their own freedom. For decades, the statehooders and colonialists have promoted the myth and fear that if Puerto Rico were to become a sovereign nation, Puerto Rico would go bankrupt, be burdened with a huge public debt, people would lose their pensions, that there would be an economic crisis, and that we would live in an anti-democratic dictatorship.

Ironically, today, all these fears have been realized under the flag and colonial government of the United States. We need to defeat all those who wish to deny us the freedom to dream and aspire to a *better* Puerto Rico, a *free* Puerto Rico. The minute that Puerto Ricans realize and are aware of their own power and strength and withdraw their consent and cooperation to such depraved colonial humiliation, the colonial house of cards *will* fall.

All we need to do is withdraw our consent to colonial rule; launch various multifaceted and ubiquitous non-violent civil resistance campaigns and actions; organize massive protests; make "citizen's arrests" of corrupt politicians who are known to have committed felonies under the law, yet are protected by the political party machines; deface and remove symbols of colonialism and post it to social media; and implement non-cooperation actions and sanctions against the pillars of support of the entire colonial regime. In the words of Alexandra Lúgaro, "*we need to transform our indignation into action.*"

With such a political crisis of legitimacy on its hands and without its crumbling pillars of support, like Sampson, we *can* bring down the temple of colonial rule and finally establish and forge our own Republic with a democratic government of the people, by the people, and for the people, where all sovereign power and authority resides, not in some faraway and foreign congressional committee presided over by indifferent federal officials, but in the Puerto Rican nation itself.

We have been chained, kneeling, and surviving for over half a millennium under despotic Spanish and United States colonial rule, and its finally time to stand up, take back our home, and clean out and uproot all the colonialist Mafiosi and corruption that has plagued us for centuries. This colonial humiliation will end because it must end. Boricuas, it's time we rise up in unity and show the world the power and force of the defiant and proud Puerto Rican nation.

Although statehooders and colonialists believe that Puerto Ricans are a passive people, throughout history, we as Puerto Ricans have fought and battled empires and armies to defend Puerto Rico and our families. As you will see, Puerto Ricans are a strong, loyal, and determined nation, and if there's something we do well, it's to defend Puerto Rico in the face of overwhelming odds.

Our Taino ancestors rose up in the *Guazábara of 1511* to free Borikén from foreign occupation and continued to fight for decades against Spanish colonialism. Our African ancestors revolted various times against slavery and the tyrannical slave masters. When invaded by foreign European armies, we Puerto Ricans rose up, battled, and expelled the British, the French, and the Dutch from Puerto Rico.

In the 1500s, Puerto Ricans from San Germán fought and defeated three French invasions of western Puerto Rico. In the 1700s, Puerto Ricans fought and expelled pirates and various Danish, Scottish, and Brandenburg-Prussian colonizers from the island of Vieques and formally made it part of Puerto Rico.

On August 5th, 1702, a small group of thirty Puerto Rican militia (mostly farmers – *jíbaros*), led by Captain Antonio de los Reyes Correa, with machetes in hand, were pitted against and defeated an entire British Naval invasion force of warships full of professional and better armed soldiers with muskets and swords at the beaches of Arecibo. Yes, in 1702, a group of thirty Puerto Ricans defeated the British Empire, the most powerful empire and naval power of its time, with machetes. It took General George Washington's American Revolutionary Army over 200,000 soldiers and 8 years to do what thirty Puerto Ricans did in one day: defeat the British Empire.

On April 30th, 1797, the British returned and attacked the walled city of San Juan. As the Battle of San Juan raged on between the British and Spanish-Puerto Rican troops and militia, a religious procession (La Rogativa) of clergy and women carrying candles and torches off in the distance convinced the British that Spanish reinforcements had arrived and they left San Juan by May 1st. Although the Spanish-Puerto Rican troops held the British at bay, it was ultimately a procession of brave *Puerto Rican women* from the mountains that saved Puerto Rico from British occupation and colonial rule.

Again, a handful of Puerto Ricans managed to defeat the British Empire. Before Spain surrendered in the Spanish-American War, Spanish-Puerto Rican militia soldiers actually defeated and halted an advance of American troops in the Battle of Asomante (1898) in the mountains of Aibonito.

For our freedom and independence, we organized and rose up in the San Germán Conspiracy (1809), Grito de Trujillo Bajo (1838), the Grito de Lares (1868), the Ciales Conspiracy (1870), the Camuy Revolt (1873), the Intentona de Yauco (1897), the Grito de Ciales (1898), and the Grito de Jayuya (1950) under the banner of the Republic and freedom. The one day of the first Republic in Lares (1868) and the three days of the second Republic in Jayuya (1950) are worth more to me than 121 years of humiliating colonial rule because, for that brief time in that specific place, we were *free*.

In 2003, after decades of protests, Puerto Ricans finally forced the U.S. Navy to evacuate the island of Vieques. We rose up again as a strong and united people in the Summer Revolution of 2019, but we now need to finish what we began. We cannot clean one room and leave the rest of our house in utter disorder and colonial filth.

We do not have the military strength to liberate our nation, but as a people, we *do* have the strength, imagination, and determination to embarrass our colonizers and destroy their prestige and image in Puerto Rico and around the world, thus forcing them to sit down and begin the transition to sovereignty. The days of being told what to do by the U.S. Congress and their colonial lackeys must come to an end. Where to begin and how?

In Old San Juan, *Calle Resistencia* needs to extend *into* La Fortaleza, not just stop at the gate. The flag of Puerto Rico needs to fly, by itself, atop La Fortaleza and El Capitolio. Massive anti-colonial protests can be reignited by showcasing and making public more acts of colonial corruption, depravity, and criminal acts so that the Puerto Rican people become so incensed and outraged as to demand an end of the colonial regime (#RenunciaColonia) because the regime itself is what is sustaining and allowing such corruption to thrive and destroy our lives.

It's a symbiotic relationship where the corrupt politicians need the colony, and the colony needs the corrupt politicians. As the colonial regime falls, so will the statehooder and colonialist corrupt politicians and their rigged colonial electoral system.

The gallery and floor of the colonial Senate need to be flooded by teachers, bikers, and *galleros*; and the chambers of the colonial "supreme" court need to be packed by truckers, taxi drivers, and pensioners. Imagine a flash mob of hundreds of Puerto Ricans entering and occupying El Morro fortress and other historic facilities with Puerto Rican flags and banners demanding the transfer of said national monuments and patrimony to the Institute of Puerto Rican Culture under the slogan of #ElMorroEsNuestro (*El Morro Is Ours*), among others. Puerto Ricans could even protest outside the offices of the U.S. National Park Service within San Cristobal fortress.

In response to the recent attempts by the statehood party to quash dissent; sell off public utilities, lands, and historic assets to foreign developers and companies; and the anti-democratic "electoral reform" (called locally the *electoral deformity*) that is being rushed and approved by pro-statehood legislators without public hearings in order for them to steal the November 2020 elections, the Puerto Rican people need to react and act fast with various protests and direct actions.

Those legislators that supported said anti-democratic changes need to be protested, shamed, and heckled where ever they go; need to be ostracized and ridiculed in public; and have thousands of Puerto Ricans mail defaced mock ballots that say *"No al Golpe Estadista"* (No to the Statehooder Coup) to their legislative and district offices every week.

Posters, decals, T-shirts, and banners with the *"No al Golpe Estadista"* and *"Dile No a la Dictadura PNP"* (Say No to the Statehood Party Dictatorship) slogans would be displayed everywhere in Puerto Rico. Other great slogans would be:

1. *"PNP: Futuro Seguro de Corrupción"* (With the Statehood Party, Ensure a Future of Corruption);
2. *"El PNP quiere un Puerto Rico sin Boricuas"* (The statehooders want a Puerto Rico without Puerto Ricans);
3. *"El PNP: Tomamos de Pend@jos Hasta los Nuestros"* (The statehooders: we even tricked our own People).

Protesters can ensure that these slogans are written everywhere in Puerto Rico, particularly around voting centers and tourist areas. Protesters need to organize, plan, and strategize to put in motion a coordinated and multifaceted plan to destroy the image, prestige, and credibility of all the corrupt colonialist politicians, officials, and judges in Puerto Rico, all of them.

All national monuments and historic buildings under federal control need to be occupied by protesters and have Puerto Rican flags hoisted on their roofs. Historic buildings under colonial government control, such as the current headquarters of the Institute of Puerto Rican Culture, that are in danger of being leased off to hotel developers need to be occupied and barricaded by protesters as well until the local colonial government annuls such shameful and harmful contracts.

This is tantamount to the U.S. President signing a secret deal to lease the Smithsonian to hotel developers or turning the Washington Mall into a golf course. Those clueless and opportunistic individuals responsible for selling off Puerto Rico's national patrimony in backroom deals, such as a former colonial governor (nicknamed Agapito) and others, must be ostracized, called out in public, and shamed everywhere they go in Puerto Rico.

There is nothing "honorable" about such individuals, and they need to realize that. Such shaming needs to occur for all of them, no matter where they are. Such pathetic and closedminded colonialists do not respect Puerto Rican culture and must be globally shamed after having squandered away and done irreparable harm to Puerto Rico's national patrimony. We must remind them constantly, wherever they are in the world, that Puerto Rico does not forget nor forgive. He will forever be known as "Agapito The Hotelier" (*Agapito El Hotelero*).

In defiance of the federal prohibition on cockfighting, the *galleros* can hold actual cockfighting tournaments right in front of the U.S. federal district court in San Juan; *galleros* could name the various clandestine cockfighting venues after the "honorable" judges of the U.S. federal district court; and *galleros* can release hundreds of roosters and chickens onto the grounds of the U.S. federal district court and take pictures and video of federal agents and employees chasing after roosters and chickens for all of social media and the world to see.

The *galleros* can also flood the congressional offices of legislators that supported the prohibition with thousands of photos of their finest roosters; and *galleros* can also hold vigils and ceremonies outside the federal district court for all the deer, quails, and bears mercilessly killed by American "sport" hunters across the United States, yet not prohibited by federal law nor the "Farm Bill" that prohibited cockfighting, among other ideas of resistance.

Protesters can also bring hundreds of roosters and chickens (*gallos patrióticos*) to the "resident" commissioner's office in Washington, DC, and release them all in the lobby, after telling security that this delivery of *gallos patrióticos* is for the Office of the Puerto Rico "resident" commissioner. For a moment, just imagine hundreds of roosters and chickens running around and rampaging through the lobby and congressional offices of the Longworth House Office Building while the *galleros* sit by with Puerto Rican flags, play Puerto Rican folkloric music, and sing *La Borinqueña*.

Another idea could be to bring various roosters into the lobby of the Longworth House Office Building and set up a quick cockfighting tournament for those Americans to see. If these Congressmen impose their federal laws on Puerto Rico, then the *galleros* can bring and impose the *gallera* (cockfighting arena) on these Congressmen at their very offices. Of course, all of these protests would be recorded and shared on various social media platforms for the whole world to see. These *gallero* protests would become news and would embarrass the "resident" commissioner and other congressional officials, helping to erode their façade of honor and prestige as they maintain colonial rule in Puerto Rico.

Being lied to, ignored, and betrayed by the statehood party and its "resident" commissioner in Washington, DC, the *galleros* can also organize and form a powerful voting bloc to deny that political party of its support in all upcoming elections. For the statehood party, allowing the cockfighting industry to die (just like Section 936 of the federal tax code) was just another way the statehooders could make Puerto Rico more in line with the fifty states. For the *galleros*, the only hope of protecting their industry and livelihoods is via the establishment of a sovereign government where no foreign entity can legislate over Puerto Rican affairs.

Imagine a massive maritime protest where hundreds of boats, jet skis, and kayaks encircle the U.S. Coast Guard headquarters at La Puntilla in San Juan Bay with hundreds of Puerto Rican flags and large banners demanding decolonization and sovereignty. Puerto Ricans can organize such a National Regata for Freedom (*Regata Nacional por la Libertad*) where hundreds of boats, jet skis, and kayaks would park themselves at the entrance of San Juan Bay for one day (strategically on a busy cargo shipping day), effectively blockading it and not allowing the U.S. Merchant Marine cargo ships and cruise ships into the harbor and establishing effective Puerto Rican control over San Juan Bay.

There are not nearly enough police marine units nor foreign U.S. Coast Guard agents and resources in Puerto Rico to stop any of these massive protests. U.S. Coast Guard personnel would just have to sit by and watch the massive protests from La Puntilla. Just like the Summer Revolution of 2019, portraits of federal and colonial officials in public buildings need to be put in the trash, recycled, or mailed back (*repatriated*) to the House Committee on Natural Resources in Washington, DC.

Puerto Ricans can respectfully establish an ongoing collection drive for American flags throughout Puerto Rico that would be mailed back (*repatriated*) to the House Committee on Natural Resources in Washington, DC, or the office of the Speaker of the House of Representatives. This volunteer collection drive could be called "*Pecosas pa' DC*". Ironically, after many statehooder rallies and events, hundreds of small American flags are strewn about the ground like trash.

Flag protesters can rescue these flags off the ground and humbly send them back to the United States, where they can be appreciated and cared for by actual Americans, not Puerto Rican colonial subjects. These offices would be receiving hundreds of boxes and packages (piling up in rooms) with thousands of used American flags being sent back to the United States from thousands of Puerto Ricans throughout Puerto Rico.

The repatriated flags should be treated with respect, not defaced, and accompanied by a letter stating that the United States flag looks better in the United States and not in Puerto Rico. The letter would also respectfully ask the United States government to begin the negotiations towards a transition to Puerto Rican sovereignty. Such flag protesters and others could even wear T-shirts stating; "*I just violated federal law Flag Code 18 U.S.C. § 700 in Puerto Rico!*"

Such open and flagrant violation of this federal law in Puerto Rico would help to erode the fear that many have regarding the federal government and its *federicos* in Puerto Rico. If the *federicos* in Puerto Rico actually begin to enforce the one-year prison penalty on Puerto Ricans for violating the U.S. Flag Code, it would cause massive protests in Puerto Rico, a surge in nationalism, and continued civil resistance.

Imagine groups of elderly Puerto Ricans joining anti-colonial phone bank brigades where they would call the offices of federal agencies, U.S. congressional offices, the colonial governor, and corrupt legislators every day 24/7 asking questions like *"when will the U.S. leave Puerto Rico?"* or *"why did you support the law that reduced my pension?"* or *"As a U.S. state, will Puerto Rico still be able to keep its National Olympic Team?"* These phone bank brigades would disrupt office communications, overburden the telephone systems, waste thousands of working hours answering such calls, and cause an uproar in federal and colonial political circles.

If just twenty elderly activists from all 78 Puerto Rican municipalities joined such an anti-colonial phone bank brigade, there would be 1,560 *abuelas* and *abuelos* working together to successfully disrupt the colonial communication system. Imagine what we can do with forty activists per municipality making such calls. If just thirty elderly Puerto Ricans from all 78 municipalities joined this anti-colonial phone bank brigade, there would be 2,340 people making calls. Now, if each of these 2,340 people made 20 calls/day, this group would collectively be making 46,800 calls/day.

In one year, this group of *abuelas* and *abuelos* would be making 17,082,000 calls to disrupt the colonial communication system and overburden their phone systems. If all of these 17,082,000 calls were directed at just five offices, each office would receive 3,416,400 calls/year. That's enough to overburden any phone system and really annoy our colonial rulers. To further annoy American office staff in Washington, DC, calls to some congressional offices could also be entirely in Spanish, day after day for months.

Are the federal and colonial authorities really going to go after and arrest all those elderly Puerto Ricans who made calls and simply asked questions? This would be a true dilemma action victory for the pro-sovereignty forces in Puerto Rico because if the authorities do nothing fearing a backlash for arresting these elderly activists, we win.

If the authorities do arrest these elderly activists for simply making phone calls, the authorities will look silly and would be humiliated and discredited on social media, thus allowing the elderly activists to claim a victory. If arrested, they would be celebrated and become instant heroes and heroines in Puerto Rico. The mugshots and photos of these handcuffed elderly activists would be shared around the world. The Puerto Rico, American, and international press would have a field day with such a story.

Truckers and school bus drivers do have the power to paralyze the Puerto Rican transportation network in thirty minutes if they wanted to. If they wanted, Puerto Rican electricity workers have the access and power to cut electrical power to La Fortaleza and the Puerto Rico colonial legislature so that they can experience the blackouts that thousands of Puerto Rican families experience all too frequently due to their corruption and mismanagement. Puerto Ricans with blue FEMA tarps still on their roofs after two years can assemble at the offices of corrupt legislators and mayors and attempt to cover and encase said offices in blue tarps.

Puerto Rican dockworkers have the access and power to hoist the flag of Puerto Rico over all the U.S. Merchant Marine ships at the port, the very ships that control and choke our economy via the detested cabotage laws. Puerto Ricans can also go and do protest sit-ins at the offices of the American maritime companies in San Juan and Jacksonville, Florida.

Protesters can write or spray-paint "**20%**" around such offices and cargo containers, in reference to the 20% price increase that these companies unjustly impose on Puerto Rican consumers by their colonial price protection racket. The "20%" symbol can become the most effective anti-cabotage law tactic because it can be written anywhere, go on stickers, T-shirts, flags, and it reminds Puerto Ricans of the 20% higher prices they have to pay to subsidize the U.S. Merchant Marine and its despised colonialist companies.

Let's not stop there. Puerto Ricans can also mock and ridicule the unelected junta members in Puerto Rico and around the world. We can start a massive social media campaign asking Ukraine to #TakeBackJaresko (#*Взяти назад Яресько*). We can establish various street theater shows across Puerto Rico, mocking and humiliating the unelected junta members in hilarious parodies that highlight their anti-democratic, sadistic, and buffoonish policies that would be recorded and shared across various social media platforms. I think the beautiful flag of Puerto Rico needs to fly alone atop the federal courthouse in Old San Juan over the heads of its "honorable" foreign-appointed judges so as to remind them that they are in Puerto Rico, not Boston.

Somehow, during the night, all of the presidential statues at the *Paseo de los Presidentes* can disappear and miraculously end up smelted somewhere into new statutes of Agüeybaná II, Betances, Albizu, Blanca Canales, Juan Antonio Corretjer, and other patriots in towns across Puerto Rico. Inspired by the Estonian Singing Revolution, Puerto Ricans can take to the streets and sing *La Borinqueña* and other patriotic songs (*Preciosa*, *Verde Luz*, etc.), en masse, every day in front of federal buildings, particularly during federal and colonial events and ceremonies.

At every 4th of July Independence Day official government ceremony, massive protests should occur demanding Puerto Rico's freedom, particularly at such ceremonies and in tourist areas. As

Puerto Ricans, we believe it is very disrespectful for the officials of the U.S. colonial regime in Puerto Rico to be celebrating their nation's freedom and independence while imposing their colonial rule and anti-democratic regime on Puerto Rico. It's like celebrating France's Bastille Day in French-occupied Algeria, - it's definitely not going to go well.

During such events, various Puerto Ricans in attendance should interrupt the speeches and begin to sing Puerto Rico's national anthem, *La Borinqueña*, and continue even as they are dragged out by security. After a few minutes, another Puerto Rican in attendance does the same thing, and so on and so on. Imagine fifty Puerto Ricans doing this staggered singing protest at such an event.

On this very day, thousands of protesters can assemble on the perimeter roads and encircle U.S. military base Ft. Buchanan, with various mounted speakers, continuously playing *La Borinqueña* very loud for the whole day so as to disrupt their official ceremonies. Even as they take refuge in the base from the hordes of chanting and singing Puerto Ricans, they will be constantly reminded that they are in occupied-Puerto Rico, not the United States.

We can even have a Puerto Rican actor dress up as a British colonial-era general on horseback and carrying the Union Jack flag lead a protest just outside the ceremony demanding the "separatist" American federal and colonial officials to kneel down and accept British rule, surrounded by cheering and laughing Puerto Ricans. There's an old adage that says that "it is hard to control and rule a people that is laughing at you."

The colonial regime may have the guns, but with the weapons of comedy and ridicule, we Puerto Ricans can laugh and make sure we show the world how ridiculous and absurd the colonial officials and agents look and act as they impose their colonial rule. They need to be humiliated day after day until they leave Puerto Rico.

Such colonialist 4th of July ceremonies need to be disrupted until they are cancelled due to the various interruptions and awkward situations created by protesters. If federal and colonial officials want to celebrate their freedom and independence from British rule, they can do it peacefully and proudly in the United States, *not* in Puerto Rico. A master should *never* celebrate his own freedom in his slave's quarters, especially if the master used to be a slave himself. It's just not right.

Regarding the interruption of official colonial events, we can also have a pro-sovereignty American actor dress up as the infamous colonial dictator Governor Blanton Winship, in full 1930s military regalia and carrying the American flag, constantly interrupt and crash official Puerto Rican colonial government events and press conferences and bark orders and insults in loud English at Puerto Rican statehooders and colonialists, asking them to help him find "nacionalistas" so he can imprison them again. This mock Governor Winship would also bark orders at the Governor of Puerto Rico and express amazement that a Puerto Rican is actually pretending to be the governor and would constantly ask officials "if they know where Albizu is."

The mock Governor Winship would also yell at and attempt to seize Puerto Rican flags from people because, for him; it is an illegal flag of seditious separatists. This protest action would be amazing to experience, and it would also allow modern Puerto Ricans to experience the indignities of being harassed by such a racist barbarian who was at one time actually the appointed American "governor" of Puerto Rico.

I would insist that all veterans and Memorial Day events and ceremonies be *off-limits* to any protest. Regardless of what anyone believes of such wars and foreign policy, Puerto Rican veterans should and need to be allowed to celebrate and honor their service in peace, with no protests whatsoever. The strategic target of the protesters needs to be the image, functions, symbols, policies, prestige, and credibility of the U.S. colonial regime, not veterans.

As one might imagine, the colonial regime in Puerto Rico will attempt to undermine and enforce a media blackout on such protests, but in the age of social media, that is virtually impossible. In order to ensure that Americans in the United States get the message of *Puerto Rican Sovereignty Now!*, hundreds of Puerto Rican activists can arrange to interrupt the singing of the U.S. national anthem at hundreds of baseball games by singing *La Borinqueña*, unfurling Puerto Rican flags, and others running onto the field with more Puerto Rican flags and signs denouncing colonial rule in Puerto Rico.

Imagine this protest happening at televised games such as the World Series or the Super Bowl. Of course, they will be dragged off the field, arrested, and probably beaten, but their mission is accomplished, which is to force Americans to *think* about Puerto Rico. Of course, all of these protests would be recorded and go viral on social media, particularly as the protesters are hailed as heroes and patriots by Puerto Ricans.

We need to become *impossible* for them to ignore and what better place to do that than at baseball games across the United States. Yes, many Americans will be angry at us for interrupting their beloved games, but we've been angry for 121 years regarding U.S. colonial rule in our country, and these Americans never seemed to mind or care.

This very act of protest, happening every day at baseball games and other sporting events (like the November 23rd, 2019 protest at the Yale-Harvard football game) for weeks and months at a time, would generate enough press and publicity regarding Puerto Rican decolonization and sovereignty all across the United States as to reverberate back to the U.S. Congress in order for them to finally sit down and seriously address decolonization and the transition to sovereignty.

Also, every night at 8 pm, the entire nation can participate in a national *cacerolazo* (banging pots) to remind the colonial regime that we aim to root out corruption and end colonialism. At press conferences and ceremonies with federal and colonial officials, hundreds of youth can quickly show up in a flash mob and start various sessions of *perreo combativo, salsa combativa,* or surround the press conference with a hundred Puerto Ricans singing La Borinqueña or Preciosa.

We can show the colonial regime that Puerto Rico has finally heard the cry of "*Coño Despierta Boricua!*" Luis Llorens Torres' *patito feo* (ugly duckling) has finally become a swan, and we are taking flight beyond the nest of apathy and despair. Puerto Ricans, the list of tactics and possibilities to resist and confront colonialism using the arsenal of non-violent civil resistance is endless and only limited by our imaginations.

I challenge all Puerto Ricans, young and old, to be creative and come up with ideas and tactics that can be used in non-violent civil resistance campaigns to further consecrate our freedom and liberation. We have the opportunity to make history and make sure that in one hundred years, the Puerto Ricans of the future will look back and thank us for our struggle and sacrifices, which allow them to live in freedom and democracy. We can do this.

From a conquered people, we must organize and rise to conquer and take our freedom, reestablish our sovereignty, embrace our national identity, and become a truly transnational, maritime, and global nation. Puerto Rico has so much potential to be great, but as a colony, our potential is limited and confined within the filthy colonial basement of the Territorial Clause of the U.S. Constitution. We cannot allow corrupt and inept colonial administrators and clueless federal officials and Congressmen to take and squander our future away from us.

There will be *no* place for corrupt officials and lackeys in the government of the Republic of Puerto Rico if we are able to establish an independent and non-partisan anti-corruption investigative service; enforce anti-corruption laws and institute long prison sentences for corrupt acts; and a serious, professional, and meritocratic Civil Service that would guarantee that only qualified, competent, and meritorious Puerto Ricans are able to work in Puerto Rico's public administration and agencies, not the inept and corrupt colonial lackeys (*batatas*) and the unqualified children of corrupt politicians (mockingly called *hijos talentosos*) that currently control these government agencies.

From the ashes of colonial rule, the Republic will help us forge a new reality for the Puerto Rican people, a reality where we are standing tall in freedom and ruling ourselves as masters of our own country, not kneeling in chains before the colonial regime and its barbaric supporters. We need to show ourselves and the world that Puerto Ricans have earned the right to live as equals with all the other nations of this planet.

There is an old Chinese proverb that says: "*The person who says it cannot be done should not interrupt the person doing it.*" For Puerto Ricans, we cannot let those statehooders and colonialists who claim that "*Puerto Rico no puede ser libre*" (Puerto Rico cannot be free) to interrupt, derail, and limit those of us Puerto Ricans who do believe that "*Puerto Rico puede y tiene que ser libre*" (Puerto Rico can and must be free).

We cannot allow those that believe that Puerto Rico should be an eternal colony or slave to stop those that believe that Puerto Rico should be a free, sovereign, and democratic country. Dr. Pedro Albizu Campos once said, "*that Puerto Rico is represented by those that affirm her, not by those who deny her.*" In the eyes of our nation and the world, those that believe in colonial rule have no standing or credibility whatsoever.

We as a people are a symbol of freedom and defiance to tyranny and barbaric colonialism the world over because we have survived and defeated *all* efforts to destroy us from the supposed most powerful country on Earth. Our mere existence is a symbol of defiance because, according to U.S. colonial policy, we are not supposed to exist, but yet, here we are stronger than ever and proudly waving our beautiful and once banned Puerto Rican flag all over the world. Paraphrasing Albert Camus in *The Rebel*, the very existence of Puerto Ricans after having defeated over a century of American assimilation policies *"is an act of rebellion."*

The U.S. colonial regime has been successful in convincing many Puerto Ricans to believe and feel that they are unworthy of freedom and that living under the colonial heel of another country is the best thing they can aspire to. The day Puerto Ricans recognize this fallacy and realize their own power and place in the world, they *will* realize and comprehend that they are worthy of freedom. No U.S. colonial regime can thrive or survive on a foundation of free, brave, and powerful Puerto Ricans. Confronted by free and patriotic Puerto Ricans, the colonial regime will collapse.

Puerto Ricans, we exist because we rebel. Every cell of our bodies encapsulates a small piece of the fury, spirit, and courage of Agüeybaná II's call for *Guazábara* and rebellion over 508 years ago. *Rebellion* has ensured our survival, and it will also ensure our liberation. Puerto Ricans, we need to finish the rebellion that Agüeybaná II began back in ancient Boriken.

Through struggle and national affirmation of the Puerto Rican nation, we not only survived, but we managed to transform our colonial damnation into our national redemption and rise as a transnational country due to our growing and determined Puerto Rican diaspora having settled large areas of the United States and North America, thus enlarging the territorial and intercontinental dimensions of the Puerto Rican nation itself beyond our original insular borders.

Puerto Ricans not only resisted and survived U.S. colonial rule, but we also began to establish vibrant and patriotic Puerto Rican communities in the major cities of the very colonial ruler itself.

We are not immigrants nor migrants, but pioneers expanding the Puerto Rican nation across the United States, one Boricua at a time.

For 121 years, the U.S. colonial regime tried to crush us into the ground with fear, violence, and terror without realizing that we were seeds that survived and grew back stronger than ever in Puerto Rico and the United States...still being proud Puerto Ricans. Our mere existence is a victory they cannot take away. We must put an end to colonial rule and forge our future as a free, sovereign, and democratic nation.

If we are ready to claim our rightful place in the international community, we must be a free and sovereign nation; there is no other way. One is either free or enslaved, and I choose freedom. On the world stage, colonies and U.S. states need not apply. We as Puerto Ricans owe it to all those brave and patriotic men and women who died and suffered in prison and endured tortures in defending Puerto Rico, our Spanish language, our national identity, our Puerto Rican flag, our Puerto Rican culture and traditions, and the ideals of freedom and democracy in the face of overwhelming odds and colonial power and repression.

These patriots died and suffered so that we can survive as a distinct people and carry on our struggle for freedom. We cannot let them nor the future generations down. Puerto Rico *will* be a Republic; it's not a matter of *if*, but a matter *when*. It's our duty to ensure that this *when* is as soon as possible if we are to save our country from more years and decades of humiliating colonial rule.

Puerto Rican, if you also despise colonial rule and wish to end such colonial humiliation, you need to support and defend sovereignty and liberty because Puerto Rico can only move forward if we are able to rule ourselves in peace and prosperity. We can all contribute to Puerto Rico's liberation from such barbaric colonial rule and cannot let opportunities of defiance and resistance pass us by.

We are a very creative, vibrant, and robust people that can pressure, cajole, and shame a colonial power into sitting down with us and start negotiating the terms of an orderly transition to sovereignty. We can do this.

Author Bio

Javier A. Hernández, born in Río Piedras, Puerto Rico, is a Puerto Rican father, author, artist, linguist, entrepreneur, pro-sovereignty advocate, and indigenous rights activist. Javier earned a B.A. in Political Science & International Relations from Florida International University; an M.A. in International Communication from The American University; and an M.S. in Education from Lehman College. Javier has also earned certificates in Diplomacy of Small States, Emergency Management, Homeland Security Planning, Global Security Issues, and Non-violent Conflict & Civil Resistance.

Javier is a recognized linguist and is currently one of the few people in Puerto Rico and the United States that are members of the International Association of Hyperpolyglots, being able to speak nine languages and read thirteen other languages.

In 2018, Javier also reconstructed and revitalized a modern variant of the indigenous Taino language of the Caribbean and published its first primer, which is being used in various indigenous school programs in Puerto Rico. Javier is a small business owner, an independent security consultant, instructor, and has experience in the federal government and the private sector.

Javier is a flag enthusiast and artist having designed in 2013 the proposed National Coat-of-Arms of a Sovereign Puerto Rico, the flag of the Puerto Rican Diaspora, the flag of Santurce-San

Mateo de Cangrejos, and various other Puerto Rican cultural and regional flags.

Along with supporting and promoting pro-sovereignty campaigns and patriotic events, Javier also supports Puerto Rican agricultural initiatives and platforms. Javier is married and has four children.

ADDENDUM

List of Ways to Support Puerto Rico's Path to Sovereignty and Democracy

1. Read up and learn as much as possible about **Puerto Rico, its history, culture, politics, geography, economics**, and other fields by reading books, taking courses, reading Wikipedia articles about Puerto Rico, and speaking with Puerto Ricans. Having read this book is a great first step in learning about Puerto Rico and the pro-sovereignty movement.

2. Watch **movies, documentaries, speeches, and interviews** about the struggle for Puerto Rican sovereignty, freedom, and anti-colonial resistance. There are hundreds of such resources on YouTube and Vimeo.

3. You can **contact your local, state, and federal representatives** and tell them about the struggle for Puerto Rican decolonization and sovereignty. You can even contact the offices of Puerto Rican legislators and government officials. Such contact can be by e-mail, letters, online petitions, phone calls, and office visits.

*__United States Congress Contacts:__ *https://www.congress.gov/contact-us*

*__Puerto Rico Colonial Government Contacts:__ *https://www.usa.gov/state-government/puerto-rico*

You can even contact your local and state politicians and representatives and ask them to support Puerto Rican decolonization and the transition to sovereignty. If you reside in the United States, register to vote and support candidates that support Puerto Rican decolonization and sovereignty. In Puerto Rico, register to vote and support parties and candidates that support Puerto Rican decolonization and sovereignty.

4. Learn about the **various Puerto Rican pro-sovereignty organizations** and contact them via e-mail, phone, or Facebook, and ask how you can help. They will be very appreciative of any assistance you can offer in helping to support and advance Puerto Rican sovereignty.

5. You can **host a fundraising event** to help boost awareness and donations for the various pro-sovereignty campaigns. You can organize one by yourself or partner with a larger group.

6. You can **organize educational events**, workshops, talks, presentations, and seminars about Puerto Rican sovereignty and decolonization at your school, university, religious institution, local community center, or at a library, among other locations. Particularly important are educational and awareness events on Puerto Rican, American, and foreign college campuses so that new generations and leaders can learn about Puerto Rico's sovereignty movement.

7. **Connect with pro-sovereignty organizations via social media platforms**, particularly Facebook, Twitter, Instagram, and YouTube. You can start engaging with people

and related groups and communities with "Likes", writing comments, and sharing engaging posts, event information, and *calls-to-action* (CTA). Protests and other direct actions need to be shared with as many people as possible, particularly on Facebook and Twitter, using the appropriate hashtags (#). YouTube videos of protests and actions need to be shared on social media as well. Doing this would help boost social media awareness of events and issues related to Puerto Rican sovereignty, decolonization, and anti-colonial resistance.

8. Make and/or share **educational pamphlets, books, and other publications** related to Puerto Rican sovereignty. These publications can be created or downloaded from websites and printed off, ready to go. These publications can be in English, Spanish, and other languages to reach out to other communities.

9. You can learn how to write a **press release to raise awareness** for Puerto Rican sovereignty or hire a freelance writer. These press releases can be about events, campaigns, protests, and calls-to-action. You can also write articles and op-ed pieces for local, regional, state, and national publications, explaining the goals and proposals of the Puerto Rican sovereignty movement.

10. **Donate resources and / or volunteer** to work with a pro-sovereignty group in Puerto Rico or the United States

11. **Decide to** *"Buy Puerto Rican"* by making a commitment to buy Puerto Rican products either in person or online so as to support struggling Puerto Rican businesses trying to operate and succeed in a colonial economy. For example, you can decide to buy all your coffee from online providers of 100% Puerto Rican coffee. Businesses can also decide to

source their supplies from Puerto Rico and Puerto Rican small businesses.

12. Along with sourcing products from Puerto Rico, you or your business can **hire Puerto Rican freelancers** and / or Puerto Rican companies for professional services and projects. Such projects can be in Puerto Rico, the United States, or any other country. A great website to shop at and support Puerto Rican businesses and hire Puerto Rican talent, experts, and professionals is **Shop+HirePR:** *https://shopandhirepr.com/*

    By hiring Puerto Ricans, you help them support their families and the Puerto Rican economy, and in turn, you benefit from Puerto Rican talent and professional services.

13. Once you learn about Puerto Rico, it's history, and the struggle and proposals of the Puerto Rican Sovereignty movement, you can **become an outspoken advocate for decolonization and sovereignty**. This book, I'm sure, will be a great resource for new sovereignty advocates. You can talk to your family, friends, and colleagues about Puerto Rican sovereignty, why statehood should never happen, and the various proposals to make Puerto Rico a stable, democratic, and economically prosperous country.

14. If you own a business or have personal resources, you can help **sponsor pro-sovereignty events**, actions, and campaigns in Puerto Rico and the United States.

15. To **support Puerto Rican farmers and other agricultural initiatives**, you can contact the various farms in Puerto Rico (via Facebook) and ask how you can help, support, or invest in their cause and business.

16. Purchase, create, or **acquire pro-sovereignty products (merch)** such as T-shirts, decals, signs, flags, pins, posters, and pamphlets with information, designs, and quotes.

17. If possible, you can **participate in protests, marches, pickets, and various other forms of protest**. You can read up on theories and tactics of civil resistance and discuss such ideas with your preferred groups in planning potential future protests and actions.

18. If you have a bank account with Banco Popular or any other large Puerto Rican bank, you can show your disgust at how these bankers and financial insiders benefited from the Puerto Rican illegal debt scandal by **closing your accounts and transferring your funds and assets to a Puerto Rican credit union**. When closing your account, remember to tell them why you are closing it and that you are disappointed in their unethical behavior and hope that their CEO ends up in prison.

    To find the nearest Puerto Rican credit union (cooperativa de ahorro y crédito), please access the following link from CooperativasPR:

    https://www.cooperativaspr.com/directorio/

19. If you are ever at an **event where a Puerto Rican or American official is speaking at and defending colonial rule or promoting statehood**, you can respectfully ask them, *"why should Puerto Ricans support colonial rule and statehood when the United States has...* (and then begin to read off the concise list of colonial atrocities and repressions mentioned in the conclusion of this book)."

    Believe me, the speakers will be taken by surprise, will not know how to respond, and will probably ask security to drag you outside (which would further illustrate to the audience the ugly side of colonial rule and its need to persecute and silence dissent).

20. You can help **promote and spread the information** on why Puerto Rico should never become a state and why

sovereignty is the best option for various American audiences, particularly liberal and conservative groups and media organizations. By doing this, you can help reverse the false "*Puerto Ricans want statehood*" narrative that pro-statehood lobbyists and operatives have been peddling for years in Washington, DC, and the U.S. media.

21. If you are Puerto Rican, **actions you can take to further consolidate, explore, and celebrate your Puerto Rican national identity** and knowledge of Puerto Rico and the pro-sovereignty struggle are:

    a. Learn about Puerto Rico and Puerto Rican culture.

    b. Learn more about your family history. Ask your parents and grandparents about family stories and anecdotes.

    c. Learn to recite and sing *La Borinqueña* (the original patriotic lyrics, not the 1952 colonial lyrics). Also, learn to sing *Preciosa*, *Verde Luz*, and other patriotic songs.

    d. Learn about Dr. Pedro Albizu Campos, read his speeches, his biography, and listen to his speeches on YouTube. Although in Spanish, many are transcribed into English.

    e. Learn and read about other inspirational and great Puerto Rican patriots such as Betances, De Hostos, De Diego, Lolita Lebrón, Juan Antonio Corretjer, Blanca Canales, Matienzo Cintrón, and so many others. Also, learn about and read books on the Puerto Rican sovereignty movement.

    f. Display the Puerto Rican flag in your home and teach your children to respect and revere the Puerto Rican flag. Teach them the history of the flag and how it used to be banned by the colonial government and that many people went to prison and suffered just so we can have and celebrate our beautiful national flag. Also, learn to recognize the flag of Lares and other municipios.

g. If you are in the diaspora, visit Puerto Rico, experience your family, meet new relatives, experience your culture, visit historic places, volunteer to work at a farm or community service project, attend cultural events and festivals, take a course and walking tour in Old San Juan, spend time in the mountains, bathe in a river, visit El Yunque, and speak with pro-sovereignty advocates and leaders.

h. Wherever you are in the world, always celebrate *El Grito de Lares* on September 23rd.

i. Learn languages. If you only speak Spanish, learn English as well. If you are bilingual, learn other languages. If you only speak English, make every effort to learn Spanish. Along with the professional, travel, global, and financial benefits of knowing Spanish (one of the top 3 global languages), Spanish will allow you to speak with Puerto Rican family and be able to read important books about Puerto Rico, which are only in Spanish.

j. Learn about and celebrate your indigenous Taino and African heritage and cultures since these are pillars of the Puerto Rican culture and experience. Also, learn about Spain, Spanish regions, cultures, and histories since they are also important in Puerto Rican culture, language, and history.

k. Learn and use Taino phrases and words in your daily life, such as *Taigüey* (Hello), *Bo-Matúm* (Thank you), and others.

l. Travel and become well-versed not only in Puerto Rican politics and geography but also in world politics and global issues, so that you can be a great ambassador for Puerto Rico when you travel abroad and engage with foreigners. It is very important that you travel the world and experience life in other countries, not just base your experiences on life within the confines, political circus, and humiliations of colonial rule in Puerto Rico.

Although you have to travel the world on a U.S. passport due to congressional decrees in 1917, remember to identify yourself as a *"Puerto Rican"* in other countries and explain the colonial dilemma if asked. As a *"Puerto Rican"*, you will surely receive better treatment from cordial foreigners and greatly reduce the chances of being the target of terrorists.

Remember, <u>there are no terrorist groups or kidnapping rings in the world that target Puerto Ricans</u>. Overseas, having a Puerto Rico flag patch on your backpack can save you from a lot of problems. Also, remember to carry a Puerto Rican flag whenever you travel, you never know when you might need to unfurl it or a photo op presents itself.

m. Learn to identify and confront the colonial mentality wherever you are. Destroy and invalidate myths and colonial fears with facts, data, examples, and proposals.

n. You can buy a property in Puerto Rico, thus establishing a legal *"land"* connection with Puerto Rico. It can be a house, an apartment, a summer or country home, a plot of land, or even various acres. This land or house could become a family property and patrimony for you and your family to enjoy, develop, and start a farm if you wanted to. Also, you would be helping to ensure that Puerto Rican land remains in Puerto Rican hands.

As you can see, there are many ways to support Puerto Rico's path to sovereignty and democracy. I'm sure there are other and more creative ways that you can think of that I did not mention. The struggle for Puerto Rico's freedom has been a long and difficult one, raging on in some form or another since 1511, but it's a struggle that *can* be won.

You, too, can contribute and participate in helping Puerto Rico achieve its long-sought out freedom so it can finally establish a free and democratic government for Puerto Ricans, by Puerto Ricans, and of Puerto Ricans. Our own free country and democratic Republic that would allow us to engage with the other nations of the Earth as equals, not as slaves or property of another nation. Puerto Ricans deserve and demand their freedom. You can help us make this happen. Join us.

A Concise List of Colonial Atrocities

When statehooders and colonialists attempt to sway you to support "statehood" or continued U.S. colonial rule and tutelage, please remember the following facts and events:

- the thousands of murdered and tortured Puerto Ricans who were victims of the policies and excesses of the U.S. colonial regime;

- the thousands of Puerto Ricans jailed over the decades for owning a Puerto Rican flag;

- the hundreds of forced female sterilizations to reduce the Puerto Rican population;

- the banning of our flag, our national anthem, and national symbols;

- the bombing and burning of homes and businesses of pro-independence leaders and supporters;

- the criminalization of "independence" and the illegal police dossiers used to persecute and intimidate independence supporters and their families;

- federal government programs, such as COINTELPRO, used to infiltrate and weaken independence and sovereignty organizations in Puerto Rico;

- the Río Piedras and Ponce massacres of 1935 and 1937;
- the attempts to destroy Puerto Rican culture via assimilation policies;
- the decades of inept and humiliating colonial rule by foreign American white supremacists who were appointed "governor";
- the use of El Morro and its sacred historical grounds as a military golfing and swimming pool area for the U.S. military;
- the radiation torture and burning of Dr. Pedro Albizu Campos by U.S. colonial authorities;
- the physical and mental tortures inflicted on independence supporters, particularly being locked up in a cell full of bedbugs that would cover the human body;
- the colonial police executions of pro-independence supporters (such as the Cerro Maravilla assassinations);
- the hundreds of kidnapped and missing Puerto Ricans because they supported independence and human rights;
- the destruction of our economy and democratic institutions;
- the abolition of our peso currency in order to plunge more Puerto Ricans into poverty;
- the attacks on our Spanish language and the imposition of the English language;
- the infection of hundreds of Puerto Ricans with diseases by U.S. doctors for medical experiments;
- the drafting of thousands of Puerto Ricans to fight in foreign wars as colonial troops;
- the Puerto Ricans who were murdered by Dr. Cornelius Rhoads via cancer injections;

- the thousands of Puerto Ricans held in concentration camps during anti-colonial revolts;
- the father who was forced to eat his own murdered son by American soldiers at the "Academy of Truth" in 1950, the electrocutions and being forced to scream "Long Live the United States" while being beaten by US soldiers;
- the deaths and damage caused by the violent pro-statehood turba mobs to terrorize Puerto Ricans;
- the imposition of the colonial mentality and a colonial educational system;
- the forced usage of expensive U.S. shipping companies via the Jones Act that takes $1.5 billion out of the Puerto Rico economy every year to subsidize American shipping companies;
- the decades of U.S. Navy abuse, violence, and environmental disasters in Vieques and Culebra; and many other atrocities.

Proposed Map of Puerto Rican Autonomous Regions

Coming Soon

Here are some of the upcoming books and publications by Javier A. Hernández and Editorial Libros El Telégrafo scheduled to be published in 2020.

El triunfo del pitirre: de dictadura colonial a soberanía democrática (Triumph of the Pitirre: From Colonial Dictatorship to Democratic Sovereignty)

Editorial Libros El Telégrafo

Editorial Libros El Telégrafo is the small boutique self-publishing label founded by Javier A. Hernández in 2018 with the aim of publishing books about Puerto Rican politics, sovereignty, democracy, culture, language, society, economics, history, human rights, indigenous communities, and national identity, among other topics related to Puerto Rico, Hispanic issues, the Caribbean, and Latin America as well.

During the Grito de Lares revolt of 1868 against Spanish rule, Puerto Rican revolutionary leader, Dr. Ramón E. Betances, arranged for a ship called *"El Telégrafo"* to sail from St. Thomas to

Puerto Rico with a cache of firearms and weapons that were to be used by the revolutionaries to free Puerto Rico. Unfortunately, the Danish authorities in St. Thomas supported Spain and took over the ship, not allowing the much-needed arms to reach the Puerto Rican rebels, thus helping to defeat the first Republic.

Today, instead of firearms, *El Telégrafo* brings knowledge and information via books and publications to help free Puerto Rico and strengthen the Puerto Rican nation. The ship in the logo represents *El Telégrafo* and the year "1868" represents the Grito de Lares.

El Telégrafo's Latin motto "*Scientia Liberabit Vos*" means "Knowledge will set you Free."

Editorial Libros El Telégrafo will always remain committed to Puerto Rico, advancing Puerto Rican authors, and provide its readers with valuable, quality, pertinent, and engaging books, publications, and resources ranging from academic books to various multilevel readers, guides, and books for younger readers.

To contact **Editorial Libros El Telégrafo,** please send a detailed E-mail to: libroseltelegrafo@gmail.com

Endnotes & References

1. "Satisfecho movimiento que impulsaba el ELA soberano". Primera Hora (in Spanish). November 7, 2012. https://www.primerahora.com/noticias/gobierno-politica/nota/satisfechomovimientoqueimpulsabaelelasoberano-720329/

2. During the 2017 status plebiscite, statehood received 97% of the vote, yet the level of support decreases dramatically when one considers that there was an electoral boycott by pro-sovereignty forces which demonstrated that statehood supporters constituted 23% of voter participation. Pro-sovereignty forces called for an electoral boycott due to U.S. federal insistence that colonial "territory" status be an option in the plebiscite, which was then complied to by the pro-statehood Rosselló administration. Due to the statehooder controlled media and resources, the media began to falsely report that 97% of Puerto Ricans chose statehood. Once the U.S. government and the international media realized that voter turnout (mainly statehooders) was 23%, the plebiscite was discredited and ignored.

3. https://www.businessinsider.com/usd-countries-use-dollars-as-currency-2018-5/

4. Current U.S. colonies are: Puerto Rico, the U.S. Virgin Islands, Guam, the Northern Marianas, and American Samoa.

5. Civil Liberties in American Colonies, American Civil Liberties Union, p.17, 1939

6. Civil Liberties in American Colonies, American Civil Liberties Union, p.10, 1939

7. http://home.epix.net/ landis/navarro.html; http://carlisleindian.dickinson.edu/images/group-puerto-rican-students; http://home.epix.net/~landis/portorican.html

8   In 1934, President Franklin D. Roosevelt appointed General Blanton Winship as governor to deal with the "Puerto Rico Problem" by consolidating colonial rule, militarizing the police, instituting a dictatorial police-state, and attempting to squash and destroy Puerto Rican nationalism by terror and murder. With Governor Winship, Puerto Rico suffered through the Río Piedras massacre, the Ponce massacre, and many other acts of terror and colonial repression.

9   "Satisfecho movimiento que impulsaba el ELA soberano". Primera Hora (in Spanish). November 7, 2012. https://www.primerahora.com/noticias/gobierno-politica/nota/satisfechomovimientoqueimpulsabaelelasoberano-720329/

10 Article IV, Section 3, Clause 2 of the United States Constitution (The Territorial Clause): "The Congress shall have Power to dispose of and make all needful Rules and Regulations respecting the Territory or other Property belonging to the United States."

11 https://www.newsweek.com/trump-once-joked-trading-puerto-rico-greenland-1455689

12 *Cangrimanes* is a play on the term "Congressman", which incidentally and mockingly sounds like the Spanish word for crabs (cangrejos). The term *cangrimanes* was coined early in the 20th century when U.S. politicians would visit Puerto Rico and tour the poverty-stricken areas, shanty towns and rural villages to see how Puerto Ricans were enjoying the "blessings of American civilization".

13 General Accountability Office (GAO) Report, *Information on How Statehood Would Potentially Affect Selected Federal Programs and Revenue Sources*, Published March 4, 2014: https://www.gao.gov/assets/670/661334.pdf

14 *Statehood Is Not The Conservative Solution For Puerto Rico*, Ross Marchand, Daily Caller, August 8th, 2018: https://dailycaller.com/2018/08/08/puerto-rico-statehood-conservative-solution/

15 "Annual Estimates of the Resident Population for the United States, Regions, States, and Puerto Rico: April 1, 2010 to July 1, 2018" (XLSX). United States Census Bureau. Retrieved December 21, 2017.

16 Trujillo Bajo was later renamed Carolina.

17 José L. Vega Santiago, "8 Atrocities Committed Against Puerto Rico by the U.S." (2012): http://listverse.com/2012/10/26/8-atrocities-committed-again-puerto-rico-by-the-us/

18 Juan Gonzalez; Harvest of Empire, pp. 60–63; Penguin Press, 2001

19 https://www.latinorebels.com/2015/02/24/how-luis-munoz-marin-and-his-addiction-to-opium-enslaved-puerto-rico/

20 https://nacla.org/article/puerto-rico-united-nations

21 La Ley 600 y la mentira del ELA, Rosa Meneses Albizu, Boletín Nacional, 2004

22 La Ley 600 y la mentira del ELA, Rosa Meneses Albizu, Boletín Nacional, 2004

23 https://caselaw.findlaw.com/us-supreme-court/446/651.html

24 Rodríguez Cancel, Jaime L., "*El Consejo de Seguridad Nacional de Estados Unidos: su Acción Secreta sobre Puerto Rico (1977 – 1980)*", Cuadernos del Ateneo (2000)

25 In colonial Puerto Rico, the "*Model Colonial Puerto Rican*" is a Puerto Rican with an English first name; who is bilingual, yet prefers to speak only in English; is ashamed of their Puerto Rican culture; admires American culture and seeks to assimilate as much as possible; denies his/her Puerto Rican identity; and is prideful that he/she knows nothing about Puerto Rico nor its history. Such Puerto Ricans actually exist but they simply cannot operate in Puerto Rican society. These are the model colonial Puerto Ricans that Americans, particularly federal officials, always hope to employ and use in Puerto Rico.

26 Civil Liberties in American Colonies, American Civil Liberties Union, p.5, 1939

27 https://adelantereunificacionistas.com/2018/03/31/los-hermanos cheo-de puerto-rico/comment-page-1/

28 Before being executed by the U.S. colonial Insular Police, Elias Beauchamp said, "Shoot, so you can see how a real man dies." (*Disparen para que vean como muere un hombre*)

29 Civil Liberties in American Colonies, American Civil Liberties Union, p.12, 1939

30 Civil Liberties in American Colonies, American Civil Liberties Union, p.16, 1939

31 Civil Liberties in American Colonies, American Civil Liberties Union, p.14, 1939

32 Civil Liberties in American Colonies, American Civil Liberties Union, p.11, 1939

33 https://ehss.energy.gov/ohre/roadmap/

34 War Against All Puerto Ricans: Revolution and Terror in America's Colony, Nelson A. Denis, pg. 179-180

35 https://www.primerahora.com/noticias/puerto-rico/nota/maribrasyatieneciudadaniaboricua-109821/

36 https://www.motherjones.com/media/2015/04/puerto-rico-independence-albizu-campos/

37 https://sanjuanpuertorico.com/castillo-san-felipe-del-morro-san-juan-puerto-rico/

38 https://www.nps.gov/saju/learn/management/statistics.htm

39 My family and I were in Mayagüez, Puerto Rico during both hurricanes that struck Puerto Rico in 2017 and experienced the disastrous aftermath, lack of communications and food, lack of electricity and water, and saw the suffering and pain of many people trying to survive.

40 https://www.bbc.com/mundo/noticias-america-latina-41422551

41 https://aldia.microjuris.com/promesa/

42 https://consortiumnews.com/2015/11/10/how-ukraines-finance-chief-got-rich/

43 Fiscal Control Board (债务重组委员会): Zhàiwù chóngzǔ wěiyuánhuì

44 "Debt to the Penny". United States Department of the Treasury. Retrieved June 24, 2019.

45 https://waragainstallpuertoricans.com/2016/03/08/new-york-times-agrees-no-more-jones-act-in-puerto-rico-2/

46 https://waragainstallpuertoricans.com/2016/03/14/puerto-rico-is-supporting-the-usnot-the-other-way-around-2/

47 https://caribbeanbusiness.com/studies-peg-cost-of-jones-act-on-puerto-rico-at-1-5-billion/

48 https://jacobinmag.com/2017/10/puerto-rico-hurricane-maria-trump-jones-act-colonialism/

49 https://historyplex.com/navigation-acts-purpose-summary-significance

50 https://legal-dictionary.thefreedictionary.com/Interstate+commerce+clause

51 https://www.lexology.com/library/detail.aspx?g=22e6346e-9f7b-4ddf-ba6f-655c6fa6a708

52 Fernández, Ronald. "A Joy Ride: U.S. Attitudes Toward Puerto Rico, Its People and Its Culture." Technical Presentations in *Violation of Human Rights in Puerto Rico by the United States*. Editor: Luis Nieves Falcón. San Juan: Ediciones Puerto, 2002. 82-88.

53 https://waragainstallpuertoricans.com/2016/03/14/puerto-rico-is-supporting-the-usnot-the-other-way-around-2/

54 https://pasquines.us/2015/09/01/sterilization-the-untold-story-of-puerto-rico/

55 https://pasquines.us/2015/09/01/sterilization-the-untold-story-of-puerto-rico/

56 https://pasquines.us/2015/09/01/sterilization-the-untold-story-of-puerto-rico/

57 https://www.pbs.org/wgbh/americanexperience/features/pill-puerto-rico-pill-trials/

58 https://repeatingislands.com/2010/03/23/attorney-claims-puerto-rico-was-unlawfully-exposed-to-experiments/

59 https://repeatingislands.com/2010/03/23/attorney-claims-puerto-rico-was-unlawfully-exposed-to-experiments/

60 https://www.military.com/daily-news/2013/09/25/groups-accuse-us-of-human-rights-abuses-in-vieques.html

61 "Census 2010 News | U.S. Census Bureau Releases 2010 Census Ethnic Counts for the U.S. Virgin Islands". 2010.census.gov. Archived from the original on February 10, 2013. Retrieved March 23, 2013.

62 https://intomybrokenmind.blogspot.com/2017/01/us-military-presence-in-vieques-puerto.html

63 https://www.christianpost.com/news/bishops-join-efforts-with-local-vieques-residents-to-end-u-s-military-occupation.html

64 https://archive.org/details/historiadepuerto00mill/page/n21

65 Translation: "We are many, and we're not afraid".

66 The *Pitirre* (Grey Kingbird), in Puerto Rican folk history is a symbol of Puerto Rico and Puerto Rico's courage to stand up to tyrants. The small *Pitirre*, in defending its nest, is known to attack and fight larger eagles and hawks without fear.

67 The territorial boundaries of these eight Autonomous Regions were modeled and inspired by the old Senatorial Districts of the Commonwealth government, with some modifications. The current Municipio Autónomo de San Juan would be divided into the restored Municipio de Río Piedras, the new Municipio de Santurce, and the new San Juan National District.

68 In my proposal, only Puerto Rican citizens who pay Puerto Rico taxes and voluntarily affiliate themselves to the *Autonomous Region of the Puerto Rican Diaspora* would have voting rights and could participate in Puerto Rico elections to elect diaspora delegates to Puerto Rico's Parliament. Puerto Rican citizens would also have voting rights to elect delegates to the PRD Regional Parliament. Although affiliated Puerto Rican nationals pay taxes and can benefit from PRD services and programs, nationals can only vote for delegates to the PRD Regional Parliament.

69 State congresses, such as a *PRD-Florida State Congress (PRD-Congreso Estatal de la Florida)*, would organize, coordinate, and be made up of all the various affiliated Puerto Rican political, community, educational, cultural, social, and business organizations within the state of Florida.

70 Due to their large Puerto Rican populations, *Comunidades Autónomas* could be established in large urban areas such as New York City, Philadelphia, Chicago, Springfield (MA), Hartford, Newark, Orlando, Kissimmee, Bridgeport (CT), Boston, and Allentown (PA), among many others. *Comunidades Autónomas* would be independent cooperative political structures that would organize community resources and promote the interests of the local Puerto Rican community. Within the internal structure of the Autonomous

Region of the Puerto Rican Diaspora (PRD), the *Comunidades Autónomas* would have the same status as *"Municipios"*.

71 "Abeyaney" is the native Taino name for the island of Caja de Muertos.

72 "Aymoná" is the native Taino name for the island of Mona.

73 The Aymoná Territorial Commission (ATC) would be the governing body and central administration of the territory. The ATC would be administered by a council made up of the Administrator and representatives of the Región Autónoma de Yagüecax-Aymáca, Ministerio de Recursos Naturales, Energéticos y del Ambiente, the national government, the University of Puerto Rico, and other environmental, scientific, and maritime agencies. The Administrator would be appointed by the Presidential Council with ATC approval.

74 Named in honor of Agustín Stahl, a famous Puerto Rican scientist and botanist.

75 https://factfinder.census.gov/faces/tableservices/jsf/pages/productview.xhtml?pid=ACS_17_1YR_DP05&prodType=table

76 https://www.therichest.com/nation/richest-countries-in-the-world/

77 https://qz.com/1388117/puerto-rico-eyes-building-the-energy-grid-of-the-future/

78 https://www.ashleyedisonuk.com/world-voltages/caribbean/voltage-puerto-rico-1141/

79 https://www.power-technology.com/features/featuretidal-giants-the-worlds-five-biggest-tidal-power-plants-4211218/

80 http://www.oceanenergy.ie/

81 An energy independent Puerto Rico could export surplus electrical energy to such nations as Senegal (864MW) and Mauretania (380MW) to help them meet their installed capacity at a lower cost since energy generation in Africa can be very expensive. Via a Puerto Rico-Africa Multinational Energy Agreement, Puerto Rico could generate profits while supplying energy to various African markets.

82 The Puerto Rican Peso Initiative that I propose would be modeled on the *BerkShares Project*, from the Berkshire Region of western Massachusetts.

83 El PNP mató la estadidad, Mario Ramos, El Vocero, Feb. 8th, 2019: https://www.elvocero.com/opinion/el-pnp-mat-la-estadidad/article_b8c1286a-b4c6-11e9-8cd8-df6eac6f0908.html

84 Comparison of a potential 10% PR corporate tax rate with the corporate tax rates of other successful economies: Australia (30%), Canada (15%), Hong Kong (16.5%), Ireland (12.5%), Singapore (17%), Mexico (30%), South Korea (22%), Israel (25%), Chile (24%), Spain (25%), and the United States (21%-35%). Thus, even with a 10% corporate tax rate, Puerto Rico would be more economically competitive than various other countries and would be able to attract foreign direct investment and new corporate subsidiaries to Puerto Rico.

85 http://www.cadtm.org/Behind-Puerto-Rico-s-Debt-Corporations-That-Drain-Profits-from-the-Island

86 The issue of U.S. citizenship in a sovereign Puerto Rico is very controversial. Statehooders use the threat of losing one's U.S. citizenship in a sovereign Puerto Rico as a major reason why one should not support sovereignty and support statehood. I detail above how one can maintain and transfer U.S. citizenship to children born overseas using U.S. policies. In a sovereign Puerto Rico, one can be a Puerto Rican citizen or a dual citizen with both U.S. and Puerto Rican citizenships.

87 A Puerto Rican National would have the same benefits of citizenship (access to healthcare and government services), but would not be able to vote in Puerto Rico elections.

88 Under the **U.S.-PR Consular Support Policy** that I propose, any U.S. citizen in an emergency situation who cannot access a U.S. diplomatic mission, will be able to receive support and protection from any Puerto Rican diplomatic mission. Any Puerto Rican citizen in an emergency situation who cannot access a Puerto Rican diplomatic mission, will be able to receive support and protection from any U.S. diplomatic mission.

89 https://www.fvap.gov/citizen-voter/additional-info

90 For example: Mrs. María Pérez, a Puerto Rican U.S. citizen born in San Juan in 1965 (prior to sovereignty) is also eligible to vote in Florida. With the advent of sovereignty, Mrs. Pérez would also be recognized by the Republic of Puerto Rico as a Puerto Rican citizen. As a U.S./PR dual citizen, Mrs. Pérez can reside in Puerto Rico and yet also vote absentee in federal and Florida

elections if she desires because she would be considered an expat U.S. citizen residing overseas. Mrs. Pérez would also have to pay annual federal and state income taxes on her global income, just like any other U.S. citizen residing in the United States or overseas.

91 https://travel.state.gov/content/travel/en/international-travel/while-abroad/birth-abroad.html

92 https://www.expatinfodesk.com/expat-guide/relinquishing-citizenship/renunciating-your-us-passport/five-steps-to-renunciating-your-us-passport/

93 https://www.expatinfodesk.com/expat-guide/relinquishing-citizenship/renunciating-your-us-passport/five-steps-to-renunciating-your-us-passport/

94 https://elcascotenews.com/oea-sobre-bolivia-no-es-golpe-de-estado-simplemente-son-militares-y-policias-tomando-por-la-fuerza-el-poder/

95 https://caribbeanbusiness.com/study-reveals-poverty-scenario-in-puerto-rico-after-hurricane-maria/

96 https://machiavelli.thefreelibrary.com/Prince/27-1

Made in United States
Orlando, FL
03 February 2025